D0359636

Hackers
Crime in the digital sublime

Paul A. Taylor

drpaul_a_taylor@yahoo.co.uk

London and New York

First published 1999
by Routledge
11 New Fetter Lane, London EC4P 4EE

Simultaneously published in the USA and Canada
by Routledge
29 West 35th Street, New York, NY 10001

Routledge is an imprint of the Taylor & Francis Group

© 1999 Paul A. Taylor

Typeset in Baskerville by Routledge
Printed and bound in Great Britain by MPG Books Ltd, Bodmin

All rights reserved. No part of this book may be reprinted or
reproduced or utilised in any form or by any electronic,
mechanical, or other means, now known or hereafter
invented, including photocopying and recording, or in any
information storage or retrieval system, without permission in
writing from the publishers.

British Library Cataloguing in Publication Data
A catalogue record for this book is available from the British Library

Library of Congress Cataloging in Publication Data
Hackers: crime in the digital sublime/Paul A. Taylor
Includes bibliographical references. 1. Computer crimes –
Netherlands. 2. Computer hackers – Netherlands –
attitudes. 3. Freedom of information – Netherlands. I. Title.
HV6773.3.N4T39 1999   99–22358
364.16'8–dc21   CIP

ISBN 0–415–18071–6 (hbk)
ISBN 0–415–18072–4 (pbk)

He was a thread of gold running straight through the pattern of a carpet woven by a madman.

(Alessandro Baricco, *Silk*)

Contents

Preface

Seldom is there an integrated socio-technical approach to the computer crime problem ... We need to establish where the social and psychological lines are drawn between normal and deviant, between allowed and disallowed, between expected and unexpected, between wanted and unwanted.

(Sherizen 1992: 40)

The English novelist and scientist, C.P. Snow, once famously observed that: 'The intellectual life of the whole of western society is increasingly being split into two polar groups. – Literary intellectuals at one pole – at the other scientists. ... Between the two a gulf of mutual incomprehension.'[1] I believe a similar gulf of mutual incomprehension exists between the computer underground and its adversaries, an incomprehension that is consistently exacerbated by the sensationalising tendencies of the modern media. This book is written in order to understand better the exact nature of the gulf by closely examining the dynamics of the vociferous disagreements it brings forth.

Background to interview material: hacking culture – the gossamer network

instead of being able to base our theories on adequate knowledge of the phenomenon we are trying to explain. It is as though we tried, as anthropologists once had to do, to construct a description of the initiation rites of some remote African tribe from the scattered and incomplete accounts of a few missionaries.

(Becker 1963: 166)

The primary research material for this study is based upon a combination of face-to-face interviews I conducted in the UK and the Netherlands between 1990 and 1993 and email-based interviews carried out from 1989–98 on a world-wide basis. The interviews were undertaken with three main groups: hackers; computer scientists; and computer security practitioners. Within the work as a whole I have endeavoured to obtain a healthy mix of both well-known and knowledgeable interviewees taking into account that notoriety and/or media appeal do not necessarily equate with knowledgeableness. Access to interviewees was obtained in the first instance via email and these initial contacts 'snowballed' to provide further contacts who were willing to meet with me in person, which, in a further iteration, led to more email contacts based upon personal referrals from those I had originally interviewed on a face-to-face basis.

Analysing the computer underground is inherently difficult. It appears as a 'gossamer framework' mixing real-world relationships and the immateriality of cyberspace with the result that its social ties are loose, even by subculture standards. In addition, it has proved difficult to pursue the main focus of this book (the relationship between the computer underground and the computer security industry), since both groups are far from being coherent and well-established given the relative youth of computing and its hectic evolutionary pace. The boundaries between groups are unusually fluid and there is no established notion of expert knowledge – since this is itself one of the sites of active contestation between competing groups. It is thus at times problematic, in choosing interview subjects and source materials, to fall back on conventional notions of what constitutes an expert or even a member of a subculture. The quotations and sources used throughout this book are individual examples of opinions I commonly encountered amongst a wide range of different hackers and members of the computer security industry. Suitable emphasis is placed upon any of those quotations that appeared to be atypical in any way.

Finally, all the acknowledged difficulties of researching the computer underground are further heightened by the climate of secrecy resulting from the fear and suspicion that arose after various legal crackdowns on hacking. The Netherlands was chosen as the main site for my face-to-face fieldwork with hackers, for example, because the deterrent effect of the UK Parliament's Computer Misuse Act quickly ruled out extensive fieldwork in the UK and, whereas hackers of other nationalities declined to be interviewed, Dutch hackers: were willing to talk; were in relatively close geographical proximity; and invariably spoke excellent English. A gap that still remains in this study, however, is the absence of an analysis of computer virus writers, consistent access to whom proved totally impracticable because even those happy to admit to illicit computer intrusion would not admit to distributing viruses.

The hawks and the doves

> from the amused concern of the cognoscenti to the hysteria of the casual user, and from the research community and the manufacturing industry to the morally aroused legislature and the mediated culture at large. Every one of these explanations and narratives is the result of social and cultural processes and values.
>
> (Ross 1991: 78)[2]

I wish to make it clear immediately that this book does not purport to be a definitive depiction of hacking culture but rather a sketch that will contribute to what I hope will be an ongoing process and debate. Other writers such as Levy (1984), Meyer (1989) and Chantler (1995)[3] have attempted to provide detailed descriptions of the origins and social organisation of hackers. This book whilst being grateful for such efforts has a different aim. It seeks (whilst maintaining a realistic sense of the above various practical difficulties associated with researching the computer underground) to provide a portrait of the phenomenon of hacking by concentrating upon the conflict between the computer security industry and the computer underground. Thus a key theme of this book is that hacking cannot be considered as a purely technical activity to be looked at in isolation from its social context. Our present perception of hacking is the direct result of a series of conflicts and contestations between various social groups.

As a broad simplification, computer *cognoscenti* are split into two camps: those who either come from or are prepared to co-operate with the computer under-ground and those to whom the computer underground is an anathema. Borrowing from the argot of the cold war, I describe the two ends of this spec-trum of opinion as the *hawkish* and *dovish* camps. Hawks advocate little or no co-operation: the computer underground should be punished in the courts. The doves, in contrast, argue that hackers represent an important stock of technical knowledge that society should not prematurely isolate itself from by adopting a 'punish first, ask questions later' approach. In recent years, however, the hawkish view has come to dominate media, legal and commercial perspectives on hacking.

Given such divergence of opinion it is perhaps time for society to take stock and ask itself if the hawkish approach is appropriate and adequate. There are a wealth of technical arguments both for and against hacking. I hope, however, that this book will highlight that the activity has a wider social and historical significance that, if paid attention to, may shed at least a weak light on our present struggle to come to terms with the full cultural implications of an increasingly networked world.

The contested term

> just about everyone knows what a hacker is, at least in the most commonly accepted sense: someone who illicitly intrudes into computer systems by stealth and manipulates those systems to his own ends, for his own purposes.
> (Dann and Dozois 1996: xii)

Whilst the moral and social aspects of hacking are hotly debated, the very meaning of the term itself is also essentially contestable. The currently accepted meaning of the word relates to the unauthorised access to and subsequent use of other people's computer systems. This is a relatively recent definition compared to its first period of common usage in the 1960s when its illicit connotation was absent. In addition, the media and computer security industry have largely succeeded in reducing hacking's connotations to computer-based activities. To members of the computer underground *hacking* still refers, in the first instance, to the imaginative and unorthodox use of *any* artefact[4] – a view pithily expressed in William Gibson's neo-Chandleresque phrase, 'the street finds its own uses for things';[5] to the lay person, the phrase is likely to conjure up sensationalised images of malicious computer geeks in darkened rooms obsessively typing away; meanwhile, to the computer *aficionado*, the phrase is more likely to be associated with its dramatic fictionalisation in the movies and the postmodern literary genre of *cyberpunk*; to the computer programmer the term may refer to some of the earliest and most imaginative people involved in programming; and, finally, within the computer security industry, the term *hacker* is likely to present a cue for opprobrium to be directed at 'electronic vandals'. This book fleshes out the commonly propagated images of hacking by paying attention to the full range of these competing perspectives[6] and examining how they interact with each other.

Media hype and hackers: the rhetoric of the digital sublime

> in the last twenty years, nothing has thrown us like the evolution of geekus digitalist ... we're still stunned by how quickly garden variety computer geeks managed to shed their pocket protectors and slide rules for leather jackets and attitude, morphing from social pariahs to techno-revolutionaries. In the hothouse atmosphere of media hype, our favorite nerds blossomed into mythic Hackers: a schizophrenic blend of dangerous criminal and geeky Robin Hood. Chalk it up to an increasingly bi-polar fear and fascination with the expanding computer culture.
>
> (Hawn 1996: 1)

A main aim of this book is to dispel the hype surrounding the phenomenon of hacking, a sentiment summarised by the cynical populist admonition: 'don't believe the hype'. The *rhetoric of the digital sublime* describes the particularly high levels of hyperbole that seem to surround computer-based technologies. In recent years the subject of hacking has been subjected to a spate of TV programmes, books, movies and newspaper/magazine articles – all with a marked tendency to sensationalise something that is ironically an inherently sedentary, repetitive and non-photogenic/televisual activity. An accurate understanding of the cultural significance of hacking is made more difficult by such hyperbolic misrepresentation and it inevitably diverts attention away from its significant social implications. Although many news stories suffer exaggeration and misrepresentation at the hands of the media, in the particular case of hacking the ubiquity and integral importance of computer systems in modern society may mean that such barriers to understanding created by the media are becoming increasingly costly.

Hacking is particularly amenable to media hyperbole because the activity simultaneously embodies (in roughly equal measure) the elements of both fear and fascination with which Western society views computing technology: hackers themselves provide the bonus of a human focus for such concerns. These attitudes to technology are heightened in the case of hacking by the fact that both the activity and its technology are unusually enigmatic. We are fascinated by the 'black box' nature of computers and the technical virtuosity of hackers who manipulate them, but at the same time we are fearful of their lack of transparency and the fact that our conventional concept of technological experts may be fatally undermined by largely anonymous, unaccountable, and potentially subversive technological whiz-kids. Fascination with the potential of computer technology complements our wider societal fondness for gadgets and technological solutions. Conversely, fear of computer technology complements our perennial cultural concern that we cannot ultimately control our technological curiosity. The perennial nature of this fear is illustrated by the historical range of cultural expressions that give it voice. It is present in the fate of such Greek mythological figures as Prometheus and Icarus; it is vividly portrayed in Mary Shelley's gothic classic *Frankenstein*; and it is present in such contemporary cultural forms as the cyberpunk novel *Neuromancer* and science fiction films such as *Bladerunner* and *Terminator*. I label this enduring cultural theme *fear of Frankenstein* and contend that it provides an important contextual backdrop to any discussion of the hacking phenomenon.

One of the main factors making hacking particularly suitable for media hyperbole is its aura of anonymity. This means that the additional threat of the unseen is added to our general *fear of Frankenstein*. Just because they cannot be easily rounded up and physically identified does not mean that a hacker community does not exist, but it does mean that the lack of a physically identifiable community provides a rich environment for uncorroborated speculation, media sensationalism and a disturbing reliance by governments and official organisations on anecdotal and/or fictionalised sources of information on hacking behaviour. It should also be noted that no single group has a monopoly on the strategic use of hyperbole. Despite their diametrically opposed arguments as to the potential social and technical benefits of hacking, both computer security figures and denizens of the computer underground occasionally manipulate and exaggerate the malevolent aspects of hacking (the former to stigmatise and isolate hackers; the latter to revel in the subsequent notoriety such stigmatisation affords).

The information revolution: the extent and pace of change

A new doctrine of criminal information is emerging in the area of legal science, founded on the still-developing concepts of information law and the law of information technology. In accordance with modern cybernetics and informatics, information law now recognizes information as a third funda-mental factor in addition to matter and energy. Based upon empirical analysis, this concept evaluates information both as a new economic, cultural and political asset and as being specifically vulnerable to unique forms of crime.

(United Nations, *International Review of Criminal Policy*: par. 85)

The underlying reason why hackers have become a technological cause célèbre ripe for media coverage can be found in the wider social and historical context of the *information revolution*. This phrase encapsulates the claim that information technologies have not only made great technical strides but also wrought great social change. This social change rests on two main elements.

The first element relates to the paradigm shift whereby the world is viewed in increasingly informational terms.[7] The marriage of information technology (IT) and genetic engineering techniques provides a vivid example of both elements of the IT-induced paradigm shift. The human body's DNA is increasingly concep-tualised as the informational 'building blocks' of life that can be programmed and re-engineered like computer code whilst the speed at which such a reconcep-tualisation has been put into practice is illustrated by the massively reduced time-scales that now exist between the dystopian fictional portrayals of genetic technologies in such works as Michael Marshall Smith's novel, *Spares* (1996), and movies such as *Gattaca* (1998) and their actual use in cases such as Dolly the sheep, the world's first cloned mammal.

The second element of the information-induced paradigm shift relates to the fact that the new conception of information has coincided with a rate of techno-logical change that surpasses the pace of previous technological 'revolutions'. Social upheaval in the face of technological change is not new. Societies throughout history have incorporated into their fabric technologies that have had profound cultural effects, the printing press being one of the more obvious examples. What is arguably significant about the information revolution, however, is the pace of the technological change it brings. A pace of change, the inexorability of which derives from its predecessor, the industrial revolution:

> for the first time in human history, the shackles were taken off the produc-tive power of human societies, which henceforth became capable of the constant, rapid and up to the present limitless multiplication of men, goods and services. ... The Industrial Revolution was not indeed an episode with a beginning or an end. To ask when it was 'complete' is senseless, for its essence was that henceforth revolutionary change became the norm.
>
> (Hobsbawm 1975: 28–9)

Technological change has now reached a speed that is increasingly difficult for both society and individuals to accommodate unproblematically, a situation evocatively expressed by the cyberpunk novelist William Gibson in his description of a typical urban environment of the near future.

> Night City was like a deranged experiment in social Darwinism, designed by a bored researcher who kept one thumb permanently on the fast-forward button. Stop hustling and you sank without a trace, but move a little too swiftly and you'd break the fragile surface tension of the black market; either way, you were gone, with nothing left of you but some vague memory ... though heart or lungs or kidneys might survive in the service of some stranger.
>
> (Gibson 1984: 14)

This *Zeitgeist* of constant change has provided the underlying impetus and basic leitmotifs for cyberpunk literature and its fictional portrayal of hackers as cyberpunks.

Conclusion: hackers as cyberpunks?

> he closed his eyes. ... It came on again, gradually, a flickering, non-linear flood of fact and sensory data, a kind of narrative conveyed in surreal jump-cuts and juxtapositions. It was vaguely like riding a rollercoaster that phased in and out of existence at random, impossibly rapid intervals, changing altitude, attack, and direction with each pulse of nothingness, except that the shifts had nothing to do with any physical orientation, but rather with lightning alternations in paradigm and symbol system. The data had never been intended for human input.
>
> (Gibson 1986b: 40)

In the context of the information revolution hackers emblematise issues of wider social significance than merely breaking into other people's computer systems. The *Zeitgeist* that hackers personify has been vividly expressed in the fictional genre of *cyberpunk*, which presents hackers as prototypical denizens of a new informational world order. Levy describes how the earliest hackers, 'attained a state of pure concentration. ... When you had all that information glued to your cerebral being, it was almost as if your mind had merged into the environment of the computer' (Levy 1984: 37). He also presciently foresaw cyberpunk's depiction of the man/machine symbiosis with his observation that: 'Real optimum programming, of course, could only be accomplished when every obstacle between you and the pure computer was eliminated – an ideal that probably won't be fulfilled until hackers are somehow biologically merged with computers' (Levy 1984: 126). Cyberpunk typically portrays hackers of the future as the ultimate extension of this idea of man/machine symbiosis making the genre a vehicle with which to fundamentally reassess the nature of humanity and its boundaries:

Certain central themes spring up repeatedly in cyberpunk. The theme of body invasion: prosthetic limbs … genetic alteration. There is the even more powerful theme of mind invasion: brain-computer interfaces, artificial intelligence, neurochemistry – techniques radically redefining the nature of humanity, the nature of the self.

(Sterling 1986: xi)

The key social significance of hackers lies in the way in which they embody in reality, even if only to a limited extent, such widespread cultural concerns over the implications of our increasing levels of interaction with rapidly changing and evolving information technologies. Such an explanation at least partially accounts for the way in which the hacker geeks and nerds of one period in time have become the Hollywood cyberpunks of another.

Acknowledgements

The original research that constitutes the heart of this book was conducted at the Research Centre for Social Sciences at the University of Edinburgh. I received help, advice and support from various staff and associates, especially from Dr Rob Procter and Dr Robin Williams (on and off the pitch).

On a medical level I would not have been around to write this book if it had not been for the skill and dedication of Prof. Stell from the University of Liverpool: thank you.

My greatest thanks and love go to my father, Richard Daniel Taylor – an emeritus professor in the 'University of Life'.

Finally, I'd like to dedicate this work to the memory of my mother who introduced me to books, Patricia Taylor, 1939–98: 'You'll never walk alone'.

Introduction

The following sections in this introduction expand upon the theme of the sensationalistion of hacking referred to in the Preface. This is done to provide a context for the subsequent analysis of hacking and is necessary groundwork for an exploration of the social processes at work in the depiction of hacking by both its opponents and proponents.

Fear, ignorance and vulnerability: hyping hacking

> The cops, and their patrons in the telephone companies, just don't understand the modern world of computers, and they're scared. 'They think there are masterminds running spy-rings who employ us,' a hacker told me. 'They don't understand that we don't do this for money, we do it for power and knowledge.' Telephone security people who reach out to the underground are accused of divided loyalties and fired by panicked employers. A young Missourian coolly psychoanalyzed the opposition. 'They're overdependent on things they don't understand. They've surrendered their lives to computers.'
>
> (Sterling 1991: 4)

Whilst the allegedly criminal aspects of hacking alone would seem enough to create a media interest in the activity, it also contains a mysterious technological element manifested in the lay person's uninitiated awe of computers' complexities and capabilities.[1] Despite the possible existence of reasons for us to welcome their maverick spirit, hackers also serve to remind us of our technological vulnerability/ ignorance. This has been manifested in the problems experienced by law enforcement officials and legislators in their encounters with the computer underground and are perhaps merely smaller-scale illustrations of some of the wider problems society encounters as it attempts to assimilate new information technologies into existing social structures. There have been various cases of alleged over-reactions to computer security incidents by law enforcement agents. A legal example is provided by the E911 case whereby a member of the hacker group Legion of Doom, Craig Neidorf, was accused of threatening the safety of residents throughout the US by having copied a document containing details of the tele-phone emergency 911 system. When the case came to trial the federal prosecutors were embarrassed when it was proved by the defence team that the allegedly sensi-tive document valued at $80,000 was in fact available to the general public for $13.[2]

The authorities' often dramatic response to hackers and their activities was perhaps most vividly manifested in the series of police raids on the homes of hackers code-named 'Operation Sun Devil' by gun-carrying US law enforce-ment officers. Officers were accused of over-reacting to the physical threat posed by hackers in their homes by entering with their guns drawn and of removing excessive amounts of computing equipment unrelated to their specific investiga-tions. Whilst such a response can be interpreted as exhibiting displaced fear it is also viewed by some as deliberate strategy that fulfils a pragmatic function:

> Where the target of the raids is an individual, usually at his or her own home, this simple approach to raid and seizure is … entirely appropriate and very effective. Hackers and paedophiles in particular are used to dealing with people and problems by means of remote connections; suddenly to be faced with by a veritable army of (in the US, gun carrying) officers is usually sufficient to persuade total – indeed, often *abject* – co-operation.
>
> (Barrett 1997: 157 [emphasis in the original])

A British perspective on allegedly over-zealous law enforcement is provided by the father of the 16-year-old London-based hacker, Richard Pryce, who was accused of hacking into the systems of US military bases:

> It was around 7 p.m. and I was watching TV when about eight cars pulled up and people started banging on the door. When I answered it, the officers came filing in … there were so many of them, I thought he must have killed someone. They burst into his room and pulled his hands away from his computer keyboard. They then stripped his room. When I went up the stairs he was sitting there in shock while they were ripping up his floor-boards. They searched his room for 5 hours.
>
> (Sterling 1991: website)

Similarly, with reference to the case of Kevin Poulsen,[3] his attorney, Paul Meltzer, argued: 'It's ludicrous, it's absurd. … They can't decide if they've got a kid playing in his garage or Julius Rosenberg'.[4] Meltzer said he was 'very disturbed by the inability of federal prosecutors to distinguish between assault with a deadly weapon and assault with a computer. I mean, c'mon, the guy's non-violent' (Fine 1995). Poulsen's own words are also instructive:

> The trouble began before I was released. I planned on living with my parents when I got out of prison, until I could find employment and live on my own. My probation officer anticipated this months before my release-date, and visited my parents. He was shocked to find that they had recently

purchased an IBM compatible computer, and he warned them that they must get rid of it before I moved in. They didn't have a modem, mind you, but as a notorious hacker I might easily fashion a modem out of ordinary household appliances. ... It got even more interesting when I was released. When I reported to my P.O., he explained to me that, not only could I not use any computer, with or without a modem, but that *I couldn't be in the same room as a computer.* ... Judge Real declined to second-guess the decisions of the probation officer, and specifically rejected the contention that I should be allowed to obtain employment that allows access to computers without modems, noting, 'Who knows what a computer can do?'

(Poulsen undated-a: website)

Justin Petersen, (alias *Agent Steal*) reinforces the claim that there is an apparent culture and knowledge gap between hackers and the legal authorities. Petersen spent forty-one months in Federal Prison for hacking into a bank's computer and transferring funds. Whilst serving his sentence he met up with Chris Lamprecht (alias *Minor Threat*), another hacker. He describes how:

The prison officials were terrified of us. They became obsessed as they read our mail, screened our magazines, listened to our phone calls, and sent informants to try and infiltrate our little group of technophiles. The only conclusion they could come to was that they had no idea what we were up to. When the computer at the prison industries plant crashed, Chris was promptly fired from his job there. It wasn't his doing, but unbridled paranoia spreads far and wide among bureaucrats.

(Petersen 1997: website)

This general fear and ignorance of the authorities towards the abilities of hackers is further evident from Chris Lamprecht's experience of the court system. His judge, Sam Sparks, stipulated in his sentencing that:

Upon release from imprisonment ... for a term of three years, the defendant cannot be employed where he is the installer, programmer, or trouble shooter for computer equipment; may not purchase, possess or receive a personal computer which uses a modem; and may not utilize the Internet or other computer networks.

(cited in Thieme 1996: 21)

From the perspective of the computer underground:

Doesn't Sparks know that anyone with a few dollars can buy a social security number in the data marketplace? Besides, good hackers are equally adept at 'social engineering.' If Lamprecht talks someone out of their social security number, should we cut out his tongue? In short, does the judge have a clue as to how life is led these days? Lamprecht's former boss, Selwyn Polit of

ODT, laughed when asked about the case. 'They're dead scared of him because of the computer stuff,' he said. 'They treat him differently because they think if he just thinks about computers, he can do magical things.' Unfortunately, Lamprecht's statements feed these projections. He plays enthusiastically to the 'evil hacker genius' image.

(Thieme 1996: 21–2)

A cultural gap is again evident in the fate of a young bulletin board operator in New Brunswick in 1985, held liable for the material posted by other users. His arrest, in 1985, led Jeffrey Fogel of the ACLU to use a forceful analogy[5] in order to claim that the youth was unfairly singled out: 'He has an electronic bulletin board and arresting him and seizing his computer amounts to seizing a printing press', Fogel said. 'It would be like if someone put a stolen credit card number in a newspaper classified. Would you close down the newspaper?' (PR Newswire 1985). Frustration from the computer underground at the perceived inappropriateness of the establishment's fear-induced responses is exhibited in the way in which metaphors are reappropriated in order to reinforce their own rhetorical points:

Denying a criminal access to computer networks is like breaking his fingers for writing a hold-up note and forbidding him to use a pen. When the crime has nothing to do with computers or networks in the first place, it's like putting him into a sensory-deprivation tank simply to punish him.

(Thieme 1996: 21)

Hacking's predominantly non-physical character and its accompanying air of mystery tends to heighten its potential for creating fear and anxiety. Its anonymity mixed with its illicit nature makes it easier for the media to portray the actions of hackers, who are rarely seen in the flesh, in such forms as 'electronic stalkers'. According to the convicted hacker, Kevin Poulsen: 'Criminal cases involving suspected unauthorized computer access, or "hacking", are frequently subject to wild, unsubstantiated, and often bizarre claims by prosecutors and investigators' (Poulsen undated-b). This claim of a tendency to over-dramatise would seem to be at least partially borne out by the ominous sounding subtitle of the book written about his exploits, *The Watchman*. This seemed designed to make a none-too-subliminal association with serial killing, being subtitled: *The Twisted Life and Crimes of Serial Hacker Kevin Poulsen*.

Hackers who hype

It was no longer enough to break into computer systems, now it was essential to break into the limelight of national media attention, as well.

(Hawn 1996: 2)

The hyperbole and mystery surrounding hacking is not always something that hackers passively suffer. They also make use of the immaterial anonymity of cyberspace in order to heighten the effects of the various on-line personae they adopt. On occasion they can revel in exaggeratedly malevolent poses: 'Cyberspace is a new world and in it the hacker is a datalord, a baudrate barbarian who takes what he wants' (Marotta 1993: 3). Under the cover of anonymity hackers project threatening personalities to the outside world and media facilitating the subsequent over-reactions of the police and legal establishment. Hacking groups generally choose colourful names such as 'Bad Ass Mother Fuckers, Chaos Computer Club, Circle of Death, Farmers of Doom'[6] and this can create a self-fulfilling prophecy in terms of the authorities' response. Anonymity allows hackers to indulge in extravagant role-playing whereby they form a dangerous underground movement with revolutionary credentials:

> Since we are engaged in Revolutionary War in Cyberspace … Our Guerilla Warfare Operating Area, (GWOA), is the Internet. … Our greatest tactical advantages are the speed of light and non location specificity. … One small voice in Cyberspace becomes global interpersonal communication at the speed of light as the net grows geometrically. Global interpersonal communication is the greatest tool for world peace our species has ever known. We have the technology to achieve virtual collective consciousness on a planetary scale. The potential of the Electronic Revolution is awesome. Instead of electing an aristocracy whose choices are packaged by mass media marketing to govern us, we have the ability to transcend the physical limitations of deceptive appearance, and illuminate the truth of being through the digitized reflection of intelligence.
>
> (Davis undated: website)

Barlow (1990), questions the actual malevolence of such poses with reference to a group of hackers who had previously frightened him with a similar sort of aggressive email posturing. When he actually came face to face with two of the hackers they:

> were well scrubbed and fashionably clad. They looked to be as dangerous as ducks. But … as … the media have discovered to their delight, the boys had developed distinctly showier personae for their rambles through the howling wilderness of Cyberspace. Glittering with spikes of binary chrome, they strode past the klieg lights and into the digital distance. There they would be outlaws. It was only a matter of time before they started to believe themselves as bad as they sounded. And no time at all before everyone else did.
>
> (Barlow 1990: 48)

Aided by the choice of deliberately provocative handles, the eventual outcome of the hyperbole caused through anonymity is the danger that hackers become victims of their own hype. Barlow's experience is a direct illustration of

Becker's observation: 'Treating a person as though he were generally rather than specifically deviant produces a self-fulfilling prophecy. It sets in motion several mechanisms which conspire to shape the person in the image people have of him' (Becker 1963: 34). Similarly, Thieme notes in relation to the New Brunswick arrest of a bulletin board operator cited earlier that: 'the case illustrates not only the great gulf fixed between those who use the Net and those who don't, but also how the image of hackers as "evil geniuses" can distort the perception and judgement of those who play into the image – as well as those who fear and misunderstand it' (Thieme 1996: 21). The result of this distortion of judgement can be profound:

> Before I first met with the computer hacker and convicted felon who goes by the handle of Minor Threat, I am warned. 'You have no idea what these people can do,' says a reporter who's familiar with the digital underground. She tells me Minor Threat and his hacking buddies are cyber sociopaths who get off on mangling credit histories, tampering with telephone lines, invading email accounts, and crashing hard drives. 'They might mess with you just because they can,' she says. 'It's a power game.' ... So I am prepared to greet Darth Vader beind the razor wire of the federal correctional institute. ... Sitting in the waiting room amid drug dealers and armed robbers, he looks more like a refugee from a college chess tournament than a high-tech supervillain. Yet Lamprecht is serving a 70 month sentence ... many who know Lamprecht and the hacking subculture say that law enforcement officials are overreacting, spooked by the harm they perceive hackers can do as much as by actual misbehavior.
>
> (Heiman 1997: 70)

In my correspondence with Gisle Hannemyr, a Norwegian computer security officer, he took exception to the idea that the media is solely used by those seeking to stigmatise hackers:

> As you point out, the media prefers the sensational to the factual, and you seem to imply that the computer security industry is in cahoots with the media to create a designer enemy. To me, it looks as if the main conspiracy is between the press and the computer underground – not between the press and the computer security industry. Why this is, we can only speculate. It is easy to understand what the media gains from the relationship (stories that sell papers), but the motivation of the computer underground is more subtle. My guess is that it is part attention-seeking (if you can't be famous, you can at least be notorious) – plus that some individuals (Chris Goggans comes to mind) have managed to make substantial profits from their notoriety as computer underground heroes.
>
> (Hannemyr: email interview)

Life after the Cold War

> 'Massive networking makes the US the world's most vulnerable target', said William Studeman, former deputy director of the CIA. Jamie Gorelick, a former deputy attorney-general, was even more blunt in her address to a Senate hearing on the subject: 'We will have a cyber equivalent of Pearl Harbor'.
>
> (*Sunday Times* 17 May 1998: 26)

A specific historical and cultural context that arguably contributed to some of the responses to hacking identified above is the post-Cold-War *Zeitgeist* where new scapegoats are sought to apportion blame for widespread feelings of vulnerability. For example, in a 1994 report on global organised crime, the Center for Strategic and International Studies, an independent research centre formerly associated with Georgetown University, asserted that 'a despot armed with a computer and a small squad of expert hackers can be as dangerous and disruptive as any adversary we have faced since World War II' (cited in Roush 95: 4). Various media accounts make full use of the cold-war imagery in order to emphasise the vulnerabilities hacking throws into sharp relief. The UK Sunday tabloid newspaper, the *News of the World*, for example, provides the following account under the headline 'I had my finger on Doomsday button':

> Hunched in a cramped bedroom in his parents' terraced house, computer whiz-kid Mathew Bevan felt a creeping chill as he gazed at the image on the screen before him. Against all the odds – and using just a £400 High Street system – the 17-year-old had hacked into the American Air Force's FLEX project ... **F**orce **L**evel **Ex**ecution. With an awful realisation he watched his twitching index finger hover over the nuclear button. One twitch more, he says, and he might have launched a Peacekeeper missile with a 150 kilotons nuclear payload. Its maximum range is 12,000 kilometres. It guarantees total devastation within a 20-mile radius of impact. With that, Bevan could lay waste to whole cities, kill millions ... and start World War III. *For a few numbing seconds his Cardiff street was mission control for the apocalypse.*
>
> (*News of the World* 23 November 1997: 43 [emphasis in the original])

Whilst the significance of the above sentiments could be played down by reference to the sensationalistic excesses of tabloid journalism, not too dissimilar sentiments are encountered in a broadsheet newspaper's account of the US's vulnerability to hackers:

> President Bill Clinton will announce plans this week to build ramparts against a new and invisible enemy threatening to spread more chaos in America than any conventional terrorist attack. He will unveil defence measures unprecedented in the history of human conflict to protect America from the potentially devastating peril posed by cyber warfare, in

which computer systems controlling airports, hospitals, traffic lights, banks and even nuclear weapons could be destroyed creating havoc. It sounds like a science fiction fantasy. But it is already happening. This month the Pentagon reported 'a series of systematic attacks' on its computer systems in an incident considered so ominous that the President was told it could be the work of Iraq's Saddam Hussein. The prospect of Saddam hiring a computer hacker to try to cripple American computer systems fills defence experts with horror: by a strange paradox, America's technological superiority and consequent dependence on computers, leave it more vulnerable than most countries to cyber attack.

(*Sunday Times* 17 May 1998: 26)

The feelings of vulnerability experienced by otherwise extremely powerful groups are caused by the potent mix of the anonymity of one's opponent (and the exaggerated perceptions such anonymity may then give rise to) and the paradox that one's own apparent strength and superiority may in fact prove to be an Achilles' heel. This combination of factors is portrayed as the new threat, coming quickly after a Gulf War which illustrated the apparent unassailability of the US's conventional military capability:

Making things even more difficult for American defence experts is not knowing who the enemy is. Whether they are disgruntled Americans, Hamas terrorists or pariah dictators such as Saddam, the attackers could wage cyber warfare undetected on any laptop computer from the Sinai desert to Singapore. Just as exasperating for the government would be deciding how to deploy its vast military. 'If you don't know who your enemy is, how can you retaliate?' said one expert. This makes cyber warfare the great equaliser, a cheap and effective weapon for any Third World rogue state or small terrorist organisation wanting to wage war against a superpower – and win. All they might need is a few million dollars to hire a handful of 'cyber mercenaries' capable of penetrating supposedly secure government systems.

(*Sunday Times* 17 May 1998: 26)

One might expect that the use of Cold-War imagery and language would be restricted to those on the right of the political spectrum. However, in a book otherwise devoted to analysing the Internet as an extension of Western imperialist practices, somewhat reactionary language is used to describe the role of those opposing the dominant system:

Cellular phone ... hackers can tap into any conversation and trace anyone almost anywhere. ... Online terrorism is not too far away and most of the early proponents of this sick art are hackers. While some hackers will be causing increasing havoc, other hackers will be tracking them down.

(Sardar 1996: 23)

The disturbing prospect is that opposition to the microcybernetic consumerist dictatorship will then find its only effective location deep underground, in the hands of zealots or fanatics who are content to destroy without bothering to dialogue. And microcybernetic technology is particularly vulnerable to just such a sort of opposition; as we have seen, hackers generally get caught only when they become brazen; and a determined band of computer nihilists, endowed with patience as well as skill, could even now be ensconced deep in the system, planting their bugs, worms and bombs.

(Ravetz 1996: 52)

The loss of the old certainties of the Cold War thus seems to affect Right and Left equally. The purported vulnerability to attack from outsiders used as part of Cold-War rhetoric is recycled here in the new context of the hi-tech world. The ability of phone-hackers to eavesdrop and trace people's whereabouts is implicitly placed on the same level of concern as that given to the 'microcybernetic consumerist dictatorship'. The ambivalence with which hackers are viewed addressed earlier in this chapter resurfaces here when hacking is emotively described as a 'sick art' whilst at the same time there is the explicit recognition of society's dependence upon such figures: 'while some hackers will be causing increasing havoc, other hackers will be tracking them down'.

Books and movies about hacking: specific examples of media coverage

Popular media's fascination with things subversive and spectacular ... has the unfortunate side effect that it hides the 'other side' of hacking, the side that involves skilled craftsmen who believe that a computer is more than a means of production – it is, among many other things an instrument for creation, communication, mastery, artistic expression and political empowerment.

(Hannemyr 1997: 2)

Given the above acknowledgement that hackers are not averse to sensationalising their activity, the widespread sensationalising of hacking by those seeking to marginalise and stigmatise hackers is, for a variety of reasons to be explored at length in the rest of this book, potentially debilitating for a society struggling to come to terms with the full ramifications of the information society and all the potentially profound changes that concept may signify for our everyday lives.[7] To illustrate briefly the media's role in sensationalising hacking, I describe below the non-fictional accounts of hacking and Hollywood's movie portrayals.[8]

Books

There is frequently in non-fictional accounts of hacking a rather curious mix of self-indulgent reliance upon seemingly trivial, tangential or simply mundane details of different hacking episodes coupled with a simultaneous and frequent resort to hyperbolic description. Voluminous biographical details are provided on hackers and their dedicated but inevitably repetitive activities are described in exhaustive and somewhat exhausting detail. In *The Cuckoo's Egg*, for example, we are given various descriptions of the author's girlfriend and seemingly irrelevant details of their shared Californian lifestyle, in conjunction with a narrative suffused with recourse to references about the excitement of detective work and the underlying menace of KGB spying. In *Cyberpunk* the authors illustrate the use of hyperbolic imagery with their consideration of the issues at stake in the hiring of a hacker for security work: 'But hire such a mean-spirited person? That would be like giving the Boston Strangler a maintenance job in a nursing-school dormitory' (Hafner and Markoff 1991: 40). An overtly sensationalist tendency is evident in a sample of the titles and subtitles of some of the best-known recent books from the spate of non-fictional and journalistic accounts of hacking published in recent years:

The Cuckoo's Egg: Tracking a Spy through the Maze of Computer Espionage (Stoll 1989);
Cyberpunk: Outlaws and Hackers on the Computer Frontier (Hafner and Markoff 1991);
The Hacker Crackdown: Law and Disorder on the Electronic Frontier (Sterling 1992);
Approaching Zero: Data Crime and the Computer Underworld (Clough and Mungo 1992);
Takedown: The Pursuit and Capture of Kevin Mitnick the World's most Notorious Cybercriminal – by the Man who did it (Shimomura with Markoff 1995);
Masters of Deception: The Gang That Ruled Cyberspace (Quittner and Slatalla 1995);
The Fugitive Game: Online with Kevin Mitnick, the Inside Story of the Great Cyberchase (Littman 1996);
The Cyberthief and the Samurai: The True Story of Kevin Mitnick and the Man who Hunted him Down (Godell 1996);
Underground: Tales of Hacking, Madness and Obsession on the Electronic Frontier (Dreyfus 1997);
The Watchman: The Twisted Life and Crimes of Serial Hacker Kevin Poulsen (Littman 1997).

The movies

Various movies have used hacking for their subject matter including: *War Games*, *Sneakers*, *Die Hard II*, *The Net*, *Hackers* and *Johnny Mnemonic*. Whilst it is perhaps unsurprising that such a topical issue with particularly appealing subject matter (high technology, a subculture of apparently rebellious and anarchistic youths, the security of the nation, etc.) the movies' representations of hacking have had a disproportionately important influence upon the legislative response to the activity. Over-reliance upon fictional portrayals of hacking[9] by the authorities has contributed to helping to create a generally fearful and ignorant atmosphere surrounding computer security, which has in turn led to the charge to be fully analysed subsequently that hackers have become the victims of a somewhat hysterical witch-hunt:

Anti-hacker hysteria had gripped the nation in 1990. Huge law enforcement efforts had been mounted against illusory threats. In Washington DC ... a Congressional committee had been formally presented with the plot-line of a thriller movie – DIE HARD II, in which hacker terrorists seize an airport computer – as if this Hollywood fantasy posed a clear and present danger to the American republic. A similar hacker thriller, WAR GAMES, had been presented to Congress in the mid-1980s. Hysteria served no one's purposes, and created a stampede of foolish and unenforceable laws likely to do more harm than good.

(Sterling 1991: 6)

That fictional movie portrayals of hacking have assumed the status of fact for key members of the establishment has rather obvious and worrying implications given their fundamentally unrealistic nature:

A Hollywood thriller film about hackers – is very much part and parcel of the Hollywood thriller film tradition. Hollywood is not in the business of journalism or social analysis; Hollywood is in the mass entertainment business. I hope you wouldn't think that Hollywood gangsters or Hollywood cops bear much coherent resemblance to the quotidian daily lives of actual gangsters and actual cops. Nevertheless, cops go to cop films and gangsters go to gangster films, and sometimes gangsters (like George Raft) even become actors. Sometimes cops (like Joseph Wambaugh) become authors whose work is filmed. Criminals tend to be unrealistic and not very bright, so a lot of them have found compelling role models in deeply unrealistic screen portrayals of dashing, snappily-dressed criminals. Teenagers are also easily star-struck, so the film WAR GAMES was a major factor in the mid-80s boom of teenage computer-hacking. But to go to a typical hacker movie and think that the thrilling cyber-derring-do on the screen is a factual portrayal of the bleak, voyeuristic tedium of actual hacking – well, don't do that. It would be silly.

(Sterling: email interview)

Hackers themselves would seem to concur with Sterling's evaluation of the factual accuracy of hacker movies:

In the recent round of "Netsploitation" films, the worst offender was most likely *Hackers*. When we got the press photos we couldn't believe that Hollywood would actually think that hackers look like that. We have never seen any hacker on rollerblades. In fact, we have never seen a hacker break sweat.

(Newton undated: website)

1 *Them and us*

The hack

It is an interesting fact that most scientific research and speculation on deviance concerns itself with the people who break rules rather than with those who make and enforce them. If we are to achieve a full understanding of deviant behavior, we must get these two possible foci of inquiry into balance. We must see deviance, and the outsiders who personify the abstract conception, as a consequence of a process of interaction between people, some of whom in the service of their own interests make and enforce rules which catch others who, in the service of their own interests, have committed acts which are labelled deviant. ... It is, of course, possible to see the situation from both sides. But it cannot be done simultaneously. That is, we cannot construct a description of a situation or process that in some way fuses the perceptions and interpretations made by both parties involved in a process of deviance. We cannot describe a 'higher reality' that makes sense of both sets of views. We can describe the perspectives of one group and see how they mesh or fail to mesh with the perspectives of the other group: the perspectives of rule-breakers as they meet and conflict with the perspectives of those who enforce the rules, and vice versa. But we cannot understand the situation or process without giving full weight to the differences between the perspectives of the two groups involved.

(Becker 1963: 163, 173)

The key focus of this work is not just the computer underground in isolation, but rather upon the *them and us* conflictory relationship that exists between the computer security industry and the computer underground. In order to understand a social group labelled as *deviant* one needs to pay due attention to its ongoing interaction with those labelling it and not just attempt to research the group being labelled as deviant:

We can construct workable definitions either of particular actions people might commit or of particular categories of deviance as the world (especially, but not only, the authorities) defines them. But we cannot make the two coincide completely, because they do not do so empirically. They belong to two distinct, though overlapping, systems of collective action. One consists of the people who co-operate to produce that act in question. The other consists of the people who co-operate in the drama of morality by which 'wrongdoing' is discovered and dealt with, whether that procedure is formal or quite informal.

(Becker 1963: 185)

It is this conflict between the computer underground and those opposing groups who seek to stigmatise it as deviant that makes hackers an intriguing exemplar of how social practices dynamically emerge within technological environments.

The contested term

In its original technological sense, the word 'hacker', coined at MIT in the 1960s, simply connoted a computer virtuoso. That's still the meaning enshrined in the 1994 edition of the New Hacker's Dictionary, which defines such a person as someone 'who enjoys exploring the details of programmable systems and how to stretch their capabilities; one who programs enthusiastically, even obsessively'.

(Roush 1995: 1)

The word hack doesn't really have 69 different meanings. ... In fact, hack has only one meaning, an extremely subtle and profound one which defies articulation. Which connotation is implied by a given use of the word depends in similarly profound ways on context. ... Hacking might be characterized as 'an appropriate application of ingenuity'. Whether the result is a quick-and-dirty patchwork job or a carefully crafted work of art, you have to admire the cleverness that went into it. An important secondary meaning of hack is 'a creative practical joke'. This kind of hack is easier to explain to non-hackers than the programming kind. Of course, some hacks have both natures.[1]

Before looking in detail at the rhetorical conflicts that have occurred between hacking's supporters and opponents, we turn to the act itself and the semantic debate that surrounds it. I seek to highlight the slippery nature of the term and emphasise that there is no one single, uncontested description of hacking. The fact it has disputed meanings and connotations for different groups is addressed in terms of group boundary formation within computing. I trace the evolution in the meaning of the term and show it to be part of a complex social process in which certain computer users have become marginalised within the wider computing community. Whether such marginalisation is justified or not is perhaps a moot point given the potentially serious implications it may have for the computers that now saturate our society, an issue I will return to in the concluding chapter.

The meaning of the term, *hacking*, has gone through several changes from its original dictionary definition: of 'cut or chop roughly; mangle: cut (one's way) through thick foliage etc.: manage, cope with': to its present definition of: 'gain unauthorised access (to data in a computer)' [The Concise Oxford Dictionary, eighth edition]. It has also evolved from the MIT days of the 1950s onwards when it was first used in the context of computing. The phrase was originally used to denote the highly skilled but largely playful activity of academic computer programmers searching for the most elegant and concise programming solution to any given problem (Levy 1984). It has since been increasingly associated with its present-day connotation of illicit computer intrusion.

The origins of the phrase, *hacking*, relate to the problems encountered with programming the early cumbersome and huge computers such as the IBM 704, described by Levy as a 'hulking giant' (Levy 1984: 25). These valve-based machines were notoriously unreliable, a factor that, combined with the relative immaturity of programming methods, led to solutions to any particular computing problem being rather haphazardly constructed (thus meeting the phrase's first connotation of something being fashioned roughly: being *hacked together*). In addition, the baroque complexity and unmanageability of early software systems can also be associated with hacking's connotations of 'managing or coping with' and 'cutting through thick foliage'. The key themes from the various definitions of hacking relate to: exploration; obsession; and ingenuity/creativity. The potentially exploratory and obsessive elements of hacking are explored in the next chapter; at this point we will concentrate upon the ingenuity and creativity said to lie behind the bona fide hack.

The hack

> Bobby was a cowboy, and ice was the nature of his game, ice from ICE, Intrusion Countermeasures Electronics. The matrix is an abstract representation of the relationship between data systems. Legitimate programmers jack themselves into their employers' sector of the matrix and find themselves surrounded by bright geometrics representing the corporate data. Towers and fields of it ranged in the colorless nonspace of the simulation matrix, the electronic consensus-hallucination that facilitates the handling and exchange of massive quantities of data. Legitimate programmers never see the walls of ice they work behind, the walls of shadow that screen their operations from others, from industrial-espionage artists and hustlers like Bobby Quine. Bobby was a cowboy. Bobby was a cracksman, a burglar, casing mankind's extended electronic nervous system, rustling data and credit in the crowded matrix, monochrome nonspace where the only stars are dense concentrations of information.
>
> (Gibson 1986b: 197)

The basis of hacking culture is unsurprisingly 'the hack'. The hack did, and still does in various quarters, refer to the performing of a neat programming trick.

Despite its present predominant connotations of illicit computer break-ins, within hacking circles it is more widely defined as an attempt to make use of any technology in an original, unorthodox and inventive way. The main bone of contention in these differing interpretations is the extent to which the ingenuity of the hack should be made subordinate to its legality. Whilst this debate will be pursued in depth later, the hack is initially presented here in its widest sense in order to assess any potential commonality that may exist between all its illegal, mischievous and legitimately ingenious forms.

Turkle (1984) provides a thorough delineation of the main elements of hacking. She conflates the wider definition of illicit hacking with the general mentality of those who hack in its sense of seeking to manipulate any technology for unorthodox means. She refers to *the hack* as being: 'the holy grail. It is a concept which exists independently of the computer and can best be presented through an example using another technology complex enough to support its own version of hacking and hackers' (Turkle 1984: 232). The example she uses is that of phone-phreaking[2] and one of its main adherents, John Draper, alias *Captain Crunch*[3]. The hack, in this instance, refers to such technological stunts as having two phones on a table; talking into one and hearing your voice in the other after a time-delay in which the original call has first been routed around the world.

Turkle interpreted this type of hack in the following manner:

> Appreciating what made the call around the world a great hack is an exercise in hacker aesthetics. It has the quality of [a] magician's gesture: a truly surprising result produced with ridiculously simple means. Equally important: Crunch had not simply stumbled on a curiosity. The trick worked because Crunch had acquired an impressive amount of expertise about the telephone system. That is what made the trick a great hack, otherwise it would have been a very minor one. Mastery is of the essence everywhere within hacker culture. Third, the expertise was acquired unofficially and at the expense of a big system. The hacker is a person outside the system who is never excluded by its rules.
>
> (Turkle 1984: 232)

The main characteristics of a hack are thus:

1 **Simplicity**: the act has to be simple but impressive.
2 **Mastery**: the act involves sophisticated technical knowledge.
3 **Illicitness**: the act is 'against the rules'.

The ubiquitous hack and *the kick*

It is important to note that a key aspect of Turkle's analysis is the notion that the essential attributes of a hack can be found in relation to artefacts other than computers. In keeping with the perspective of some hackers she highlights the eclectic pragmatism with which hackers characteristically approach all technologies. Hacking has traditionally involved such diverse activities as lock-picking and model-railway maintenance (and the accompanying tinkering with gadgetry that this involves).[4] Hackers themselves express the wide range of their potential targets:

> In my day to day life, I find myself hacking everything imaginable. I hack traffic lights, pay phones, answering machines, micro-wave ovens, VCR's, you name it, without even thinking twice. To me hacking is just changing the conditions over and over again until there's a different response. In today's mechanical world, the opportunities for this kind of experimentation are endless.
>
> (Kane 1989: 67–9)

The heterogeneous range of technological targets considered 'hackable' is described by R., a Dutch hacker, who argued that hacking is not just about computer break-ins but should be defined so that it does not:

> only pertain to computers but pertains to any field of technology. Like, if you haven't got a kettle to boil water with and you use your coffee machine to boil water with, then that in my mind is a hack. Because you're using the technology in a way that it's not supposed to be used. Now that also pertains to telephones, if you're going to use your telephone to do various things that aren't supposed to be done with a telephone, then that's a hack. If you are going to use your skills as a car mechanic to make your motor do things it's not supposed to be doing, then that's a hack. So, for me it's not only computers it's anything varying from locks, computers, telephones, magnetic cards, you name it.
>
> (R., Utrecht interview)

Hackers' brushes with the criminal system have led to vivid illustrations of the ubiquitous nature of their activity and the extent to which it consists of an ability to adapt to the circumstances one finds oneself in. There is, for example, Kevin Poulsen's account of his time in prison:

> 'I've learned a lot from my new neighbors', Poulsen, the quintessential cyberpunk ... who describes hacking as performance art, said from behind the glass of the maximum security visitor's window. 'Now I know how to light a cigarette from an outlet and how to make methamphetamine from chicken stock'.
>
> (Fine 1995: website)

The phone network was the archetypal system for the early precursors of hackers, the *phone-phreaks*, the Internet providing the next complex technical system ripe for exploration. In addition to such examples of hands-on hacking, which involve ingenious manipulations of whatever artefacts are at hand, hacking can also refer more abstractly to the 'system' one is confronted with. A US hacker using the sobriquet, *Agent Steal*, for example, published an article from Federal Prison entitled: 'Everything a hacker needs to know about getting busted by the feds', the theme of which centres around the notion that the legal system, like any other system, is there to be hacked:

> The criminal justice system is a game to be played, both by prosecution and defense. And if you have to be a player, you would be wise to learn the rules of engagement. The writer and contributors of this file have learned the hard way. As a result we turned our hacking skills during the times of our incarceration towards the study of criminal law and, ultimately, survival. Having filed our own motions, written our own briefs and endured life in prison, we now pass this knowledge back to the hacker community. Learn from our experiences ... and our mistakes.
>
> (Petersen 1997: website)

Two Dutch hackers, Rop Gongrijp[5] and M.,[6] in relating some of their activities illustrate how broad the desire to technologically explore can be. M. claimed to have physically explored the subterranean tunnels and elevator shafts of Amsterdam including Government nuclear fall-out shelters (Utrecht interview). Gongrijp, similarly, related how he had entered the out-of-bounds areas of buildings such as banks by pretending to accompany legitimate tour groups and then took the first opportunity to wander off on his own, assessing the security of the site and then somewhat cheekily informing the security staff of that assessment. The 'technology', which is the subject of their curiosity in these cases, simply being the architecture and security features of buildings that they found interesting. Gongrijp described in a further example of the heterogeneity of hacking, how 'the Wageningen agricultural university a couple of years ago had a couple of students doing a project enhancing the genes of marijuana plants, to me that's gene-hacking, it's more than science, it's just somebody gets a kick out of it'.[7] He argued that hacking is a frame of mind, a sort of intellectual curiosity that attaches itself to more than just one type of technology or technological artefact: 'for me a hacker is more all-round than to some people, I think a hacker is not a real hacker unless he has a basis in two or three skills, not just hacking Unix systems but also a little bit of something else, electronics, audio hacking or something general' (Amsterdam interview).

This heterogeneity of hacking's targets fuels *the kick* gained from satisfying the primary urge of technological curiosity:

> in the early days of say the uses of electricity and how to generate it, were first developed, I think Tesla and all the people who were playing with it then were as much hackers as most computer hackers are now, they are

playing on the frontier of technology and all those hefty experiments were not only done for science, they were done because they got a kick out of it.

(Gongrijp: Amsterdam interview)

The *kick*, thus gained, crucially depends upon an element of inventiveness that serves to distinguish 'true' hacks from those that could be labelled as acts of *Nintendo Perseverance*, that is to say, hacks who exhibit large amounts of concentration and dedication rather than ingenuity. Methods of hacking entry may become widely publicised by means of the various branches of the hacker grapevine, for example, electronic and paper-based specialist magazines, or even word-of-electronic-mouth. From such sources, hacking 'cook-books' of prepackaged instructions result. Those that predominantly, or exclusively, use such sources of information for the illicit use of a technology could be labelled hackers since they fulfil the main requirement of the pejorative definition of hacking: the illicit use of a technology. The Dutch hackers I spoke with, however, were keen to differentiate themselves from such people, by imparting their concept similar to Turkle's description of the Holy Grail type hack.

Using the example of phone-phreaking phone calls Gongrijp illustrates this distinction between a technical and a 'true' hack:

it depends on how you do it, the thing is that you've got your guys that think up these things, they consider the technological elements of a phone-booth, and they think, 'hey, wait a minute, if I do this, this could work', so as an experiment, they cut the wire and it works, now THEY'RE hackers. Okay, so it's been published, so Joe Bloggs reads this and says, 'hey, great, I have to phone my folks up in Australia', so he goes out, cuts the wire, makes phone calls, leaves it regardless. He's a stupid ignoramus, yeah? The second situation is another hacker reads this and thinks, 'hey, this is an idea, let's expand on this'. So what he does is go to a phone box, he cuts the wire, puts a magnetic switch in between, puts the magnetic switch up against the case, closes the door again and whenever he wants to make a free phone call, he puts a magnet on top, makes the wires disconnect, and he has a free phone call, goes away, takes the magnet away and everybody else has to pay. Now he's more of a hacker straight away, it's not a simple black and white thing.

(Gongrijp: Utrecht interview)

Chris Goggans, a US hacker, makes a distinction between hackers and what he terms computer criminals. He says:

People have been trying to come up with these 'hacker-cracker knick-knack paddywacker' tags, but here's the difference: a hacker is someone who is interested in computer systems and networks and wants to take them to whatever possible reach they can go. A cracker is someone who breaks software copy protection.

(Goggans: email interview)

A computer criminal, meanwhile, at least according to one definition has a 'specific goal of targeting someone's mail or research, or going after other information considered proprietary' (Lange 1996: 3). Thus in the definition favoured by self-styled 'real' hackers a true hack should involve an element of originality reflected in the unorthodox subversion of any given technical situation. There are various forms a hack can take, and a hacker tends to be defined not just by what he does but by how he does it. Gongrijp, for example, mischievously pointed out to me, as we walked through an Amsterdam housing estate, startlingly vivid yellow paint on road over-pass supports. He explained that it was indelible anti-graffiti paint and observed wryly that people could cause havoc if they used such paint for graffiti purposes (Amsterdam interview).

Criminal activities of hackers

Alongside the more contestable categories of hacking activity with their own purported ethic and *kick* there are some more straightforwardly criminal variants of technological endeavour that should perhaps be acknowledged early on. Whilst most of the emphasis placed upon criminal types of motivation for hacking comes from figures within the computer security industry, conventional criminality was also recognised by several of the hackers I spoke to, one of whom, D., whilst claiming it was only to see if it could be done, demonstrated on the table of the café in which the interview took place his prototype magnetic credit-card copier:

> By the way, this is the card-copier, I'm proud of it. [So what does it copy?] Everything. [Everything with a magnetic strip?] Yeah, I'll let you hear how a credit-card sounds, the trick is you take two cards, you slide them through here at the same time, yeah well it gives the same sound but then it copies from this one to this one, you can also use this for credit cards, there's a different sound, I can hear what kind of card it is through the ear-phones.
>
> (D.: Utrecht interview)

Similarly, whilst interviewing at a hacker group's flat in Amsterdam I was also shown their latest prototype touch-tone dialler that they were in the process of miniaturising further, and which was being used as a means of phreaking free phone calls by emulating electronically the switching tones of the international digital phone systems:

> Well, I can show you something, this device, this chip, is also available in a very small package, it will fit into this whole thing [a small touch-tone dialler case]. This whole prototype will be in here [large sandwich board of electronics], he [a colleague] is working on the board now. What this basically does is, it's a touch-tone dialler that has extra features which mean you can make tones which are called C5 to control the phone system and to tell phone switches in other countries that they should complete calls without

charging you for it, so with this system you can make free phone calls, and it's all going to be in a little dialler this big, it's pretty nifty … you can have it make these tones and try things at different times, there's all these protocols for in-band telephone signalling in there, it's fully programmable. … We make our phone calls with this type of technology so it doesn't cost anything.

(G.: Amsterdam interview)

Whereas G. and his colleagues were not, or would not admit to being, interested in the potential commercial aspects of this activity, D. was much more forthcoming. When I asked him about monetary reward being a possible motivating factor behind hacking, he related how:

A friend of my brother … is only concerned with the money he gets for it, [and] all kinds of schemes he has to make things. Free phone calls, there's a lot of business in it. They sell cards, copy cards and things like that. Car phones: they change the chip with the ID of the car phone, things like that.

(D.: Utrecht interview)

He then proceeded to give more details of his own personal involvement in a scheme aimed at funding an excessively large phone bill that had been accumulated as a product of his hacking exploits:

The first system we attacked was the Spanish telephone system, it was about seven years ago, we didn't have a meter to check the costs, later we found that when we called Spain, there was one special tone which activated the computer and we had a phone bill of 10,000 guilders, so we made little boxes, blue boxes, and me and my brother went to Spain with the boxes. Well, we first sent the taxi driver to pick up the boxes and then waited to see if the taxi driver came back without the police and then we took the boxes and sold them to all kinds of people, dealers of cars and such like, it was very hard to deal with the Spanish people because they can't get money from the banks very easily, they have to show where the money is going, per box we asked 1,500 guilders, so after ten boxes we paid the bill and got back to Holland.

(D.: Utrecht interview)

D. believes that there is the possibility that hacking expertise will become more widely used by criminal elements in society:

If you keep it illegal then I think in the future there will be more people who will be interested in it, really malicious people, right now there aren't so many people who want to sell it to espionage or companies or whatever, but I think in the future there will be more people, you always see people who are interested but they don't have the means to hack themselves. There was a hackers' party, the 'galactic hackers' party' in Amsterdam and we were trying to make free phone calls and always someone behind you, some foreigner from Egypt 'free phone calls, free phone calls'. The only thing he could say in Dutch was 'free phone calls', and they offer a lot of money to make free phone calls and stuff: often companies if they want to know something else about other companies – like a friend of mine had an account that would check out all companies, they were offered money to check out other companies but when they wouldn't do it, they would get in trouble.

(D.: Utrecht interview)

R., another Dutch hacker, also gave his perspective on monetary-induced hacking. In an attempt to quantify a perhaps inevitably vague area, I asked him to give me a percentage figure for the number of hackers that hack for monetary gain, he replied:

No, you can't say it in percentage, I'd guess it's about five persons in the whole of Holland that do it for the money. For instance I had a hack and somebody wanted to publish it, he gave me money for it. Now, did I do it for the money? No, not initially, initially I did it for the kick, not because it was illegal but for the kick. Okay, so I earned a little money with it, big deal, I didn't do it for the money, and another reason is convenience, pure convenience. It is very convenient if you can make free phone calls, it is absolutely convenient if you can pull copies off magnetic cards, it is very easy if you can get your TV at home without a de-scrambler, things like that. And it's not a kick, it's not a thrill, it's not that it's illegal, it's just pure convenience.

(R.: Utrecht interview)

One group in the early 1990s that was much more criminal-minded, and recognised as such by G., D. and R., were known as the *Amiga Kids*, after the computers they used most. When discussing viruses D. described how:

There are a lot of viruses in the Amiga world. That's one of the groups they have to get rid of, the Amiga Kids, that's a real pain in the arse. Also for hackers, if we hack a system and they find out about it, like making free phone calls, they spread it. It's incredible, those guys are really destructive, because when they use something they use it for software, we use it occasionally for hacking or making calls but they use it twenty-four hours a day for software, they'll do anything for software, they use and abuse credit cards and things like that. Anything for software, and a few of them, I know, are the ones that write viruses to combat other groups, to put viruses in the programs of other groups, I hate those guys. Yeah, here in Utrecht there are a lot of these groups and they card a lot of stuff, you know carding? Using credit cards to get stuff, but illegally. They wear Rolexes, little kids on the street with Rolexes around their wrists it's incredible.

(D.: Utrecht interview)

Whilst the hackers that formed the basis of this study were at pains to disassociate themselves from such groups, they recognised the potential for hacking-related activities to branch into criminal activity. A hacker called Maelstrom related how:

> In 1989 a local friend put up a world headquarters BBS for the West German group Red Sector Inc. They were into writing Amiga demos, and were one of the top ten groups in the world, which got us a lot of interesting and well-known callers. We obtained a voice mailbox and put up a codeline on it, which was very popular for a long time. RSI made me an offer: if I would give them stolen AT&T calling-card numbers to enable them to call the USA, they give me all the hardware I needed to have the ultimate computer system. I was offered computers, high-speed modems, hard drives, and software ... the only catch was their method. Using CBI or TRW's computer, some people use credit-card numbers to steal merchandise, and by having stolen stuff sent to West Germany, they were able to escape detection when the theft was discovered since the post office there didn't keep records. This was against my morals, and I dropped out of the scene for a while.
>
> (Maelstrom: email interview)

Finally, for obvious reasons, it was difficult to look in any depth at hacking conducted solely for criminal or monetary purposes, or even to check the absolute validity of claims such as D.'s above. What I did see of the above instances seemed to be real methods of fraud, and the hackers I spoke with, with the exception of the Zoetermeer group, all had knowledge of each other and seemed to verify each other's claims and accounts. Hacking with criminal intent or for monetary gain of some sort appeared, from my interviews in Holland at least, to be conducted on the fringes/margins of mainstream hacking and then only in order to fund their activity rather than for express monetary gain. The pressure to commercialise their activity may, however, be increasing as techniques become more widely desired by traditional criminal groups.

2 Hacking culture

The hacking generations

> The 'original' hackers were computer professionals who, in the mid-sixties, adopted the word 'hack' as a synonym for computer work, and particularly for computer work executed with a certain level of craftmanship. ... Then in the seventies, assorted techno-hippies emerged as the computerized faction of the counterculture of the day. ... What characterized the second wave hackers was that they desperately wanted computers and computer systems designed to be useful and accessible to citizens. ... Finally, in the second half of the eighties the so-called cu emerged, appropriated the terms 'hacker' and 'hacking' and partly changed their meaning. To the computer underground, 'to hack' meant to break into or sabotage a computer system, and a 'hacker' was the perpetrator of such activities.
>
> (Hannemyr 1997: 2)

In the most seminal piece of work on hackers to date Levy (1984) describes three generations of hackers who exhibited to various degrees qualities associated with the hacking's original connotation of playful ingenuity epitomised by the earliest hackers, the pioneering computer *aficionados* at MIT's laboratories in the 1950s and 1960s. These *aficionados* formed the first generation of hackers defined as those who were involved in the development of the earliest computer-programming techniques. The second generation are defined as those involved in bringing computer hardware to the masses with the development of the earliest PCs. The third generation refers to the programmers who became the leading lights in the advent of computer games architecture. The phrase *hacker* is now almost exclusively used to describe an addition to this schema: the fourth generation of hackers who illicitly access other people's computers.

To the fourth generation of hackers can also arguably be added a new group: the *microserfs* identified by Douglas Coupland in his novel of the same name.[1] This generation represents the co-optation of hacker skills by commercial computing. Whilst there were still elements of this commercial acumen in hacking's second and third generations, they kept the positive connotations of the hacker sobriquet because their activity still retained the pioneering qualities and associated romanticism of ground-breaking technological endeavour.[2] *Microserfs*, in contrast, are portrayed as having had their ingenuity subordinated to the requirements of advanced capitalism in the form of the Microsoft corporation.

This study predominantly concentrates upon the fourth generation, who are now vilified by the Establishment, but who claim to represent a continuation of hacking's original values. The first generation of hackers was active in the development of the earliest software; the fourth generation have been criminalised by the passage of anti-hacking legislation. This evolution in the perception of hacking from being largely positive to predominantly negative within both computing and society at large is explained in this study with reference to a process of boundary formation and stigmatisation. It accounts for the public's worsening perception of hackers despite claims that the fourth generation share some important attributes with their antecedent generations:

> it should be noted that the ... hacking communities are not completely disjunct. The hacker of the sixties was not beyond appreciating lock-picking skills, both those addressing physical locks barring access to computer rooms, and software protection schemes such as password files and encryption schemes, and he also believed that information was born to be free – including the source code he had written and the knowledge he had about the inner workings of various systems. ... As far as politics go: Today's generation-x anarchist hackers share with their artisan and activist hacker predecessors a distrust in authority, a libertarian attitude and a tendency to position themselves outside bourgeoisie society's norms and values.
>
> (Hannemyr 1997: 2)

Hacking's decline in social acceptability is obviously the result of the predominance of a largely negative and hawkish attitude to hacking over a more ameliatory and dovish response. Contained within this general move towards more hawkish attitudes, however, lie internal conflicts both within the computer security industry and the hacking community. Whilst this study predominantly concentrates upon the internal conflict that exists within the computer security industry, there is also evidence of conflicts within the computer underground.

The hacker ethic and internal boundary formation

> In the middle of Stanford University there is a large concrete-and-glass building filled with computer terminals. ... If you go further inside, you can discover the true addicts: the members of the Establishment. These are the people who spend their lives with computers and fellow 'hackers'. These are the members of a subculture so foreign to most outsiders that it not only walls itself off but is walled off, in turn, by those who cannot understand it. The wall is built from both sides at once.
>
> (Zimbardo 1980: website)

Fuelling the hack and setting the ideal standard of hacking morality within the culture of hacking is the ethos of the first generation of early MIT hackers. Its main tenet was: 'Access to computers – and anything which might teach you something about the way the world works – should be unlimited and total. Always yield to the Hands-On imperative!' (Levy, 1984: 40).

More specific elements of this hacker ethic consist of the following five points:

1 'All information should be free.'
2 'Mistrust Authority – Promote Decentralisation.'
3 'Hackers should be judged by their hacking, not by bogus criteria such as degrees, age, race, or position.'
4 'You can create art and beauty on a computer.'
5 'Computers can change your life for the better.'

(Levy 1984: 40–5)

An illustration of the hacker ethic is provided by a group set up in 1982 and who called themselves the *Inner Circle*, an élite group of hackers who sought to trade information amongst themselves without passing it on to less ethical hackers liable to use it for nefarious ends. The need for such a group had arisen due to the huge increase in the amount of hackers at this time, itself attributable to the increased diffusion of personal computers. Typically for hackers and the informal nature of their culture, whilst claiming to be an ethical group, no attempt was made to formally draw up a specific code of behaviour. If such an attempt had been made, the leader Bill Landreth argued it would have been as follows:

> No Inner Circle member will ever delete or damage information that belongs to a legitimate user of the system in any way that the member cannot easily correct himself. No member will leave another hacker's name or phone number on any computer system. He will leave his own on a system only at his own risk. All members are expected to obtain and contribute their own account information, rather than use only information given to them by other members.
>
> (Landreth 1985: 18–19)

The most important underlying principle behind this purported code of behaviour was respect for other people's property and information: 'We were explorers, not spies, and to us, damaging computer files was not only clumsy and inelegant – it was wrong' (Landreth 1985: 19). In later chapters we will examine the accusations that hackers are actively excluded from mainstream influence within computing. We can see even at this early stage, however, that whether hackers are unfairly stigmatised by society at large or not, the ethos of groups such as the Inner Circle indicates that they operate their own set of ethical and aesthetic values, which serve to differentiate for hackers a perceived difference between 'real' hackers and the 'wannabes'. Boundary formation often takes the form of clear differentiations between 'good' and 'bad' hacking activities. A specific example is provided by the following disparaging comment upon a spate of 'email bombings' by a character known as the 'Unamailer':

> The annoying thing is that these vandals are really not using any real skills to accomplish these feats. It's the equivalent of speed-dialling a phone number over and over – very aggravating but uninspired. ... It is a shame today's batch of hackers have taken such a foul turn – tarnishing the image of what was once a great hobby to many of today's major players in the industry. Today's hackers are even worse than the virus writers, who at least have enough talent to impress us with mutating engines. Email bombing and ISP spoofing reminds me of the joke where a kid calls you in the middle of the night and asks you if your refrigerator is running. You are supposed to reply, 'I think so' and they respond, 'Well, you better go catch it'. Anyone can play the joke (or email bomb or ISP spoof), but only kids do it.
>
> (Baker 1995: website)

I saw a similar mode of group differentiation practised by the Dutch hackers who privileged those who demonstrate originality over perseverance and/or the unimaginative copying of other people's techniques.

The community of hackers

> Cultures have (1) Technology (2) Institutions (3) Language (4) Arts. By this measure, what is 'Catholic Culture'? It is heavy on Institution and weak on Technology. Hacker Culture is obviously very technological. Hacker Language is based on jargon that separates it from mainstream English.[3] Hacker Arts would be centred on Star Trek and fractals. But you would be hard-pressed to find a reason for saying that Classical or Electronic New Age Music is 'hacker' since some probably enjoy Rap far more.
>
> (Marotta: email interview)

The main and most obvious point to be made about hacker culture is its dependence upon technology. Much more than this is difficult to describe uncontentiously; descriptions of what constitutes the computer underground are inevitably subjective.[4] This is because it is difficult to readily identify an obviously structured group acting as a computer underground culture in an open fashion. Analysis is further complicated by the fact that whatever the 'culture' of the computer underground is, it exists in a non-traditional computer-mediated environment widely known as cyberspace and which has a lack of the basic physicality we commonsensically associate with our more conventional day-to-day cultural interactions:

To find "Hacker Culture" you have to take a very wide view of the cyberspace terrain and watch the interactions among physically diversified people who have in common a mania for machines and software. What you will find will be a gossamer framework of culture. Come back in 100 years and you may see more.

(Marotta: email interview)

Given these difficulties, this book explores hacking's 'gossamer framework of culture', developing its two primary underpinning aspects: the hack and the hacker ethic. From these fundamental elements of hacking has sprung what is difficult to define unequivocally, but what is generally recognised as a hacking culture.

Hacking culture: specific elements

Given the various difficulties faced when trying to define 'hacking culture', the following help to make up a picture painted with broad brush strokes.

Technology content

Hacking culture is epitomised by its easy relationship with technology. For the first time, a new generation of young people are growing up completely at home with computers and their capabilities:

What we are confronted with is a generation that has lived with computers virtually from the cradle, and therefore have no trace of fear, not even a trace of reverence. To me, a computer is still, well, something to be revered. When I started my career in computing, there wasn't really computing at that time ... there were about three of them, you had one shot at a run a day if you were lucky. It was sacrosanct, it no longer is to those kids, you go in, have a bash at the keyboard, they're convinced by experience that nothing much can go wrong.

(Herschberg: Delft University interview)

We have already seen how a crucial element of hacking resides in the innate curiosity with which hackers approach a diverse range of technological artefacts. Such a quality has existed throughout history, but the mass diffusion of computing and telecommunication equipment has meant that curiosity can more easily utilise technological artefacts for purposes, or by people, not originally intended in the initial design of the objects. The advent of cyberspace has created the conditions necessary for co-operation between previously geographically dispersed (and hence isolated) yet technologically adept and curious people.

The secrecy and fluidity of hacker culture

> There is no organized structure in the computer underworld, no mysterious chairman of the board to run things. The underground is anarchic, a confederation of phreakers/hackers and virus writers from all over the world whose common interests transcend culture or language. Most hackers have two or three handles and operate on a number of boards. They change ID's, aliases, sites, their methods, targets and gang membership as rapidly as the authorities track them. Stamping out hacking is like trying to pin down mercury.
>
> (Clough and Mungo 1992: 18)

Due to its illegal nature, a major characteristic of hacking is its secrecy. This causes obvious difficulties for any attempt at describing its culture; for example, its true size is largely unknown and even if a snap-shot figure could be obtained, the community has fluid boundaries, its loosely structured environment evolving and mutating rapidly:

> People come and go pretty often, and if you lay off for a few months and then come back, almost everyone is new. There are always those who have been around for years, but you can weed out the amateurs by comparing two lists of names acquired several months apart from each other. ... I would consider the hacker community a very informal one. It is pretty much anarchy as far as rule-making goes. The hacker ethic is not always applied, unfortunately (and that's why hacking has such a bad name). The community was structured only within the framework of different hacking 'groups'. Legion of Doom would be one example of this. A group creates its own rules, and usually doesn't have a leader. ... The groups I've been in have voted on accepting new members, kicking people out, etc.
>
> (Goggans: email interview)

Commentators from both the computer underground and its opponents in the computer security industry tend to rely upon educated *guestimates*:

> Some professional informants ... have estimated the hacker population as high as fifty thousand. This is likely highly inflated, unless one counts every single teenage software pirate and petty phone-booth thief. My best guess is about five thousand people. Of these, I would guess that as few as a hundred are truly 'elite' – active computer intruders, skilled enough to penetrate sophisticated systems and truly to worry computer security and law enforcement.
>
> (Sterling 1992: 77)

The following description given by Robert Schifreen, a 'reformed' UK hacker[5] helps to account for some of the very practical difficulties in drawing a detailed picture of hacking culture. He described the immediate impact on his local hacking group when he related how recent legislation appeared to have forced hackers underground:

> There used to be a hacking community in the UK, the hackers I used to deal with 8 or 9 years ago, were all based in North London where I used to live and there were 12 of us around the table at the local Chinese restaurant of a Friday night, talking about lots of things and getting through lots of Diet Coke ... within about 20 minutes of me and my colleague Steve Gold being arrested: end of hacking community. An awful lot of phone calls went round, a lot of discs got buried in the garden, and a lot of people became ex-hackers and there's really no-one who'll talk now, it's difficult.
>
> (Schifreen: London Interview)

An example of this suspicious and anxious atmosphere was provided by Mofo, a hacker I encountered via email, who since he was using somebody else's account adopted his pseudonym as a precaution against identification. He asked me to: 'Tell me more about yourself, but wait about a week to respond as I use this account only with the "permission" of the real owner and login only occasionally. I login on this account very infrequently as I do not want to get the rightful owner any undue attention' (Mofo: email interview). He proceeded to describe in the following manner, his views and interpretation of the significance of the actions of Robert Morris jr.:[6]

> BTW, I think that you might be interested to know that I and many others have used the UNIX sendmail bug to access many, many systems throughout the world (without damaging data in any way) until that stupendous asshole, Robert Morris, royally phucked everything up for us. I've known about the print f () sendmail bug ever since I got access to source. Only a dummy would publicize something as good as that by doing something completely phucking stoopid like what Morris did. His idiocy cost hackers/phreakers more than anyone can imagine.
>
> (Mofo: email interview)

Mofo's words vividly portray how 'true' hackers depend upon secrecy and trust each other not to act in any way that might incur a clamp-down from the law enforcement agencies. It also illuminates part of the process whereby hackers differentiate amongst themselves between those who pursue hacker ethics in secrecy and those that clumsily blow their cover. Fear of establishment clamp-downs has thus acted as cultural binding agent for those on the margins of mainstream computing. On an official level, it has led to the formation of such representative bodies as the Electronic Frontier Foundation (EFF), whilst further underground, the antipathy caused by the perceived over-reaction of various agencies to computer underground activity has led to increased feelings of 'them against us' and more secrecy.

During the late 1980s and early 1990s there was a series of 'crackdowns' in the form of legislation and arrests by Secret Services/Police forces.[7] Sources, such as the *Computer Underground Digest* (*CuD*), have repeatedly drawn attention to the belief, commonly held within the underground community, that the establishment has been guilty of paranoia and over-reaction in their pursuit of hackers. The stereotypically portrayed image is that of secret-service men raiding adolescent, bespectacled hackers' homes with guns drawn. Such operations are known as 'stings' and have such colourful names as 'Operation Sun Devil'. The establishment's reaction also takes less dramatic forms. I was informed by a Dutch programmer that one of the Dutch hackers interviewed as part of this study was under surveillance by the security services, and Schifreen describes how he came to give up hacking after having had his equipment seized by the police at the start of their investigations into his hacking activity:

> When I got it back, I'd sort of lost the inclination and I was sort of scared as well, because when you're on bail, it's not a good idea to carry on doing it. Plus the fact that it's pretty certain that my phone was being tapped.
>
> (Schifreen: London interview)

Disembodied anonymity

> In many ways, the world of cyberspace is more real than the real world itself. I say this because it is only within the virtual world that people are really free to be themselves – to speak without fear of reprisal, to be anonymous if they so choose, to participate in a dialogue where one is judged by the merits of their words, not the colour of their skin or the timbre of their voice. Contrast this to the 'real' world where we often have people sized up before they even utter a word.
>
> (Goldstein 1993)

Part of the hacker ethic is the assertion that 'Hackers should be judged by their hacking, not by bogus criteria such as degrees, age, race, or position' (Levy 1984: 43). The egalitarianism of such a principle within the hacker culture is aided by the non-physical[8] nature of computer communication, which generally fails to differentiate on the basis of conventional social hierarchies:

> power and prestige are communicated neither contextually (the way secretaries and meeting rooms and clothes communicate) nor dynamically (the way gaze, touch, and facial and paralinguistic behaviour communicate; Edinger and Patterson, 1983). Thus charismatic and high status people may have less influence, and group members may participate more equally in computer communication.
>
> (Dunlop and Kling 1992: 334)

Stemming from the disembodied characteristics of computer-mediated communication (CMC), email correspondence generally has a de-personalised quality; the reception of an email message occurs without any accompanying indicators. Even with non-interactive and inanimate means of communication such as traditional letters, important information can be transmitted from aspects such as the letterhead. Email, in contrast, is blind as to the social position or mood of the sender, which would normally be conveyed by facial expressions and general demeanour. The experience of the French introduction of the *Minitel* chat system,[9] is one *risqué* and vivid illustration of the way in which the status-stripping qualities of email can reduce traditional social barriers and people's expressive inhibitions.

A less positive aspect of this blindness to normal social cues is the tendency of many emailers to drop some of the conventions and propriety that are normally expected in more traditional forms of communication. *Flaming* is a term used to describe the particularly vituperative tirades of insults that can result when an email discussion or disagreement becomes heated. The anonymity it produces also means that 'exploration' by hackers may make them slow to accept moral responsibility for their actions.[10] It is shown later when we discuss hacking and gender issues that such anonymity may play a large part in producing the 'locker room atmosphere', which is claimed to intimidate female users and deter them from playing a full part in the culture of the computer underground. Anonymity also has important effects upon the nature of officialdom's response to the computer underground and its activities, tending to exacerbate perceptions of its threat thereby increasing its underground status. The least that can be said is that the anonymity of cyberspace allows people to adopt vague identities and that hackers were some of the earliest electronic revellers to make use of this property.

Youth, the generation gap and the seeds of antipathy

He was twenty-eight, Bobby, and that's old for a console cowboy.

(Gibson 1986b: 197)

Poor Agent Baxter didn't know a ROM chip from a Vise-grip when he arrived. ... You know things have rather jumped the groove when potential suspects must explain to law enforcers the nature of their alleged perpetrations ... he took to ... saying 'My eight year old knows more about these things than I do.' He didn't say this with a father's pride so much as an immigrant's fear of a strange new land into which he will be forcibly moved and in which his own child is a native. He looked across my keyboard into Cyberspace and didn't like what he saw.

(Barlow 1990: 53–4)

A significant issue affecting the hacking community and other groups is the issue of age. Hackers I interviewed who were in their mid-twenties complained of the fact that they were viewed as has-beens by the constantly replenishing stock of new younger hackers and those most vocal in their opposition to the computer underground are of an overwhelmingly older generation. For the first time, a new generation of young people are growing up completely at home with computers and their capabilities.

The generation gap and the misunderstandings and antipathies it gives rise to provides a major impetus for the stigmatisation of the computer underground by its opponents, one manifestation of which is vividly described by John Perry Barlow in 'Crime and puzzlement'. The hacking community, having grown up with computers almost 'from the cradle', stands in opposition to law enforcers largely ignorant of computing. Ignorance in turn leads to mystification of the opponent; for example, in Barlow's dealings with hackers he described how:

> I have since learned that while getting someone's TRW file is fairly trivial, changing it is not. But at that time, my assessment of the crackers' black skills was one of superstitious awe. They were digital brujos about to zombify my economic soul.
>
> (Barlow 1990: 47)

Barlow proceeds to describe the implications of such fear and ignorance when it emanates from the establishment. He was interviewed by an FBI agent, Agent Baxter, in connection with the 'stealing' by a hacker of proprietary Apple Macintosh source code on behalf of a group opposing the commodification of software: the Nu Prometheus League. Agent Baxter's lack of knowledge was typified by his frequent references to the 'Nu Prosthesis League'.

Hacking culture and gender: the unexplained statistic

> A hallmark of the event [Hack-Tic computer club's 1993 Summer Conference] was the male to female ratio: running at roughly 100:1, it did not bode well for the demise of the anorak. Even so there was some emergence of a hacker chic, with one of the few women sporting jewellery made from watch parts and hair decoration courtesy of an eviscerated floppy disk.
>
> (Goodwins 1993: 11)

> Not that many women frequent the underground, and most that do come into it as transients while they are dating a hacker or as press to do a one-time story. On IRC, about two dozen women hang out with hackers regularly; I'd imagine three times that many go to 2600 meetings or to Cons but do not frequent IRC. I have met more than a thousand male hackers in person but less than a dozen of the women.
>
> (Gilboa 1996: 106)

This section looks at the possible reasons for hacking's gender bias, and thereby introduces the next chapter's theme of the motivations lying behind hacking.

Faced with the above difficulties of establishing a coherent hacker culture, one characteristic that does stand out is the male dominance of the activity. Examples of women, active in or at least associated with related activities, are: Susan Thunder, an associate of Kevin Mitnick, described in *Cyberpunk*; during an American radio phone-in programme on hacking,[11] a woman called Anna proclaimed herself to be a phone-phreak; and in *Approaching Zero* the authors describe how:

> Leslie Lynne Doucette was once described as the 'female Fagin' of the computer underworld. In her mid-thirties, she was considerably older than the 150 or so adolescent Olivers she gathered into her ring. As a woman, she has the distinction of being one of only two or three female hackers who have ever come to the attention of the authorities.
>
> (Clough and Mungo 1992: 148)

Keller states that:

> In the course of a career in computing which spans 20 years in industry and academia in the United States and Great Britain I have met several people I would call *hackers* ... I have never met a female hacker. No one I know with whom I have discussed hacking can recall an instance of meeting or hearing of a female hacker. ... [and in a footnote] The *Hacker's Handbook, 3rd Edition* mentions one, but at one point puts *she* in quotes, as though to denote irony or uncertainty about that particular hacker's true gender.
>
> (Keller 1990: 57)

There are arguably three main factors that discourage women from computing and that cause it to be, in general, a largely male-dominated environment:[12]

1　Societal factors – e.g. the sexual stereotyping of young children, where boys are given technical playthings whilst girls are given cuddly toys and plastic tea-sets.
2　The masculine environment – computer science is dominated by men and therefore this creates a general 'locker room' climate in which women feel threatened or uncomfortable.
3　Gender in language – the male gender bias in the language used in computer science reinforces points 1 and 2. Even if the above reasons for the minority status of women within computer science are accepted, there are still sufficient numbers of women with computing qualifications to suggest that statistically one would expect the existence of a much greater number of female hackers. For example, in the US in 1991, 'women received a third of the bachelor's degrees in computer science, 27% of master's degrees, and 13% of PhDs' (Spertus 1991: i)

The unexplained statistic

Societal factors

The people I interviewed for this book found it difficult to provide conclusive arguments for the general absence of female hackers. They identified several possible reasons, such as general social trends that discouraged women from computing, but not the claim that hacker environments were threatening, misogynous environments. Often such social explanations were conflated with tentative views that women are somehow psychologically less likely to have the qualities required to make good hackers. Males are said to exhibit tendencies towards 'hard mastery' and females tend towards 'soft mastery':

> Hard mastery is the imposition of will over the machine through the implementation of a plan. ... Soft mastery is more interactive ... try this, wait for a response, try something else, let the overall shape emerge from interaction with the medium. It is more like a conversation than a monologue.
>
> (Turkle 1984: 102–3)

Whilst men tend to be overwhelmingly 'hard masters', females are generally 'soft masters':

> In our culture girls are taught the characteristics of soft mastery – negotiation, compromise, give-and-take – as psychological virtues, while models of male behaviour stress decisiveness and the imposition of will. ... Scientific objects are placed in a 'space' psychologically far away from the world of everyday life, from the world of emotions and relationships. Men seem able, willing and invested in constructing these separate 'objective' worlds, which they can visit as neutral observers. ... We can see why women might experience a conflict between this construction of science and what feels like 'their way' of dealing with the world, a way that leaves more room for continuous relationships between the self and other.
>
> (Turkle 1984: 107, 115)

Hacking does seem to convey a feeling of power that arguably appeals to males more than females:

> The deep attraction of this sensation of elite technical power should never be underestimated. 'Technical power' is not for everybody; for many people, it has no charm at all. But for some people, it becomes the core of their lives. For a few it is overwhelming, obsessive; it becomes something close to an addiction. People – *especially clever teenage boys* whose lives are otherwise mostly powerless and put-upon – love this sensation of secret power and are willing to do all sorts of amazing things to achieve it.
>
> (Sterling 1992: 19 [emphasis mine])

Whether or not there are innate gender-based differences that account for the overwhelmingly male nature of hacking is a $64,000 question; the biological and the cultural seem to be inextricably mixed.

For example, Krista Bradford, a female American journalist who has had an interest in computing for almost thirty years, began by referring to social reasons and then slipped into an explanation more reliant upon innate differences:

> I think you have to go back to the day women are born and the kind of social conditioning we get ... I believe the culture discourages women from pursuing math/science. The computing process/logic seems much more 'male' to me personally – more linear than circular thought (somehow my Macintosh seems friendlier and therefore more 'female') ... more Spock than Captain Kirk.
>
> (Bradford: email interview)

Jean-Bernard Condat, President of the French Computer Chaos Club, also conflates innate and cultural differences in the genders' approaches to computing:

> In France, the boys play computers and bicycles and/or skate-board, and the girls are at home. Technology is for a long time in my country an uni-sexual one. The notion of male/female criteria is not an important one. It's the cognitive aspects of the hacker ... and a tradition factor. The long concentration of the hacker's spirit on a particular problem is, perhaps, possible only for French boys!
>
> (Condat: email interview)

Mercury, a male hacker, meanwhile contended that:

> When Adam delved and Eve span ... who was then the gentleman? Well, we see that Adam delves into the workings of computers and networks and meanwhile Eve spins, what? Programs? again, my wife programs and she has the skills of a hacker. She has had to crack security in order to do her job. But she does it AS HER JOB, not for the abstract thrill of discovering the unknown. Eve spins. Females who compute would rather spend their time BUILDING a GOOD system, than breaking into someone else's system.
>
> (Mercury: email interview)

A somewhat different emphasis was placed upon the potential psychological differences between men and women by a security manager, Bob Johnson:

> Most men see a problem or puzzle as a direct challenge. They keep attacking it until it's solved, and then brag about it. Women will fuss with a problem for a little while, decide it's too hard, and will drop it. I've heard

about experiments where students were given puzzles with varying degrees of difficulty, including some that were unsolveable. Men tended to keep fighting with the unsolveable puzzles and get quite frustrated and angry. Most women simply gave up. In discussing this question, I got some other thought-provoking questions. How come you don't see women working for hours on puzzles like the Rubik's cube? How come you don't see women sitting in front of a Nintendo game for days on end? How come there are many more men in prisons than women? Psychological make-up? Ethics? Sociological pressures? Peer pressure? Different maturity levels? Western cultural roles? Who knows?!?

(Johnson: email interview)

In a two-part newspaper article that describes the contrasting approaches a husband and wife take to playing the video game, *Tomb Raider II*, purported differences in the male/female approach to computer games playing/computing are explained more confidently. After recounting his first experimentations with the games, *Doom II* and *Quake*, the husband describes his wife's subsequent involvement:

Then she too started playing them, particularly after a hard day at work. Bang would go that monster. Splat would go that goon. But while I would take three or four months to go through to the very end – and this is where the pattern was set for the future – she soon gave up. It wasn't that it was too tough. She couldn't be fagged with all that button pushing. Me, I was a trained killer now. I had no choice. Only final victory was good enough. So I played on. This is also because I am very, very sad.

(Rayner 1997:11)

In summary, whilst psychological mastery-based arguments risk charges of being biologically deterministic, they at least offer a succinct explanation for the statistical expectation yet non-appearance of female hackers.

The masculine environment: the Wild West and cybersexism

Women often feel about as welcome as a system crash.

(Miller 1995: 49)

Generally the women are there as groupies. There's even a T-shirt that says 'Fuck me, I'm in LOD' referring to the elite hacking group Legion of Doom. ... Most of the women have been stalked on- and off-line by at least one hacker, and some of them are regularly harassed in real life by several. One woman had her phone turned off by a hacker she would not have sex with. Another woman had sex with a hacker, and they hit it off so badly that the police and her university got involved more than once.

(Gilboa 1996: 107)

The editors of a collection of fictional short stories with hacking themes use the Wild West trope to describe their ambivalent view of the qualities of hackers and their overall impact. Hackers are described as:

> the kind of restless, impatient, sometimes amoral or egocentric spirit that chafes at any kind of restriction or boundary, the kind of spirit (either 'free' or 'outlaw', depending on how you look at it) that bristles resentfully at other people's laws, rules, regulations, and expectations, and relentlessly seeks a way to get over or under or around those rules. The something that does not love a wall. In other words, very much the same sort of spirit that drove the people, who, for good *and* ill, opened up the American West, the kind of spirit that produced far-sighted explorers as well as cattle rustlers and horse thieves, brave pioneers as well as scurvy outlaw gangs, and that built the bright new cities of the Plains at the cost of countless thousands of Native American lives.
>
> (Dann and Dozois 1996: xiii)

The association of the Wild West with cyberspace has been evident since the earliest days of the latter term's popular usage. Three pages into the main text of William Gibson's novel, *Neuromancer* (the source most responsible for popularising the concept), for example, the first brief description of the cyberspace matrix is immediately followed by Case, the protagonist, bemoaning the fact he 'was no console man, no cyberspace cowboy' (Gibson 1984: 11). The 'maleness' of the cyberspace environment is reinforced by the language used to describe it. The Wild West association seems to encourage the projection of machismo personalities by hackers: 'the actual natives are solitary and independent, sometimes to the point of sociopathy. It is of course a perfect breeding ground for outlaws and new ideas about liberty' (Barlow 1990: 45). Barlow communicated with various hackers during an on-line conference, his initial sympathy for crackers diminished 'under a steady barrage of typed testosterone' (Barlow 1990: 46), a machismo that is exaggerated by the nature of the medium within which they 'electronically travel'. This frontier-like status is seen as facilitating the pre-existing penchant adolescent males seem to have for exploration, be it physical space or increasingly immaterial cyberspace: 'But then teenage boys have been proceeding uninvited since the dawn of human puberty. It seems hard-wired. The only innovation is in the new form of the forbidden zone and the means of getting in it' (Barlow 1990: 48).

Laura Miller has identified this implicitly masculine sexual aspect of the frontier metaphor as crucial for developing an understanding of the gendered basis of cyberspace:

> The psychosexual undercurrents (if anyone still thinks of them as 'under') in the idea of civilization's phallic intrusion into nature's passive, feminine space have been observed, exhaustively elsewhere. The classic Western narrative is actually far more concerned with social relationships than

conflicts between man and nature. In these stories, the frontier is a lawless society of men, a milieu in which physical strength, courage, and personal charisma supplant institutional authority and violent conflict is the accepted means of settling disputes. The Western narrative connects pleasurably with the American romance of individualistic masculinity; small wonder that the predominantly male founders of the Net's culture found it so appealing. When civilisation arrives on the frontier, it comes dressed in skirts and short pants.

(Miller 1995: 52)

With the borrowing of such frontier-based concepts the computer underground has been accused of providing a home for blatant anti-female sentiments. In an article printed in the *CuD* and entitled 'Sexism and the computer underground' Liz E. Borden writes:

skewed participation transports the male culture of values, language, concerns, and actions, into a new world and creates models that women must conform to or be excluded from full membership ... BBSs, especially those catering to adolescents and college students, are frightening in their misogyny ... sexism is rampant on the nets. The alt.sex (bondage, gifs, what-have-you) appeal to male fantasies of a type that degrades women.

(CuD 3:00 1991: file 4)

Miller, in contrast, however, warns against such a 'women as victims on the Net' construing of cyberspace relations. She argues that such a perception may in fact play into the hands of those who wish to recycle social sexual stereotypes:

In the Western mythos, civilization is necessary because women and children are victimized in conditions of freedom. Introduce women and children into a frontier town and the law must follow because women and children must be protected. Women, in fact, are usually the most vocal proponents of the conversion from frontier justice to civil society. The imperiled women and children of the Western narrative make their appearance today in newspaper and magazine articles that focus on the intimidation and sexual harassment of women on-line and reports of pedophiles trolling for victims in computerized chat rooms. If on-line women successfully contest these attempts to depict them as the beleaguered prey of brutish men, expect the pedophile to assume a larger profile in arguments that the Net is out of control.

(Miller 1995: 52)

Anonymity and misogyny

From one male's perspective, at least, the anonymity previously identified as a key component of hacking culture facilitates misogyny by empowering men who would otherwise feel powerless. In the debate that followed the above Liz E. Borden posting, a man replied that the misogyny in the computer underground is:

> a sad reflection of how our society has created values by way of mass media … First, when measured against the standards of today's society, 'six foot, 180 lbs of tanned muscle, a full head of perfect hair, and gorgeous eyes', few computer freaks measure up preferring the 'safeness' of their computers … Computers don't turn you down for a date. As a result, a growing misogyny appears and manifests itself through computers where the individual can remain basically formless through either pseudonyms, or just the relative anonymity that comes from no-one knowing what they 'look like'.
>
> (CuD 3:01, 1991)

Freiss, a German hacker, concurred with this assessment of the role anonymity plays in increasing misogyny in computing:

> What often happens when a female appears on the network is that the male majority 'jumps' on her. The fact that many networks allow a user to hide his real name, i.e. cloak a user in anonymity, seems to cause many males to drop all semblance of civilization. Sexual harassment by email is not uncommon, both in universities and commercial institutions [not excluding the company I work for].
>
> (Freiss: email interview)

Whether or not sexual harassment occurs via email, it is perhaps easier to show that the anonymity provided by the Internet arguably encourages a loosening of sexual mores and inhibitions, which may discourage some women from participating fully in cyberspace. An illustration of the uninhibited sexual imagery cyberspace gives rise to is provided by the following poem:

Does she do the Vulcan mind meld on the first date?

'I want your bra size, baby,
Fax number, Email address,
Modem com code, ID,
Phone machine access.

Give me your thumb print, password,
Blood type and credit check;
Give me your anti-body spectrum,
Your immune response spec.

Let's break bread together baby,
Exchange cryptographic primes;
Let's link up our parallel ports;
And go on-line in real-time.

Let's indulge in covalent bondage;
Let's communicate in C.
Let's merge our enemy bodies
And bob in the quantum sea.

I wanna swim in your gene pool, mama;
Snort your pheromones up close range;
Tune in your neurotransmitters,
Introduce you to Doctor Strange.

I wanna surf in your quantum potentia;
Mess with your thermostat;
Wanna tour your molecular orbits;
Wanna feed your Schrödinger cat.

Let's surgically merge our organs;
Our kidneys, our lungs and our hearts;
Let's read our physics journals together
And laugh at the dirty parts.

Let's Bell-connect our bellies
With some quantum-adhesive glue;
Let's do new stuff to each other
That Newton never knew.

I wanna feel your viscosity, honey,
Melt my rheological mind;
Let your female force-field vortex
Deform my male spacetime.'

(Nick Herbert)

Finally, when not suffering from directly misogynous behaviour, cyberspace's appeal to women may suffer as a result of the paradoxical fact that their small numerical presence produces threatening situations inadvertently caused by the disproportionate interest and friendliness from male computer hobbyists keen to meet a female peer. Mercury relates how, 'My wife runs a couple of AT&T 3B2s and so she belongs to a UNIX user group. She never lacks for attention when she goes to meetings! So you can't say that hackers are "anti-female"' (Mercury: email interview).

Psycho-sexual theories of hacking

man becomes, as it were, the sex organs of the machine world, as the bee of the plant world, enabling it to fecundate and to evolve ever new forms. The machine world reciprocates man's love by expediting his wishes and desires.

(McLuhan 1964: 46)

Our fascination with computers is more erotic than sensuous, more deeply spiritual than utilitarian. Eros, as the ancient Greeks understood, springs from a feeling of insufficiency or inadequacy. While the aesthete feels drawn to casual play and dalliance, the erotic lover reaches out to a fulfilment far beyond aesthetic detachment. The computer's allure is more than utilitarian or aesthetic; it is erotic. Instead of a refreshing play with surfaces, as with toys or amusements, our affair with information machines announces a symbiotic relationship and ultimately a mental marriage to technology.

(Heim 1991: 61)

Technological endeavour has been portrayed as a sublimated libidinal process in various cultural expressions through the ages. This tradition ranges from the Greek myth of Pygmalion and Galatea[13] to Mary Shelley's evocative and perennially resonant novel and warning to Enlightenment thought: *Frankenstein*. It is perhaps not surprising therefore that claims have been made about the purportedly erotic charge underlying computer activity and by extension hacking. Psycho-sexual perspectives provide further, if somewhat more speculative, lines of reasoning that could account for the apparent absence of female hackers active in the computer underground. Men are represented as seeking either erotic fulfilment or an artificial short-cut to paternity through their non-human creations:

The computer underworld is populated with young men (and almost no women) who live out their fantasies of power and glory on a keyboard. Most are single. That some young men find computing a substitute for sexual activity is probably incontrovertible. Just as a handle will often hide a shy and frightened fifteen-year-old, an obsession with computing to the exclusion of all else may represent security for a sexually insecure youngster. The computer is his partner, his handle is his real self … and the virus he writes is the child of his real self and his partner. A German virus writer once said: 'You feel something wonderful has happened when you've produced one. You've created something which lives. You don't know where it will go or what it will do, but you know it will live on'. He was talking about his new virus.

(Clough and Mungo 1992: 8)

A spokesman for a hacker group calling themselves the *Toxic Shock Group* seems to add weight to the idea that hackers may hack in order to fulfil some subconscious, sexually based desire to penetrate and violate, with his rather 'orgasmic' description of hacking:

It doesn't happen like Wargames shows it. Oh no, it is so much different. The geek in the movie … he had it so easy. No real hackers would exist if it was that easy (perhaps therein lies the solution to the 'problem'). No, we hack and hack at a system like a man on safari, clearing away the vines of the jungle with his machete, trying to forge ahead to a destination he cannot yet see. We keep on, torturing our brains and pounding our fingers on the keyboard until at last ... oh at long, sweet last ... we are in.

(Toxic Shock Group 1990: file 4)

The characterisation of hacking as an essentially masturbatory pastime further explores the sexually based motivational explanation of hacking initiated by the Toxic Shock Group:

In the sense that hacking is a solitary and non-constructive activity, it might be termed *masturbatory*. The pleasure or interest is confined to the activity itself, and has no object, such as a lover, and no objective, such as a demonstration of affection.

(Keller 1990: 57)

This view is in keeping with a popular perception of hackers as sexually inadequate, obsessive individuals, who lacking the social skills necessary to converse with other people and especially women, prefer the company of their computers to social interaction.[14]

In contrast to the negative portrayals of hackers suffering from too much testosterone, machismo, or misplaced libidinal energy, one imaginative psychoanalytical explanation of the male predominance of cyberspace relies upon a reversal of the Freudian concept of *penis envy*:

The expression 'cyborg envy' has been used to talk about the inversion of the classical 'penis envy' taking place in the longing for cyberspace. Stone notes that the cybernetic mode 'shares certain conceptual and affective characteristics with numerous fictional evocations of the inarticulate longing of the male for female'.[15] In 'cyborg envy' we long to become woman. In the cybernetic act, 'penetration translates into envelopment'. In other words, to enter cyberspace is physically to *put on* cyberspace. To become the cyborg, to put on the seductive and dangerous cybernetic space like a garment, is to put on the *female*.[16]

(Moreiras 1993: 198)

Finally, preferring a less academically Freudian approach, Amnon Zichroni, the defence lawyer for Ehud Tenenbuam, an Israeli hacker accused of accessing sensitive areas of NASA and the Pentagon's computer systems, returns us to the machismo-orientated explanation of hacking: 'In the past we used to boast about the girls we had. Nowadays kids boast about their ability to hack into computer systems' (*Guardian* 26 March 1998 [*On-line* section]: 3).

3   The motivations of hackers

Introduction

An increasingly criminal connotation today has displaced the more innocuous, amateur-mischief-maker-cum-media-star role reserved for hackers until a few years ago. In response to the gathering vigour of this 'war on hackers', the most common defenses of hacking can be presented on a spectrum that runs from the appeasement or accommodation of corporate interests to drawing up blueprints for cultural revolution: (a) Hacking performs a benign industrial service of uncovering security deficiencies and design flaws. (b) Hacking, as an experimental, free-form research activity, has been responsible for many of the most progressive developments in software development. (c) Hacking, when not purely recreational, is an elite educational practice that reflects the ways in which the development of high technology has outpaced orthodox forms of institutional education. (d) Hacking is an important form of watchdog counter-response to the use of surveillance technology and data-gathering by the state, and to the increasingly monolithic communications power of giant corporations. (e) Hacking, as guerilla know-how, is essential to the task of maintaining fronts of cultural resistance and stocks of oppositional knowledge as a hedge against a technofascist future.

(Ross 1991: 82)

This chapter predominantly explores the *internal* account of hacking and thereby helps to illuminate the community/boundary-building techniques used by hackers themselves. This exploration provides an introduction to the analysis in subsequent chapters of the boundary formation processes that occur due to the conflicts and negotiations that take place between various hacking and non-hacking groups within computing: the conflict between the *internal* and *external* accounts. The fact that hacker culture predominantly exists in an informational rather than a conventional physical environment means that, in the absence of the community qualities that come from shared physical space, articulations of what it is to hack and why people do it may have a disproportionate role to play in community formation within the computer underground and in influencing the perceptions of those external to the activity.

Alleged motivations thus become an important focus for defining the commitment and status of members or opponents of the purported community of hackers, depending on whether one subscribes to or opposes the values implicit in them. Because of this the reasons hackers offer as motivational and justificatory explanations for their actions can tend to be put forward in a rather defensive manner. This and later chapters show how articulations of hackers' motivations are tied up in an ongoing rhetorical debate between those for and against hacking. Within this context it is difficult at times to separate cleanly the *ex ante* motivations of hackers from their *ex post* justifications. This chapter's investigation of the motivations lying behind hacking begins with an overview of the predominantly psychological theories put forward by academics. These theories are then set against the account given by hackers themselves. Further perceptions from non-hackers are explored in subsequent chapters giving rise to a dynamic of competing accounts.

Hacker motivations: academic theories

> Wherever computer centres have become established … bright young men of dishevelled appearance, often with sunken glowing eyes, can be seen sitting at computer consoles, their arms tensed, and waiting to fire, their fingers, already poised to strike at the buttons and keys on which their attention seems to be as riveted as a gambler's on the rolling dice. When not so transfixed they often sit at tables strewn with computer print-outs over which they pore like possessed students of a cabalistic text. … They exist, at least when so engaged, only through and for the computers. These are computer bums, compulsive programmers. They are an international phenomenon.
>
> (Weizenbaum 1976: 125)

Academics have theorised about the possible psychological motivations of hacking. Weizenbaum's portrayal (above) of the act of hacking provides a seminal description of what several writers deem to be its intrinsically obsessive elements. From this perspective, hackers are those programmers who love the computer not as a tool that is a means to an end, but rather as an end in itself. Compulsive programming can take the form of extreme psychological identification with the computer, which can become a type of emotional mirror or even soul-mate. The motivation of the compulsive programmer/hacker is portrayed in terms of a wish to escape from the contingencies of the real world in order to revel in the hygienic safety offered by the computer. Thus Turkle describes, in language similar to that used by Shallis in *The Silicon Idol*, how:

> Like Narcissus and his reflection, people who work with computers can easily fall in love with the worlds they have constructed or with their perfor-

mances in the worlds created for them by others. Involvement with simulated worlds affects relationships with the real one.

(Turkle 1984: 78)

Whilst hacking provides examples of some obsessive characteristics these may in fact also be shared by other intense academic pursuits:

> There is no one field in particular in academia that has a monopoly on production of single-interest people, and this practice can exist almost anywhere. There is the political power seeker, all-consumed by climbing up the bureaucratic rungs. There is the stereotyped pre-med, ignoring all but his MCAT scores. There is the compulsive artist or writer, forever lost in his work. Narrowness is widespread. But there is one field that seems to be more consistent in this practice. ... The computer is a modifier of personalities. It is highly addictive. People who gain this addiction for a period of several months tend never to give it up. And the symptoms are very sad. ... Eating and sleeping are completely rearranged to fit the addiction. The typical hacker thinks nothing of eating one meal a day and subsisting on junk food, or of sleeping from 4 a.m. to noon almost every day of the week.
>
> (Zimbardo 1980: 64)

Such an analysis recognises the dangers of overplaying the obsessional/addictive qualities of hacking. Whilst computing, along with lots of other activities, may have its element of compulsive *aficionados*, other research suggests that hacking and computer addiction are not mutually inclusive. Shotton (1989), for example, focuses upon the personalities of 'computer dependants' who may or may not be hackers, but who are characterised by the disproportionate amount of time they devote to computing. She concludes that portrayals of computer enthusiasts as socially inadequate addicts is inaccurate:

> Early readings about 'computer junkies' and 'hackers' suggested that if I pursued this research I might spend my time with people who were barely human and who were unable to converse with others on any meaningful level. How untrue this proved to be. I met some of the most fascinating people of my life. They were intelligent, lively, amusing, original, inventive and very hospitable. ... They were pursuing an interest which not only provided intellectual challenge, fun and excitement in infinite variety, but one which enabled many of them to improve their career prospects considerably. Many used computers not only at home but also at work, and true fulfilment must come to those who are able to combine their hobby with a means of earning a living.[1]
>
> (Shotton 1989: Preface)

It can be argued that hacking is too important a phenomenon to dismiss as compulsive programming. 'The hack' may provide a kick that is comparable to other forms of addiction but the imaginative and ingenious elements of hacking perhaps make it somewhat more important: few conventional drug addicts, for example, are perceived as posing a potential threat to national security as a direct result of their activity.

Hackers' descriptions of why they hack: the internal account.

> 'Hacker' to me is a term which defines an individual who succumbs to his/her thirst for knowledge (and the computing power that accompanies that knowledge). A 'hacker' will not ever maliciously commit or condone an action of destruction (be it physical or electronic) of computers or data. A vandal rejoices in his/her ability to wreak havoc upon systems run by ignorant individuals. Most often such a vandal will not seek to maintain accessibility to systems that he/she has compromised. Instead, seeking to destroy data or make life generally more difficult for users and administrators. Vandals feel the need for power as manifested in the microcosm of the machine.
>
> (Mofo: email interview)

We have already seen how the term hacking is essentially contested. The motivations offered by hackers for their activity frequently seemed influenced by their sensitivity to the agendas of the various groups that oppose hacking. The computer security industry, for example, is accused of over-emphasising the vandal-orientated motivations and pathological aspects of hacking. The limitation of such approaches is argued above by the hacker *Mofo the Clown* and the clear distinction he makes between hackers and 'vandals'. The motivations lying behind hacking, according to the internal account, are categorised into six main areas:

1   Feelings of addiction.
2   The urge of curiosity.
3   Boredom with educational system.
4   Enjoyment of feelings of power.
5   Peer recognition.
6   Political acts.

Despite this classificatory approach, it should be recognised that in reality there is a degree of fluidity between categories. Thus, to deal with just two, there seems to be a rather fine line between the levels of curiosity necessary for a competent hacker and the charge that such curiosity has stepped over the boundary into addictive behaviour. A pertinent example is that of a university student, Paul Bedworth, who was acquitted whilst charged under the UK's 1990 Computer Misuse Act on the basis of the defence's argument that he was addicted to computers. The six categories thus form part of a complex interrelation of factors that influence hackers, a mix of factors playing a variable role in the motivation of any one hacker.

Feelings of addiction

> still he'd see the matrix in his sleep, bright lattices of logic unfolding across the colorless void ... he was no console man, no cyberspace cowboy. Just another hustler, trying to make it through. But the dreams came on in the Japanese night like livewire voodoo, and he'd cry for it, cry in his sleep, and wake alone in the dark, curled in his capsule in some coffin hotel, his hands clawed into the bedslab, temperfoam bunched between his fingers, trying to reach the console that wasn't there.
>
> (Gibson 1984: 11)

One of the most intriguing aspects of hacking is the way in which its apparently obsessive aspects give rise to pejorative portrayals of nerdishness yet, simultaneously, the practical implications of the knowledge gained are still potentially important enough to promote continued public interest in the activity.

Obsessive hacking

> Damn kid. All he does is play games. They're all alike. And then it happened ... a door opened to a world ... rushing through the phone line like heroin through an addicts veins, an electronic pulse is sent out, a refuge from the day-to-day incompetencies is sought ... a board is found. 'This is it ... this is where I belong'.
>
> (The Mentor 1986: phile 3)

> We are addicted to information and knowledge, and our drugs are withheld from us. We are forced to seek our precious information and knowledge elsewhere. We have to find challenge somewhere, somehow, or it tears our very souls apart. And we are, eventually, forced to enter someone's system.
>
> (Toxic Shock Group 1990: file 4)

The use of the language of addiction and obsession to describe hacking is not just limited to its opponents but also the hackers themselves. Thus, Jean-Bernard Condat, President of the French Computer Chaos Club, describes how:

> All the hackers that I know in France, have (or have had) serious problems with their parents. Some speak only by computer or only the computer matters. Hacking for a real hacker is the only reason to live! Without background ideas. Like drinking water for a human body. The lack of computers/software to hack make the hacker ill at ease.
>
> (Condat: email interview)

Maelstrom described his urge to hack in a manner that, in addition to making use of addictive imagery, also lends weight to Turkle's theory that hackers may use the computer as some sort of psychological prop:

> I just do it because it makes me feel good, as in better than anything else that I've ever experienced. Computers are the only thing that have ever given me this feeling … the adrenaline rush I get when I'm trying to evade authority, the thrill I get from having written a program that does something that was supposed to be impossible to do, and the ability to have social relations with other hackers are all very addictive. I get depressed when I'm away from a networked computer for too long. I find conversations held in cyberspace much more meaningful and enjoyable than conversing with people in physical-reality real mode. For a long time, I was extremely shy around others, and I am able to let my thoughts run free when I am alone with my computer and a modem hooked up to it. I consider myself addicted to hacking. If I were ever in a position where I knew my computer activity was over with for the rest of my life, I would suffer withdrawal.
>
> (Maelstrom: email interview)

The addictive aspects of hacking, however, only partially describe an activity that has an array of intermingled motivations. Feelings of addiction are not the *sine qua non* of the activity. Johnson approached the question by making a distinction between intellectual curiosity and compulsion. His analysis, however, implies that there is a fine and somewhat blurred dividing line between the two:

> An automobile mechanic when fixing a motor should find the problem, replace broken parts, and complete the job. If he indulged his intellectual curiosity, he might take apart some of the motor, in order to see how it works. … If the mechanic tears the motor completely apart, or goes home and spends every waking moment tearing down and rebuilding car motors, then his behaviour has become compulsive. Will it make him a better mechanic in the long run? Probably, if he doesn't burn out (or his wife doesn't kill him). If he starts sneaking into his neighbour's garage at midnight to 'work on' his neighbour's BMW, something's dreadfully wrong.
>
> (Johnson: email interview)

Johnson argues that compulsion does not have to necessarily equate with hacking. The compulsion that *some* hackers show causes a mystique around hacking simply because computers appear to the public as more esoteric than most other technological artefacts with which they have more knowledge and everyday contact:

> We have seen the same kind of compulsive curiosity with Nintendo video game systems here in the States. Kids will literally spend days playing a single game, until they master it. There is nothing inherently compulsive in

computers, any more than in booze, drugs, television, food, work, art or anything else. Compulsive behaviour is found in people, not in things. A person can be compulsive about anything. It's just more interesting when a person is compulsive about computers, than if they're compulsive about clothes or cars. Hackers are not necessarily compulsive. Computer addicts are not necessarily hackers.

(Johnson: email interview)

John Butler (a University of Edinburgh computing officer), related how some university course administrators had asked him to deny Internet access to certain students because they had become 'NewsNet Junkies'. He felt that students became addicted to the non-physical aspects of computing and the fact that it offers 'an alternative reality and there's a disconnection between it and the real world' (Butler: Edinburgh interview). A specific reason why hackers may be viewed as compulsive by outsiders to their 'alternative reality' was described by M., a Dutch hacker, who argued that the speed of change of the computing environment, identified earlier as a distinctive part of hacking culture, means that they have to approach their pastime with above-average application:

No, it's not compulsive, but if you stop, if you don't do it for one week then things change, the network always changes. It changes very quickly and you have to keep up and you have to learn all the tricks by heart, the default passwords, the bugs you need. If you want to get into a system you have to try anything, so you have to know every bug.

(M.: Utrecht interview)

Hackers, therefore, arguably have an immediate temptation to involve them-selves with their alternative reality to a greater extent than that contemplated by more 'nine-to-five-minded' computer people.

Addiction as a defence: the Bedworth case

COMPUTERS TURNED MY BOY INTO A ROBOT
(*Daily Mirror* 18 March 1993: newspaper headline)

The following is the editorial response of the UK newspaper, the *Independent*, to a well publicised hacking incident: the prosecution of an Edinburgh University Student, Paul Bedworth, the first prosecution under the 1990 UK Computer Misuse Act. The case ended in an acquittal on 17 March 1993:

It was agreed that Mr Bedworth had broken into numerous computers in Britain and abroad by calling from the BBC microcomputer in his bedroom; that he had changed the data inside those computers; and that he had made more than 50,000 calls for which he had not paid. But his counsel found an expert witness to convince the jury that the hacker had no intent to commit the crimes, because he was so addicted to his computer that he was no longer responsible for his actions.

(Harris 1993a: 1)

This case provides a good illustration of the association of hacking with addiction. Bedworth's barrister, Mr Alistair Kelman, argued that: 'Mr Bedworth was ... someone who had grown up with computers and been damaged by them. "When a kid's best friend becomes a computer rather than a member of their family then you are courting trouble"' (Harris 1993a: 1). The extent of this trouble was illustrated in the following description taken from the Edinburgh-based newspaper, the *Scotsman*:

> Paul Bedworth is small and slightly built but he was strong enough to push his mother down a flight of attic stairs when she tried to stop him using his computer. ... So great was Paul's obsession that the only way Mrs Bedworth could force him to take a break was by switching off the electricity supply at the mains. ... Only sheer exhaustion would force Paul to stop. His mother would find him slumped across the keyboard or face down on the carpet where he had collapsed. 'It was so worrying because he would be lying there with his nose in the carpet looking like he had fainted or was dead.'
>
> (Harris 1993b: 3)

Professor Griffith-Edwards, from the Addiction Research Unit in London, was called as an expert witness. His description of Bedworth was 'One is looking at a young man with monstrously abnormal behaviour. I would classify him as suffering from a mental disorder, as distinct from a mental illness, but a very serious one' (Harris 1993b: 3). The response to the Bedworth case, although predominantly emphasising his obsessional nature also added weight to Johnson's previously quoted assessment of compulsive hacking being a particular example of a single-mindedness apparent in various otherwise harmless endeavours. Professor Osborne from Swansea University Psychology department, consulted after the verdict, argued that: 'Computer addicts may sit in their bedroom for long hours but I am not sure there is any different personality trait here than in a compulsive gardener' (Harris 1993b: 3), whilst the author of a book about computer addiction, Mary Shotton, responded to the accusation that hackers tend to be disproportionately introverted, by replying that: 'This is quite normal behaviour. Not all people are gregarious and raving extroverts. Heaven help the world if everyone was' (*The Times* 18 March 1993: 5).

Curiosity: humans and technology

What a hacker does primarily is relentlessly pursue an answer. Computers naturally lend themselves to this sort of pursuit, since they tend to be patient when asked a lot of questions.

(Goldstein 1993: file 1)

The computer underground of today is the group that would have been the HAM RADIO operators of yesteryear. These radio operators could have made public radio impossible to hear if enough 'EVIL' HAM radio operators would have decided to do this. In the long term commercial radio won out, because everyone benefited by the law and order that developed. The computer underground is just the group of people that always test the limits of the developing advances. They are the Lewis and Clark or Buzz Aldrin of this new territory. How we draw the maps, rules and laws of the future will depend on how and what they find.

(Forbush: email interview)

Leading from the previous discussion of hacking's allegedly addictive qualities is the extent to which seemingly obsessive behaviour can be alternatively reinterpreted as a less pejoratively portrayed curiosity-driven and relentless pursuit of the answer to a technical problem. In this light, hackers emphasise how such innate curiosity is the fundamental basis from which most technological improvements and adaptations are ultimately derived. The 'hacker mentality' therefore is seen as a positive attribute that drives forward technological development:

Oppression is our only reward ... yet if it were not for people like us, all of you who wake up each day to an alarm clock, or drive to work in your fine new car after cutting on your security system, while drinking that cup of coffee you didn't have to get up to prepare, would still be living in a cave, somewhere near Africa, grunting and reproducing, eating the raw meat of some beast you hunted down with clubs, trying to ignore the cold that seeps in through the animal skins you wear, and wondering why some curious person with some intelligence, creativity, and ingenuity would come along and invent the wheel.

(Toxic Shock Group 1990: file 4)

In a somewhat less provocative manner and underlining this positive element of hacking, Knightmare, a US hacker, recognises the difficulty of separating iconoclastic and idiosyncratic redrawing of technological boundaries that can potentially benefit society from 'irresponsible' hacking that is harmful to society:

I don't think I'm doing anything bad; I really don't. And I have a high sense of moral values. I'm not an 'anarchist techno-guerrilla', and I'm not recommending nor suggesting nor teaching that behavior. If everyone in the world were hackers in the broadest sense, we'd be more independent, more curious, and more concerned with the world – because we would realize what control we individuals can have over it. But I'm talking about people who hack responsibly. If people start World War III or insert your favorite hacker horror story ... then obviously we've got problems.

(cited in Marotta 1993: 2)

Boredom aspects

There's no sense getting in a pissing contest with a thousand idiots who have time on their hands.[2]

In contrast to, and as a result of, the hacker penchant for exploration is a low threshold of boredom for computing activities not of their own choosing. One of the most common complaints I encountered when talking with hackers was that they were bored with the computing education they received in a formal learning setting such as university or college. The following quotation illustrates the depth of feeling hackers have concerning the extent to which they feel orthodox education methods have failed to address their needs:

we've been spoon-fed baby food at school when we hungered for steak ... the bits of meat that you did let slip through were pre-chewed and tasteless. We've been dominated by sadists or ignored by the apathetic. The few that had something to teach found us willing pupils, but those few are like drops of water in the desert.

(The Mentor 1986: phile 3)

Related to these feelings of being educationally circumscribed are those that result from, one, lack of mental stimulation in computing courses and, two, from inadequate access to computing facilities.

Lack of mental stimulation

The Dutch Zoetermeer group of hackers claimed to have been singly under-challenged by their assignments at university. For others, once their boredom is removed and they are given responsibility, the urge to crack may stop. John Draper claimed that this was also his experience when he was made the manager of a system and needed to discourage students from destructive acts. The experience of the hacker, *Faustus*, seems to verify the idea that removing boredom from the minds of hackers means that their abilities can be more productively utilised. He relates how:

kids are bored and feel powerless in a system run by often unfriendly adults, and cracking is their only way to assert themselves. Very often a clever cracker is made into a system manager, and this is a good way to make him stop cracking, since once he is 'part of the system', the frustration that is the reason for attacking it disappears. When I was a kid (i.e. 16–18) I spent some time trying to crack systems, but nothing serious. I quickly became a 'manager type' and haven't had any motivation since then to mess with security.

(Faustus: email interview)

Thus added responsibility may limit the need to hack but may still not satisfy the illicit thrill associated with unauthorised intrusions. J.C. Van Winkel, a Dutch software engineer and researcher, who has worked in various *tiger teams* used to test the security of various sites, relates how:

I did hacking because for me it was a way to learn more about the system, curiosity and not anything else, I wanted to learn more about it and they didn't give me enough information. I mean I was pretty good at that time, I got high grades and didn't have to do anything about it, so I was bored if I didn't do anything and together with a couple of colleagues we wrote programs that were far from what the normal scientists wrote ... I think a lot of it's boredom and people like to have puzzles, I mean why do people do crosswords? ... it's the same thing with hackers. ... We took the most difficult assignments because we liked to do it, on the other hand, curiosity will never be satisfied.

(Van Winkel: Appledorn interview)

There is perhaps the intractable problem that, whereas hackers seem to need their curiosity and intellects satisfied, it is likely that, for some people at least, such curiosity is insatiable.

Lack of access

It is my contention that if Robert Morris had a legitimate venue for exploration, he would not have launched a virus on the Internet. If the Dark Avenger (who wrote a virus of the same name) had been given some guidance, he would not have launched the virus (I have met him and am now convinced that he is being turned 'to the good side' by several caring people who saw his plight and are spending the necessary time with him). I know that many of the 'hackers' I knew when I was younger would gladly have done their work with permission, but the paranoia and maniacal attitudes of those in the computing community prevented the legitimate exercise of their interests.

(Cohen: email interview)

A common complaint encountered from hackers, and more sympathetic members of the computer security industry, was that even when computer courses do stimulate, they are frequently accompanied by a lack of access to systems. The contention is that a lack of cheap access to mailing facilities and Internet news groups etc. is a major cause of hacking. Critics of hacking, in contrast, would question the right of hackers to make use of other people's telecommunication systems without paying for the privilege. The hackers I interviewed had no ethical qualms in using facilities they would not otherwise be able to afford. They argued that the nature of communication technologies is such that the marginally increased use of the system by hackers does not lead to increased prices for other consumers. Maelstrom applied this argument to both communication systems and software copyright protection:

> I've learnt a bit about the Unix and VMS operating systems, have made many friends via TALK and PHONE utilities, and now know a lot more about computer security than I ever thought I would. I will have no moral or ethical qualms whatsoever about system hacking until accounts are available to the general public for free. MSU's $460 per year charge for an Internet connection for telenetting just doesn't cut it for a high school or college student who is strapped for cash. ... For a computer enthusiast to go by the law would be to spend hundreds of dollars per month on programs and various accounts on systems. Hacking will always exist in some form or another until a person can do things without losing his shirt.
>
> (Maelstrom: email interview)

James Carlson, from a commercial computing perspective, regarded most underground activities as due to a lack of access to adequate facilities:

> Nearly all are benign. I did some of this kind of hacking myself when I was in high school. I think I did it mainly because there were few facilities available for my use ... and the only ones that were available (at school) were highly restricted. ... How about just providing better facilities and access for new users? Why can't ALL people get electronic-mail? Why can't everyone have access to open systems? These things would provide a more-than-necessary distraction for the average hacker.
>
> (Carlson: email interview)

Goggans, in addition, argues:

> If people were given legitimate access to the systems they wanted to learn about, and were given the ability to send mail and communicate with each other interactively, much of the hacking would subside. Having a legal Internet account is what has saved me. I can still blab with my peers on IRC, I can send mail to everyone, and I can snoop around via FTP completely legally on a UNIX VMS or NOS! That in addition to the

systems I am given limited permission to access via clients' contracts, my needs are fulfilled completely, and I have no desire to access systems which are forbidden to me. I think if people were given this type of arrangement early on, it would curb the urge to break into other sites.

(Goggans: email interview)

Rop Gongrijp further argued that the technical knowledge of increasingly young hackers sits uneasily with the lack of opportunity that those young hackers have to exercise that knowledge. They are aware of the Internet, which will not be accessible to them until they are aged nineteen to twenty:

I mean I know a few kids that I associate with, they have no option, they are 14, they can't wait, what do I tell them? 'Well, just be good for a while, put up with the fact that they have nothing but boring assignments for you, and it'll be five years before you have any assignments at all. ... And then in five years you might be able to work in a completely censored environment. ... Am I supposed to say that to 14 year olds that want to explore? Great prospect, so I tell them, go ahead, hack, don't break anything but explore what you want to explore, grab your computer and modem and see what's out there, I mean if that takes breaking into systems that they don't want you into for the next five years, do it. I think there is a moral right for that kid to go out and explore, keeping people away from technology or anything that long does not work'.

(Gongrijp: Amsterdam interview)

The specific experience of an academic, Brian Thompsett,[3] further illustrates the complaint regarding adequate access to facilities. He experienced what he perceived to be a limitation of access to computing facilities from Edinburgh University Computing Service (EUCS). The dispute centred on whether or not his work fulfilled the EUCS regulation of computing access only being given to those whose requirements satisfied the criteria of 'reasonable usage'. After a drawn-out dispute Thompsett was given a machine to do with as he pleased; he further related how:

Now I had the computer I began to realise that I wasn't the only victim of the strange rules on computer usage. I decided to run the donated machine on a laissez-faire basis. This is working well. The basis of the arrangement is that people can explore computers on my machine. It acts as a honey-pot principle. If we let them burn out their nasty tendencies in my sand-pit then they leave the rest of the EUCS machines alone. If they mess around in the sand-pit the other kids push them out. Works so far. So it boils down to this. I have a machine on which lots of users might be considered 'naughty boys' elsewhere, but on my machine they get to play without monster nanny breathing down their neck. They manage to mature quite nicely in a year or so. Some of my kiddies have now evolved into quite responsible people.

> Several important machines in the UK are now managed by some people in my user community.
>
> (Thompsett: email interview)

Thompsett's open-access machine became known as 'The Tardis', and privileged users/supervisors becoming known as 'Time Lords', one of whom, Malcolm Campbell (Edinburgh interview), concurred with Thompsett's opinion that the project helps to mature computer users who might otherwise turn to electronic vandalism. The argument, similar to those used in 'real world' acts of vandalism, contends that users who have a stake in a computer system are unlikely to jeopardise their user rights. The sanction of exclusion from the Tardis system proved to be an effective-enough deterrent for would-be malicious hackers.

Enjoyment of feelings of power

> 'Power and knowledge' may seem odd motivations. 'Money' is a lot easier to understand. There are growing armies of professional thieves who rip-off phone service for money. Hackers, though, are into, well, power and knowledge. This has made them easier to catch than the street-hustlers who steal access codes at airports. It also makes them a lot scarier.
>
> (Sterling 1991: 4)

Linked to the previously mentioned notion of machismo in hacking culture is the motivational factor of power. Journalistic investigations of hacking have tended to concentrate on this particular element of hacking activity. Without doubt, however, feelings of power do complement the main motivation of curiosity; in the book, *Beating the System*, Edward Singh is reported as confessing that:

> Part of it was a sense of power. You were running an informal network of about 250 computers and no-one else outside your close circle of friends knew about it. The final goal was total world domination, to have everything under control. It was the ultimate game on the ultimate scale. You got a thrill out of knowing how much power you had. It was possibly hitting back at society. There was a sort of political anarchism involved. The main thrill was beating the system.
>
> (Bowcott and Hamilton 1990: 42)

From Singh's rather dramatic analysis of his own actions, Bowcott and Hamilton derived the title for their book. In keeping with the typically fluid nature of hackers' motivations, immediately after the above 'confession', the authors admit that on another occasion Singh accounted for his actions as being primarily motivated by intellectual enjoyment. To a limited extent, among the hackers I spoke to, power was accepted as a motivating factor. Thus Thom Van

Os of the 'Zoetermeer gang' of hackers commented, 'Most of the hackers do it for the kicks, I suppose. Breaking into a bigger or more important system, or acquiring root-status can give you a real feeling of power and you seem to have proved yourself better than the system administrator' (Zoetermeer interview). The issue of power as a possible motivation of hacking was raised with Kevin Mitnick: 'the dark-side hacker' portrayed by the media as a nefarious benefactor of the power computers offered over other people. Mitnick denied the suggestion that he was ever motivated by any sinister factors such as strong yearnings of power, but recognised that some hacking is carried out for criminal gain. Rather than for feelings of power, he claimed to hack because:

> You get a better understanding of the cyberspace, the computer systems, the operating systems, how the computer systems interact with one another, that basically, was my motivation behind my hacking activity in the past, it was just from the gain of knowledge and the thrill of adventure, nothing that was well and truly sinister such as trying to get any type of monetary gain or anything.
>
> (Mitnick: telephone interview, Holland–US)

Albert Moreiras provided the following much more theoretical explanation of the power issues that relate to hacking:

> Knowledge, then … is utterly immanent and implicated in the forms and technologies of instrumental power, and readable only to the extent that we have the power to decode it. How we are known and what we know constitute a matrix of unjustly distributed power, except that there is no one reliable panopticon. The matrix is too complex and fragmented to offer itself to any one unifying gaze – a notion that does not seem entirely reassuring to me. … Hence, the attraction of the cyberspace addiction: to jack in is briefly, thrillingly, to get next to the power; not to be able to jack in is impotence. Moreover, the cyberspace addiction, the hacker mystique, posits power through anonymity. One does not log on to the system through authorized paths of entry; one sneaks in, dropping through trap doors in the security program, hiding one's tracks, immune to the audit trails that were put there to make the perceiver part of the data perceived. It is a dream of recovering power and wholeness by seeing wonders and by not being seen. But what a strange and tangled dream, this power that is only gained through matching your synapses to the computer's logic, through *beating the system by being the system.*
>
> (Moreiras 1993: 198 [emphasis mine])

Such a close identification with the 'system' was recognised by a hacker in terms reminiscent of Chapter 1's identification of the abstract nature of hacking's appeal that is just manifested in the manipulation of specific artefacts:

> 'There's a real love-hate relationship between us and the phone company.
> We don't particularly appreciate the bureaucracy that runs it, but we love
> the network itself', he says, lingering on the word 'love'. 'The network is the
> greatest thing to come along in the world.'
>
> (Colligan 1982: website)

Another example of hackers deriving what could be labelled as an intellectu-
ally abstract, as opposed to a practically malevolent sense of power, is their
collection of potentially destructive information for the simple act of collection
rather than any particular use to which it could be put.[4] *Hack-Tic* shares with
such publications as *Phrack* and *TAP*, the characteristic of containing much
esoteric, yet potentially dangerous, information. Thus throughout issues of *Phrack*
are instructions on how to make various explosives such as nitro-glycerine. To
most people outside the hacking world, the promulgation of such information
would seem, at best, of dubious value, and, at worst, extremely irresponsible.
The fact that hackers spread, but would be extremely unlikely to use such knowledge for any concrete purpose, is indicative of their general ethos that purports
information to be of value or interest in its own right. This may partially explain
the fact that much hacking activity does not seem to have any 'useful' eventual
purpose. The activity is an end in itself and the intellectual exercise of gaining
knowledge is its own justification. Rop Gongrijp explains this tendency of his
magazine and those like *Phrack* of disseminating diverse forms of technological
knowledge irrespective of the possible uses or value of that information, as
follows:

> the information is out there and the people who are going to make bombs
> have the information anyway, if you want to make a bomb you can get all
> the information on how to build a nuclear bomb if you want to, you just
> look in the library, and it's just that so many people enjoy reading about
> something they will never do just for the sake of reading about it. I mean if
> I publish a scheme on how to rob ATMs (automatic telling machines) and I
> make the scheme real elaborate, where it takes video cameras and organisa-
> tion, nobody's probably going to do that except the people that already
> knew how to do that anyway. It's only for the sense of adventure of the
> people that read that and think 'wow! this is great: a sense of power'.
>
> (Gongrijp: Amsterdam interview)

The informational content of such magazines as *Hack-Tic*, however, can be of
practical use. It is generally concerned with electronic gadgetry and 'blue-box
technology' for phreaking free phone calls. The magazine has, for example,
gained some notoriety by giving details of how to make free phone calls from
public pay-phones, and this has called into question some of the above claims of
the disinterested publication of information.

Peer recognition and hacking culture

> Although the stereotype image of a hacker is someone who is socially inept and avoids people in favour of computers, hackers are more likely to be in it for the social aspects. They like to interact with others on bulletin boards, through electronic mail, and in person. They share stories, gossip, opinions, and information; work on projects together; teach younger hackers; and get together for conferences and socializing.
>
> (Denning 1992b: 60)

The final motivational category is that of a sense of peer recognition. One example of an individual looking for recognition outside of a group of hackers is that provided by the account of Gerry Santoro from Penn State University:

> About two years ago a teaching assistant (T.A.) for my Computing in the Humanities class figured out the password for one of my mainframe disks. He then proceeded to copy files from me, including a file that listed all students and their passwords. When the T.A. was caught he denied having done this, claiming that he didn't know how he got the files. At the same time, other members of the student computing community reported that he was bragging about how he had 'outsmarted' the computer center and that no files were safe from his intrusion if he desired. I believe this particular student did it for the peer-group status that it afforded. This particular student did not have much of a social life outside of classes, and therefore this was a realistic route for obtaining (in his mind) a positive self-image.
>
> (Santoro: email interview)

Hackers themselves admit to this element of peer-encouraged behaviour. Maelstrom admitted that:

> Peer recognition was very important, when you were recognised, you had access to more. For instance, on chat systems where private channels could be set up and people could only enter by invitation, you had to be known and respected before you got to join the discussion. Also, many people hacked for fame as well as the rush. Anyone who gets an informative article in a magazine (i.e. Phrack, NIA, etc.) can be admitted to bulletin boards. Finding new user passwords requires only a few contacts, and contacts can be found on chat systems (even public non-hacker ones).
>
> (Maelstrom: email interview)

The Zoetermeer group's activity was largely based upon their contact with each other at university, and their individual hacking was encouraged by there being a receptive audience amongst both an inner and outer group of admirers:

Hacking can be rewarding in itself, because it can give you a real kick sometimes. But it can give you a lot more satisfaction and recognition if you can
share your experiences with others. Next to that it is very useful if you
operate in a group, because many know more than one alone. I think the
group nature is important because of the recognition you can get from the
group; doing bigger and better hacks clearly distinguishes you from other
people. Here at my school the group nature is also very important in
providing a competitive environment which proves very motivating. Without
this group I would never have spent so much time behind the terminals
digging into the operating system. Our group consists of a core of about
6/7 people and lots of people hanging around (in blind admiration ;-)).

(Zoetermeer: email interview)

The peer recognition aspects of hacking have been explained by recourse to
the concept of machismo. Keller explains how:

hacking is an aberrant behaviour related to *machismo*. ... *Machismo* is an
exaggerated form of male posturing designed to demonstrate a high degree
of masculinity through the accomplishment of acts of proof, with the object
of exciting the admiration of others and (perhaps also) demonstrating
contempt for the less masculine.

(Keller 1990: 58)

Using this definition of machismo to explain and conceptualise the activity of
hacking is problematic, however. In addition, Keller attempts to argue that
hackers succumb to the macho vice of only enjoying glory that accrues to the
individual and is unshared. She compares hacking to bull-running at Pamplona
and argues that, 'It is necessary to act alone, to dare the bull as an individual,
without the help of others. As I have observed, the hacker is also solitary' (Keller
1990: 59).

This does not fit well, however, with evidence that hackers use well-organised
teamwork to achieve their ends. Counter to Keller's argument, Mathew Bevan, a
UK hacker tried and acquitted of conspiracy charges after hacking into a US
Air Force base in 1993, claims: 'It's all about teamwork. I may be a good hacker
but I don't know everything', he says. 'With six or seven people, there's a pool of
expertise covering lots of different mainframe systems and telephone networks'
(*Guardian* 26 February 1998: 5 [*On-line* section]) In addition, two of the Dutch
hacking groups I interviewed face-to-face also exhibited this close-knit collective
approach to their activity, each hacker tending to have their own delineated
areas of specialisation that contribute to the overall group effort. With this and
the fact that bulletin boards, conventional and computer-mediated conferences,
group meals (stereotypically Chinese according to Levy [1984]), etc. are all used
to help generate peer recognition amongst hackers, there does not seem to be an
innate need to appropriate solely individual glory. Keller also claims that
hackers, in a fashion similar to that of serial killers, generally seek recognition of

their cleverness from such establishment figures as the law enforcement people seeking to catch them. The Dutch hackers, Gongrijp and Ralph, however, both argued that the most accomplished hackers are those whose exploits are least known. The hackers who are most publicised tend to be those who have been caught through technical carelessness and are sneered at by others in the hacking community for such carelessness.

Political acts

Some hackers claim that they are a principled force within society dedicated to opposing the re-establishment of traditional values in the newly emerging information society. They argue that such traditional values are based upon physical property rights and are increasingly anachronistic in an emerging information society predicated upon the bodiless transportation of data streams. To the extent to which hackers rhetorically revel in the vestigial new information age, hacking culture can thus be construed as offering potentially novel paradigms for living most effectively in this new order. Members of the Dutch hacking group, Hack-Tic, voiced their concern that encryption methods are not used frequently enough to ensure the privacy of email communications, and that the available encryption keys have been compromised by the US National Security Agency's requirement that they be breakable.[5] Such concern over privacy rights was also voiced by Martin Freiss, a hacker from Paderborn in Germany:

> 'information freedom' is the slogan of most hackers over here (including the notorious CCC, chaos computer club). We already have a situation where electronic communications are unsafe, i.e. governments may legally tap data lines and make copies of electronic mail. Plus, the suspicion of 'hacking' alone (i.e. no evidence) is sufficient to get search warrants or to impound equipment. What hackers (not the kind that wilfully destroys data for the fun of it, but the real hackers) are fighting for, is something of a battle of principles. They want to keep the new electronic media as safe or even safer than regular paper mail from intrusion by government agencies.
>
> (Freiss: email interview)

Opposition to the commodification of information and anti-bureaucratic rebellion

> It's as if big companies and their suck-up lawyers think that computing belongs to them, and they can retail it with price stickers, as if it were boxes of laundry soap! But pricing 'information' is like trying to price air or price dreams.
>
> (Sterling 1992: 85)

Whilst the ultimate counter-cultural status of hacking is open to debate, what is less ambiguous is the way in which they turn on its head the usually negative response to technological progress found in most counter-cultural groups: instead of demonising artefacts, they prefer to use them to their fullest advantage. Hackers' more specific claims to be an alternative culture rest with their instinctive dislike for Government information-gathering bureaucracies, and their opposition to what they perceive as the unjustified privatisation of information. The complexity and difficulties encountered by the market economy in attempting to impose intellectual property rights are reflected in its struggle with hackers. Information and its specific, and in some respects unusual, economic properties give rise to a conflict where different groups struggle and negotiate over whose view of information will ultimately prevail. The opposition to market pressures to commodify information and enforce property rights can be seen in two distinct realms: software production and computer systems intrusion. The more obvious form of hackers' oppositional status is their failure to respect the copy protection methods used to assert it. As early as 1986 the Software Publishing Association estimates that software producers lost approximately $1 billion per year in sales as a result of unauthorised copying (both for profit and for personal use).

An aspect of the modern technological order is the individual's perception of anonymity in the face of large commercial entities, acts that manage to express individuality become valued as human blows struck against dehumanised and unaccountable bureaucratic structures:

> [Hacking can be seen as] the necessary evil that will always be there; humans, by nature, will attempt to break the rules placed over them. And the anonymity of much of the computer underground activities make it that much more attractive.
>
> (Kehoe: email interview)

Richard Stallman identified this anti-authoritarian stance; when asked if he thought that some hacking was undertaken in a spirit of political rebelliousness he replied: 'I don't see a connection directly with abuse of power by governments, but abuse of power on a smaller scale by sysadmins seems directly relevant' (Stallman: email interview). He emphasised as a contributory factor behind hacking the behaviour of grass-roots system managers and administrators, and he contended that it is not enough just to prosecute and/or fix holes that hackers draw attention to, because: 'neither of these would eliminate the motive for cracking. The way to do that is to stop the fascist behaviour which inspires blind resistance to stop treating disobedience as if it were evil' (Stallman: email interview).

Hacking as a form of anti-bureaucratic rebellion can take both macro and micro forms. On a macro-level Steve Hardin argues, 'most law-abiding people fantasize about breaking the law big-time and getting away with it. We 'ordinary folk' are intrigued by the little guy who beats the big corporations or governments' (Hardin: email interview). The anti-authoritarian outlook of hackers that is needed as part of their 'free information' ethos tends to encourage little empathy with governmental agencies. The president of the French Chaos Computer Club, Jean-Bernard Condat, who partially began his career as an act of political rebelliousness, relates how:

> When I was 16½ years old, I finished the 'lycee' and passed without any problem my 'bacculauret'. I go from Beziers to Lyon (middle of France) for my University ... and discover that all the information will easily be available on a host in Palo Alto (California, USA). I try to connect me from my University-room and work on my poor $53.00-TTY-terminal all the nights. One night, I have the visit of the great DST service (anti-spy service) that ask me kindly 'Explain us how you do for connecting you ....' I never answer correctly to this question, and enter the same day in the CU.
>
> (Condat: email interview)

The dislike many people have for large 'faceless' bureaucratic organisations adopts a specific manifestation with hackers whose failure to have ethical qualms about obtaining free communication services is encouraged by what they perceive to be the unjustified level of the firms' monopoly profits (Sterling 1992: 62). Activities that involve the avoidance of payment for communication services are further encouraged by a belief that no 'real' cost is being incurred by the victim company. Ralph and Maelstrom both emphasised that any pecuniary losses attributable to their activities were carried not by individuals but by an unscrupulous monopoly power. Maelstrom, for example, in describing the activities of the German hacking group Red Sector Inc., mentions the use of stolen AT&T card numbers but qualifies the use of the word 'stolen' by contending that:

> You can't 'steal' a number without stealing the whole card; you can only copy it. The rationale was that the customer whose card is being abused won't have to pay the bill, AT&T will absorb it and give him/her a new one. And AT&T deserves to absorb. After all what does it cost to make a phone call? The lines are already in place, and the electrons don't care how far they travel. The voltage is going through your lines whether you use it or not. So you're not really ripping anyone off. Big companies like AT&T just like to make it seem that way so they can get more money.
>
> (Maelstrom: email interview)

On a more micro-level, the Dutch hacker, G., points out how hacking can be in response to the bureaucratic inconveniences imposed on computer users:

> I gave you the example of the VMS system where the operating system itself has all these little windows and forms built in ... many for the sake of the internal bureaucracy and if you program around that, you can hack the system, because one of the many purposes of those windows is to keep you

out, but the other advantage of programming around that, and that's been done quite a lot by very respectable programmers, and the techniques are used in most professional pieces of software, especially for IBM machines. If you hack around that window, that whole bureaucratic system, your file access becomes faster, you can do more things with the system, you can write software that genuinely looks more impressive, because it's much faster than anything that's written in the official way, and in DOS that's very, very well known.

(G.: Delft interview)

The exploits of people such as *Captain Crunch* give rise to the tacit respect and recognition that the technologically unversed majority hold for acts involving illegal but technically dextrous methods. Respect tends to be afforded for any non-violent feat that involves a technological artefact being used to defeat a technological system, especially if that system is part of '*the* system'. Human individuality is perceived as threatened by the anonymity of modern technological systems; those that are seen as striking back against that anonymity are perhaps more difficult to view as criminals than would those acting against identifiable individuals using less technological means.

Conclusion

There are a lot of people interested in playing around at hacking out of sheer curiosity and a small group whose interest is motivated out of mischief and malevolence. There's a macho prowess to hacking, it's a challenge.[6]

In sum, the attraction of phreaking and its attendant life-style appear to center on three fundamental characteristics: The quest for knowledge, the belief in a higher ideological purpose of opposition to potentially dangerous technological control, and the enjoyment of risk-taking.

(Meyer and Thomas 1989a: 14)

The descriptions of hacking as a form of compulsive programming emphasise how it is often pursued at the expense of the ability to conduct 'normal' social relations. The stereotypical 'computer geek', therefore, is someone who finds refuge from what seems to be a hostile world in the safety of the esoteric computer knowledge they have chosen to master. The complex mix of motivational factors exhibited by hackers in this chapter complicates the task facing those seeking to combat hacking. The 'boredom' excuse, for example, may be answered by finding various ways to increase the interest quotient of the courses hackers complain about at college, but such measures will necessarily have little effect on the incidence of hacking caused by anti-bureaucratic attitudes. It would seem that no one solution aimed at eliminating hacking will succeed in addressing the mix of possible motivations that fuel the act. The analysis in this chapter of the reasons put forward for their activity by hackers themselves has aimed to compensate for the limitations of those accounts that define hacking predominantly as compulsive programming. The aim has been to provide a fuller, more well-rounded picture of the full complexity and significance of hacking in its various guises. It is important to have this fuller, more balanced understanding of what motivates hacking, especially if policies are to be developed with which to reduce it or to at least tap and/or channel its ingenious qualities in other directions.

4 State of the industry

Introduction: the invisible crime and the state of the industry

> the term 'dark figure', used by criminologists to refer to unreported crime, has been applied to undiscovered computer crimes. The invisibility of computer crimes is based on several factors. First, sophisticated technology, that is, the immense, compact storage capacity of the computer and the speed with which computers function, ensures that computer crime is very difficult to detect. In contrast to most traditional areas of crime, unknowing victims are often informed after the fact by law enforcement officials that they have sustained a computer crime. Secondly, investigating officials often do not have sufficient training to deal with problems in the complex environment of data processing. Thirdly, many victims do not have a contingency plan for responding to incidents of computer crime, and they may even fail to acknowledge that a security problem exists.
>
> (United Nations *International Review of Criminal Policy*: par. 30)

This chapter examines the state of security within computing and the reasons for the security weaknesses that allow hackers to access other people's computer systems. The chapter outlines the extent to which security flaws exist; the reasons they are not eliminated; and the potential role hackers might have as correctors of such faults. It analyses the notion that computer security is relatively unstructured and under-theorised, and describes the subsequent problems associated with producing verifiably secure computer systems and how those problems can be related back to a concept referred to as the *software crisis*. The next section describes the problems encountered in producing reliable statistics for computer crime. Because of these problems, I prefer to concentrate in this chapter upon some of the underlying basic reasons for the existence of security weaknesses in principle rather than the scale and frequency of actual breaches.[1]

Computer systems are intrinsically insecure in the sense that they cannot be guaranteed, a priori, to be totally impervious to intrusions. The reasons given for computer security flaws are both technical and commercial. Commercial pressures are such that there is a tendency to skimp on the security measures and procedures that do exist and in addition education about computer security suffers from a low profile in both the academic and business sectors. Once it has been established that there is a fundamental need for security improvements within computing, this chapter looks at hackers' claims that they have real technical knowledge that could be used to help provide them. The question then arises as to why co-operation between the computer security industry and the computer underground does not occur on a larger scale and why hackers do not now have the level of acceptance enjoyed in their early MIT days.

The first hackers were largely tolerated because their knowledge was valued and useful despite its often unusual methods of acquisition. What was once tolerated in the academic pursuit of knowledge, however, seems to be no longer tolerable in the increasingly commercial environment of computing, the changing nature of which has led to a hardening of attitudes towards hackers. As a result the computer underground's expertise in security is not generally utilised by the computer security industry despite the fact that a generally poor quality of security within computing coexists with their potential to produce technical fixes. This leads to the assumption that hackers are being marginalised away from a core of influence within computing and that this is due primarily to social rather than technical reasons.

Lies, damned lies, and statistics ... and guestimates

In the business sector ... reluctance [to report computer crime] is related to two concerns. Some victims may be unwilling to divulge information about their operations for fear of adverse publicity, public embarrassment or loss of goodwill. Other victims fear the loss of investor or public confidence and the resulting economic consequences. Some experts have suggested that these factors have a significant impact on the detection of computer crime. ... International studies have examined the relation behind this reluctance, evident particularly in the financial sector, to report computer crime. Loss of consumer confidence in a particular business and in its management can lead to even greater economic loss than that caused by the crime itself. In addition, many managers fear personal repercussion if responsibility for the infiltration is placed at their door. Victims have complained about the inconvenience of lengthy criminal investigations and indeed have questioned the ability of authorities to investigate the crime.

(United Nations *International Review of Criminal Policy*: paras 31 and 223)

It is inherently difficult to compile reliable statistics pertaining to the absolute size of the computer security problem. Mirroring the relatively vague and anonymous nature of the computer underground, it is likely that official statistics under-report hacking incidents. One reason for this is that the companies and organisations affected may be totally oblivious to security breaches that have occurred, because the innately reproducible and immaterial nature of the information contained within the computer systems targeted by hackers means nothing physical may actually be missing. Even assuming that the crimes are detected, there is also the additional problem of the non-reporting of incidents; large organisations are unsurprisingly reluctant to admit to security breaches when they do occur. A further complicating effect that in contrast is likely to lead to overestimates of computer crime is the tendency for both computer security figures and hackers to hyperbolise the situation. The former are keen to maximise the perceived need for their services and the latter may wish to exaggerate their 'electronic lethality'.

These problems associated with dark figures create a tendency, in the absence of definitive statistics, to rely upon *guestimate* figures. The Internet Worm[2] is an example of an incident that received large-scale attention and suffered large-scale exaggeration as a result of press interest:

> The incident received world-wide press coverage. Along the way the extent of the damage was magnified. One of the first estimates – from John McAffe, the ever-quotable chairman of CVIA – was that cleaning up the networks and fixing the system's flaws would cost $96 million. Other estimates ran as high as $186 million ... McAfee's estimate of $96 million was dismissed as being 'grossly exaggerated' by Cornell University's subsequent report on the incident.
>
> (Clough and Mungo 1992: 98)

This vagueness of figures relating to computer crime appears to be a common quality compounded by the boastfulness of some hackers, and also stemming from a reluctance of the victims of the crimes to report their vulnerability. This produces subsequent difficulties when trying to collate reliable and meaningful data about security breaches. Dr Taylor, a computer security consultant, gives the following account of this:

> There's lots of media hype but it all comes back to the number of facts and occurrences, what I'd say is that there are very few virus incidents that are discussed in public which is due to a very simple reason. If ... a company gets hit hard with a virus because somebody's been negligent in checking for example in-coming discs or in-coming software, then the next time there's a general meeting of that company, then all the share-holders of that company will go for the chief-executive or his henchmen and just roll the lot of them and put in a new board. It's a job-losing incident, so whenever there's a security incident not just involving viruses, anything involving hacking, fraud, forgery in any plc which has got public share-holders, there's a big whitewash job done ... I would say, I've got to guess, but I would say there's probably ten to twenty serious security incidents in public companies a year, all of which are whitewashed, otherwise the management are accused of negligence.
>
> (Taylor: Knutsford interview)

The widespread reliance on *guestimate* figures by the press and trade journals results from the initial reluctance to report incidents but has far-reaching effects. The subsequent use of estimated figures increases fears of computer crime by exaggerating the perceptions of the potential harm hackers can commit. This process then directly contributes to the 'them and us' stigmatisation process and a concomitant sense that a legislative response is required to solve the problem – both of these reactions are shown in subsequent chapters to be of the potentially knee-jerk rather than the considered type of response that is required if society is to find constructive ways to deal with hacking and its associated costs.

Hacker exploits

I have been in more systems than one can imagine, ranging from military installations, financial installations, to soda companies. I have seen insider-trading information, had access to transferable funds, had the ability to manipulate credit information and have had complete control over phone networks.

(Goggans: email interview)

I obtained a whole slew of accounts on Eastern Michigan University's VAX/VMS system. I've also gotten into very critical test-creation accounts at colleges and universities. It's amazing how easy it often is to get into important accounts that many instructors access.

(Maelstrom: email interview)

The US hacker, Chris Goggans, illustrates the relative ease with which unauthorised access can be gained to computer systems. In his description of several of his break-ins, he claims to have seen:

The advertising campaign outlines for 'new' Coke months before its release; insider stock trading information in mail on Citibank computers, electronic fund transfer systems; military systems with 'sensitive' non-classified information, phone company computers that allow you to listen in on any telephone call in that area; credit computers; the ministry of treasury system in South Africa (whose MOTD [Message Of The Day] changed to 'end apartheid now' as if by magic).

(Goggans: email interview)

Maelstrom and Goggans also both described the way in which their phone-phreaking activities combined with their computing knowledge to enable them to enjoy free international teleconferencing, in addition to the ability to eavesdrop at will on other people's telephone calls. Maelstrom recounted how he:

learnt to use the Michigan C/NA (Customer Name and Address) bureau, which allowed me to dial up a computer and, after entering a passcode, use touch tones to get information on the owner of any Michigan telephone number. Some of my friends from around the world would start AT&T Alliance teleconferences every so often, and we would talk throughout the night, sometimes for as long as 12 hours at a shot (which was probably not good for grades at school). On one memorable conference Cellular Phantom demonstrated a REMOB number (REMote OBservation) which allowed us to listen in on any phone line in the country at will ... I learned quite a bit about how much privacy people REALLY have as opposed to what they THINK they have.

(Maelstrom: email interview)

Similarly, Goggans said:

I know all too well how simple it is to view and alter consumer credit, to transfer funds, to monitor telephone conversations etc. ... I can monitor data on any network in existence, I can obtain root privileges on ANY Sun Microsystems UNIX. If I, a 22 year-old, non-degreed, self-taught individual can do these things, what can a professionally taught, profit motivated individual do? THERE IS NO PRIVACY. ... People need to know the truth about the vulnerabilities of the computers they have entrusted their lives to.

(Goggans: email interview)

A particularly vivid example of the alleged insecurity of computer systems was recounted by a computer security officer from a US military site:

Back in 1989, another nearby facility was penetrated, and the intruder gained control of an industrial process. The product of this process is so specialized that there is no other source. Fortunately, it was local enough that we could trace him. He was still playing with his new 'toy' when the police broke down his parents' (!) door. The raw materials he used were worth more than one million U.S. dollars, and everyone involved thought it was a minor miracle that he hadn't destroyed the plant! [It really happened, I was there, believe it!]

(Z.: email interview)

To add to the alleged vulnerability of systems to outsiders is the added danger of hacking from insiders intimate with the working details of particular systems. Several interviewees (who asked to remain anonymous because they did not want their employers to become aware of the fact that they hacked) concurred with the view that concern over the vulnerability of systems to outside intrusion generally fails to take into account intrusions from people working inside systems.

The existence of security weaknesses

> A computer security industry survey calculated last year that 550 of America's biggest corporations, government agencies and universities had lost more than $100m to computer-related financial fraud, copyright theft and data sabotage.
>
> (*Sunday Times* 8 February 1998: 26)

There seems to be a general consensus of opinion within both the computer security industry and computer underground that there are large and continuing security faults in many systems and that often computer crime highlights rectifiable security weaknesses rather than any special abilities of hackers. The fact that computer systems are vulnerable to attack is ironically underlined by the fact that hackers have been criticised for seldom, if ever, making use of original, previously unknown security weaknesses:

> computer criminal behavior cuts across a wide spectrum of society, with the age of offenders ranging from 10 to 60 years and their skill level ranging from novice to professional. Computer criminals, therefore, are often otherwise average persons rather than supercriminals possessing unique abilities and talents. Any person of any age with a modicum of skill, motivated by the technical challenge, by the potential for gain, notoriety or revenge, or by the promotion of ideological beliefs, is a potential computer criminal.
>
> (United Nations *International Review of Criminal Policy*: par. 34)

The Internet Worm, for example, was often referred to as 'an accident waiting to happen' and the official Cornell University report into the incident downplayed the technical brilliance of the Worm's author:

> although the worm was technically sophisticated, its creation required dedication and perseverance rather than technical brilliance. The worm could have been created by many students, graduate or undergraduate, at Cornell or at other institutions, particularly if forearmed with knowledge of the security flaws exploited or similar flaws.
>
> (P.J. Denning 1990: 256)

To compound matters and in addition to the charge of unoriginality, even when specific technical fixes have been produced for some of the threats posed by hackers, the incremental nature of much software development is such that hackers can make use, not only of technical weaknesses in systems, but also the logistical problems encountered in attempting to fix them:

> Hackers rarely exploit the full spectrum of IT risks! (Apart from a few instances, such as worm technology and stealth viruses), hackers actually use rather primitive methods to access systems, program and data. E.g. the

NASA hack exploited a hole in a DEC VMS version when this hole was in principal already patched; while DEC customers had received (and hopefully installed) the patch when the attack was undertaken, the hackers used a second-hand system (not bought directly from DEC) whose existence was not known to DEC, and where the patch was not sent!

(Brunnstein, University of Hamburg: email interview)

Reasons for security weaknesses: the problem of anticipation and the role of testing

Intrinsic insecurity and serendipity

The difficulty of anticipating *a priori* threats to security helps hackers expose security weaknesses by 'testing the limits of the developing advances'. Subcultural groups are often associated with the cutting edge of technological developments, for example, Sterling (1992) describes how the new communications technologies were largely pioneered by criminals, so much so, that: 'In the early years of pagers and bleepers, dope dealers were so enthralled by this technology that owning a bleeper was practically prima facie evidence of cocaine dealing' (Sterling 1992: 183). That security weaknesses in systems are seemingly inevitable is reflected in the experience of hackers' serendipitous opportunism. Robert Schifreen, for example, was known as the 'Prestel hacker', for hacking (along with his associate, Steve Gold) into the Duke of Edinburgh's private electronic-mail box:

> I was playing with some software one day and found out that if you typed ten 2's for an id number on Prestel it was a valid account. *Just by pure chance*, I was just testing some terminals, I wasn't actually trying to get in. I hit the 2 button, ten times and it said 'yeah, fine what's the password?', so I thought 'this is easy, I know passwords are four characters so I'll try 1234', tried 1234 and it let me in and it turned out to be an internal BT account that let me access loads of closed areas on the system.
>
> (Schifreen: London interview [emphasis mine])

Schifreen's experience illustrates a serendipitous aspect of gaining access to other people's systems. What he perceives as attributable to chance, however, is largely based upon such basic security failings as inadequate user identification log-in procedure. Once he had gained initial access, subsequent entry to privileged accounts became possible because security was not maintained throughout the system. Information that allowed further progress was left lying around on the assumption that no one could have gained access because of the initial security measures. Making a system relatively secure requires security measures at different levels of a system, and assuming that some of the first-level security measures may be broken. However, even if systems are designed with this assumption that at any one stage previous security barriers may have been broken, total and 'pre-emptive' security for some artefacts may still be effectively impossible. It is arguably in the nature of security that weaknesses cannot always be foreseen. They may only come to light as a result of the imaginative manipulations of hackers. The heterogeneous and ubiquitous curiosity of hackers allied with their 'instinct' for security flaws results in them eventually finding security loopholes in all kinds of technological artefacts. Thus Mike Dell, a Dutch hacker, relates how he always keeps his eyes open for a hacking opportunity:

> If I work or am on holiday I also see things where I think, 'hey yeah, that's possible, last year I was in Miami and I found a way to park for absolutely free ... just by chance I found that if you put a dime in and turn the parking meter all the way up, as far as possible, and let it go all at once, because of the speed the meter goes, for one dime you can park the whole day. You develop an intuition, an instinct.
>
> (Dell: Utrecht interview)

It is this instinct for serendipitous discovery that conventional security theory may always be struggling to contain, since the initial security breakthrough may not be due to the type of logical strategy that can be most easily anticipated within formally conceived security measures. One commentator described in the following manner the unpredictable and refractory nature of computer security:

> Take a computer and put it in a bank vault with ten-foot-thick walls. Power it up with an independent source, with a second independent source of backup. Install a combination lock on the door, along with an electronic beam security system. Give one person access to the vault. Then give one more person access to that system and security is cut in half. With a second person in the picture, [a computer hacker] could play the two against each other. She could call posing as the secretary of one person, or as a technician in for repair at the request of the other. She could conjure dozens of ruses for using one set of human foibles against another. And the more people with access the better.
>
> (Konstantinou 1995: 49)

The ubiquity of hacking

An important contributing aspect to the vulnerability of systems is the generic nature of hacking. That is, often the ability to hack into one computer system can be applied to a whole class of systems. Professor Herschberg, from the Computer Science department of Delft University in The Netherlands, pointed out that when he accepts a documented hack as a Master's Thesis, the penetration described within the thesis should be for a class of systems as opposed to just one individual system: 'it's always a class ... hack one, hack all, otherwise it doesn't count, proper penetration is generic' (Herschberg: Delft interview). This generic nature of hacking, however, also causes great concern for the computer security industry due to the fact that, unlike traditional intrusion with generic hacking, once a flaw has been found in a system it is then vulnerable not just to local hackers, but to the world-wide community. Goggans related how: 'today hackers have everything documented for them on the usage of a plethora of systems by past hackers' (Goggans: email interview). Holbrook, a US security practitioner, explains why this situation can cause concern about security threats to assume paranoid proportions:

> I would go back to the analogy about physical trespass. In that realm, the amount of damage that an intruder can use is usually related to how much effort they put in, how much expertise they have, and so forth. People are very comfortable with what kinds of threats exist in the 'real world' and how to deal with them. There is no similar comfort level in the computer world. With the breakdown of physical barriers surrounding computers that the network brings, organisations have equal risk from malicious local users and from crackers half way around the world. Intruders can compromise and damage a system with information that could be found on a cracker bbs. Most computer systems don't have any levels of security. Any gap is sufficient to compromise the entire system. So some paranoia is warranted!
>
> (Holbrook: email interview)

The generic quality of hacking, in addition, may exacerbate the vulnerability of systems to damaging security breaches, over and above the deliberate damage of malicious hackers because of the tendency of non-malicious but careless system intruders to inadvertently cause damage. In the words of Chris Goggans:

> In my own experience, I was VERY cautious in the early days. I didn't just barge in to a system like the stereotypical 'bull in a china shop' and I imagine most people keep this level of alertness. Even with this heightened sensitivity to the potential disasters, some people still executed programs they shouldn't have, edited sensitive data, etc. ... Today it seems many hackers just don't care, but then again, today hackers have everything documented for them on the usage of a plethora of systems by past hackers, so perhaps armed with these instructions they feel overly confident from the onset.
>
> (Goggans: email interview)

The state of computer security knowledge and education

Contemporary insecurity and unsafety are basically built into today's IT architectures, but only very few people understand this (there is *no theory of secure and safe systems*!). Some hackers deliberately intend to demonstrate the apparent insecurity of contemporary systems (e.g. CCC), while others produce negative impact during unconscientious experimenting with parts of the technology (e.g. Morris' INTERNET worm) ... we have serious problems to understand what security and safety means, and we have *no theory of safe and secure systems*.

(Brunnstein: email interview)

Indicative of the security weaknesses of systems is the perceived widespread lack of knowledge in the field of computer security. Computer security ignorance is compounded by the tendency of those within computing to regard its effects as being overwhelmingly positive. This seems to be reflected in the way in which the technology is approached by software engineers:

> The general taboo behind contemporary IT is that everybody regards these systems as *positive*; only few users and even fewer experts realize that there is a positive side of the coin ('useful': hip, hip Hurrah!) connected with a negative one (bugs, viruses ...). Following the implemented moral categories, engineers regard technology as 'morally neutral', and they do not feel responsible for faults or misuse as they regard these as tasks of the users; unfortunately, users cannot understand today's very complex systems (mega bits of data/programs/data flow ...) to control the adequacy of IT results!
>
> (Brunnstein: email interview)

A general lack of education in the knowledge that does exist contributes to the continued existence of security weaknesses that could otherwise be repaired. Comparing it to a 'leaky sieve' Dr Cohen argues:

> The leaky sieve comes from the fact that OS designers don't know about protection, and treat it as an afterthought. Like most afterthoughts, the retrofit doesn't really fit. Why don't they know? Because they aren't taught about it in school. Universities rarely teach anything about protection. The average computer science graduate has only 15 mins on protection – that in an OS course where they are taught how to keep processes separate in memory. On the other hand, about 4% of the GNP is lost each year in most industrialized nations due to computer integrity problems. (According to some Lloyd's underwriters and several confirming research studies). Ignorance is not bliss – it is suicide.
>
> (Cohen: email interview)

Dr Cohen describes the effects of poor education on the quality of security in industry:

> Crackers do not provide a service by breaking in – we know the situation is bad, and we know why – it is because computer professionals are ignorant and the fault should lie squarely with our educational system. ... Computer security issues are ignored – or worse misstated by our teachers, and as a result, we have many people going in random directions making 20 year old

mistakes. ... Most crackers are simply using trivial holes left by ignorant programmers. I think any computer professional should be taught the limitations of computer systems and be given assignments to demonstrate these flaws in school. The situation now is like teaching how to fly airplanes but not teaching pilots that engines sometimes fail. Your system depends on your knowledge for its proper operation, just as an airplane does. We don't accept pilots that can't handle minor mechanical failures, why do we accept computer professionals that can't handle minor protection problems?

(Cohen: email interview)

The consensus amongst hackers also emphasises the poor state of the conventional education system. They frequently describe their knowledge of computing and its security features as being self-taught or peer group-derived. Schifreen, for example, describes the autodidactic nature of his own computer knowledge:

I didn't go to university, I did computing at school until o-level and that was basically the only computing education I got, the rest of it was self-taught for enthusiasm ... the knowledge you need for a computing job doesn't correspond to the course work you've done at University or College. They're not teaching the things that are right for jobs.

(Schifreen: London interview)

Calls for hands-on experience

The perceived failure of the education system and the computer security industry to fully address security and operational weaknesses has led to calls for more practical 'hands-on' security knowledge. It is claimed that hacking may provide practical experience and a *de facto* education in computing and its security measures.[3] Professor Herschberg, for example, defends hacking's status as an intellectual exercise that contributes to both theoretical and practical knowledge:

Well, before I became a professor I was given many opportunities to do it myself, but that was in the very early days. The last time I attacked one with my own lily-white hands must have been about 13 years ago, so I'm certainly to be counted amongst the first generation of hackers, as to being sympathetic, yes, I do accept, a technically satisfactory piece of hacking in lieu of the formal oral exam, providing it's well documented, providing it's not a trivial system and provided no harm has been done ... the proof of the pudding is in the hacking.

(Herschberg: Delft interview)

Herschberg is an example of those who believe that hackers' expertise at breaking into systems could be utilised in order to improve security knowledge. He and his students have been invited by various Dutch companies to attempt to access their systems and to give a full report of any security weaknesses found.

His seemingly idiosyncratic views on the benefits of hacking are fuelled by the contention that computing is in great need of a combination of both academic theory and hands-on direct experience of computer security. He describes how he has:

> a continuous trickle, it's not more than one or two firms at a time, who want me to investigate the only way there is, which is penetration. As an academic, I have one continuous complaint about security: there is no theory; almost no theory. There is some theory, there is cryptography which is quite respectable academically and therefore has a great deal of worthwhile interesting theory, there are a few other areas, say inference from systems one may interrogate interactively. Again, the problem lies, as Dorothy Denning has pointed out, that, by putting the right questions the user may reach information or may infer information he was not meant to possess. That at least has the beginnings of a theory behind it. For the rest, let's say the general penetration attempt is hardly covered by the theory, so that the only way to find out about it is to take the experimental approach: wade in, do it.
>
> (Herschberg: Delft interview)

Thus, Professor Herschberg argues that the theory will only come through the lessons gleaned from practice, 'wading in', and, like Rop Gongrijp, he sees computing and the hacking of systems as still very much a frontier activity. The best comparison to be made:

> would be with the early days of say radio. Marconi successfully transmitted across the Atlantic before there was a theory of terrestrial radio-wave propagation. The Wright brothers flew by the seat of their pants, theory came much later. I think it's fair comment that any new technology must go through the stage in which theory lags far behind practice. It is true for security except for shreds and patches, so I see no other way than actually to attack a system in order to make a valid statement about its penetrability.
>
> (Herschberg: Delft interview)

The actions of hackers, whether deliberate or not, serve to illustrate security weaknesses in an area where theoretical knowledge tends to be subsumed under the exigencies of practical applications and interactions of programs and computer systems:

> As the importance of IT will grow further, we will need better understanding of risks inherent in IT (e.g. concepts of inherently safe and secure systems), as well as risks from its use and misuse. Only IT-inherent risks may be analysed independently of its application; the terms 'safe' and 'secure' (which are semantic categories, rather than syntactic ones!), may only be

defined in terms of an application, and therefore a theory of safe and secure applications may only be defined after hands-on experiments.

(Brunnstein: email interview)

The call for more 'hands-on' and less formally structured approaches to computing has arguably been reflected in the computer security industry in recent years where there has been:

A movement away from the 'Rainbow Books' to more practical security approaches. The 'Rainbow' series reflected a concern with formally provable security, which was based on being able to demonstrate that the system was always secure, no matter what the order of security-related actions. Unfortunately, that meant that security had to be centralized and single-threaded to ensure that could be shown. Modern systems are distributed and need some other approach. This was first recognized with the publication of the 'Red Book', where the review comments identified a long list of hard problems. Modern security is based instead on a more effective and realistic 'onion' model, with multiple layers using different security technologies in each layer.

(System administrator [anonymity requested]: email interview)

The knowledge gap

An illustration of the perceived need for more hands-on experience is the alleged knowledge gap that exists between the computer security industry and computer underground. To the extent that computer security is lacking in a theoretical grounding, the only true way to test security is to actually attempt to breach a system. This requirement for practical knowledge has put pressure upon some of the conventional 'experts' in the field of computer security. In this area, theoretical knowledge tends to be gained at the expense of detailed specific knowledge. Often a security expert with a good grasp of the general tendencies of most computer systems is at a disadvantage when it comes to the question of the finer details of specific systems. A hacker will research his narrowly defined area of specialisation in an exhaustive and comprehensive manner, in an amount of time and to a degree not feasible for a computer security consultant. Detective Harry Onderwater from the Dutch Criminal Research Institute recognised this and pointed out that it was impossible to know everything about every system, and, in his job, he relied heavily upon networks of specialists to obtain the exact information he needed. This highly detailed level of knowledge is much sought after in the hacker community and is arguably much more difficult to obtain for computer security professionals working within the confines and demands of a conventional job structure. Kevin Mitnick (referred to in the press as 'the dark-side hacker'), when asked whether hackers tended to have an edge in their skirmishes with the computer security industry, described how:

They've got the motivation and don't forget, computer security people go to their job from nine to five, for hackers it's a hobby. You dedicate more time to that hobby than you would a job, when you're done with your job, you want to get out of there, go home to your wife, play golf, go work out at the gym. You don't want to sit there and deal with it, usually. But hackers, on the other hand, devote hours and hours to learning, so a lot of them are more talented in maybe that narrow area of computers.

(Mitnick: telephone interview, Holland–US)

This type of knowledge gap between the specific knowledge of the hacker and the general knowledge possessed by the computer professional is reflected in their different interpretations of particular incidents, and the lack of shared values between the professional security experts and the hacker. Professor Spafford has been described as one example of a well-known and influential figure on the Internet who, amongst the hackers I spoke to, was repeatedly referred to in derisive terms.

Schifreen describes what I would term as an essential *knowledge gap* between the computer underground and computer security industry that he believes should be reached across more often:

I'm bridging the gap because that's the way it's got to be done. Yes, you've got the security consultants like a big-city accounting firm that will come and talk to you, and they know the theory because they've read the books and talked to the manufacturers and certainly they can give you some good advice. But they're not involved in the real world, they sit at their desks writing articles, books and reports, they don't talk to hackers, they haven't been on the end that I have. They don't keep their ears to the ground, they don't know what's going on, they know what's going on by reading product reviews and certainly there are management principles that you can go around telling people and they are always relevant, but unless you've got the mind of a hacker and you think as a hacker thinks, you won't realise where the loopholes are in people's security systems.

(Schifreen: London interview)

The 'knowledge gap' is thus rooted in the difference between theoretical concepts and guidelines to security and the 'nitty gritty' of real-world computing situations where security weaknesses flourish in the interstices of continually expanding and evolving computer systems.

Commercial pressures and long-neglected security holes

James V. Christy II, director of computer crime investigations for the Office of Special Investigations at Bolling Air Force Base in Washington, D.C. ... tells of a young Washington-area hacker who had pleaded guilty to breaking into a Pentagon computer system. 'We asked him to help us out', Christy says. 'I sat him down in an office at Bolling and had him go in and attack as many Air Force systems as he could get into. We wired this kid up so that everything he did was recorded. Within 15 seconds he broke into the same computer at the Pentagon that he was convicted for, because its administrators still had not fixed its vulnerabilities. I had to go back the next day and tell the emperor he still had no clothes'. The unorthodox operation continued for three weeks. 'During that time he broke into over 200 Air Force systems', Christy recounts. 'Zero victims reported that they had been hacked into. Not one'. Christy used these embarrassing results to press information-security officers throughout the Air Force to patch over long-neglected security holes.

(Roush 1995: 5)

One of the underlying reasons for the level of ignorance described in previous sections is the perennial problem of scarce resources. Professor Spafford, for example, complains that education in security issues tends to be an essential but often neglected expense:

We're producing students that don't know enough about software engineering, about safety of software systems ... I have to teach them on equipment that is very often several years out of date, that is underpowered, that is lacking in basic tools that they will be using when they go out into industry ... there are institutions that are producing students whose sole education is done either on PC's using MS-DOS or some kind of batch-operating system, I know of places that are still using punch cards.

(Spafford: email interview)

The scarcity of resources is also evident at a commercial level and contributes to the continued existence of security holes:

It's because the bottom line in any company today is making profit, you've got no time to do anything that doesn't bring you money or makes you profit. British industry in general is in a hell of a mess and in particular all the staff who could be squeezed out of work in any enterprise, have been squeezed out. There's no time for non-productive work which is the security issue ... everything in the computing industry like everywhere else is done in a hell of a hurry to get it done yesterday. A lot of rather poor programs get written.

(Taylor: Knutsford interview)

Thus, in addition to the security weaknesses, hackers have gained prior and exclusive knowledge over and which thereby helps constitute the *knowledge gap*; there are a large number of well-known bugs and security holes. Specifically, the following factors create conditions conducive to the continued existence of security holes.

Commercial pressures: job structure and low profile of security

Commercial pressures are evident with respect to the way in which computer security jobs are structured. Detective Harry Onderwater, of the Dutch Criminal Research Institute's Computer Crime Squad, complained that computerisation has taken place within companies with scant attention being paid to adequately educating those given jobs involving close contact with computers. He described the informal and *ad hoc* way in which he found himself involved in the issue of computer security:

> I got system manager next to my job at the Drugs Squad, because there was no system manager and I was the only one who could work with computers, so I did the computing ... I think if there had been somebody specialised then, they could have done the job better than I. It's hobbyism of the guys who work there, it's a problem also with the money involved ... they won't make a system manager but leave you at your old job and do that next to it. Courses are very expensive ... it's a job you do next to your own job, a lot of functions should be divided over more people, maybe a system manager should never be the same man as a database administrator, but because it's a small firm, the guy is a system manager, a database administrator, a security officer and he's also the book-keeper.
>
> (Onderwater: Hague interview)

Schifreen also draws attention to the *ad hoc* way that jobs are structured for security personnel, arguing that this contributes to the generally security-ignorant nature of computing in industry:

> apart from most people not knowing what they're doing ... another problem is that, let's say you've got a large company and they suddenly read a book and it says 'make sure you've got a security manager'. And they think, 'right, who's next in line in promotion to manager? So and so down the corridor. Get him in, congratulations, you're now a manager. 'What of?' 'Security: go and read this book'. The average security manager according to recent research, as they say, has been in the job for eight months, so there's no way that they've got the experience to know what the risks are, and reading a theoretical book is not going to tell you where the risks are.
>
> (Schifreen: London interview)

In addition to the prevalence of under-qualified personnel attempting to deal with security problems, many organisations make do with poor administration practices:

I am forced to agree that most computer managers are just about as incompetent as most crackers; they merely apply 'formula' solutions to problems with no real understanding of what they are doing. To the extent that crackers are exposing this lack, perhaps they are doing a service to the industry and perhaps we will eventually see truly professional computer managers and security staff hired by companies, rather than the 'clerks' that they use now.

(Bickford, US security practitioner: email interview)

The reason why those in charge of security are often particularly unsuited to the job is the result of the low esteem in which security work is often held. Computer security in the commercial sector adopts an inevitably low profile because any successes are negatively defined. If a conscientious security officer presides over a trouble-free system, then it:

unfortunately creates the impression, a very negative impression, of no actual achievement to point to. The proof of the achievement, if any, is in the absence of penetrations or penetrations come to light, which is a different thing ... virtually everybody's successes are more visible than those of the security officers. Therefore, it is good for your career development, not to be the security officer or whatever title he may bear in the organisation.

(Herschberg: Delft interview)

Tozer, a UK security practitioner, expressed his constant frustration at the lack of care organisations take over their security, and the negative impact job structure tends to have on the provision of security:

I still blame a lack of professionalism amongst Data Protection (DP) managers, for allowing things to occur. It's their job ... but you get very few DP people at the board level anyway, even though DP penetrates everywhere. So even if they do know what they're doing they don't even get a chance to put it at the same strength as the others. ... For years I've been trying to find out what's needed to trigger people's minds in the right channel. Last week for example, I got a phone call from a very well-known company. Could I give a course, a data-protection course? ... he said these are people at the top, so I said it shouldn't be too difficult ... I'll send you a sheet and fill in a few questions and we'll see how long it'll take. 'Oh, well, they've only got two hours! ... I mean a day, yes, for senior people, but two hours?'

(Tozer: Hawarden interview)

The constant need to update

Most individual sites are not in a position to fix bugs. Even if you have source, you generally don't want to make any more changes to the distributed system than are absolutely necessary. I'm speaking here from my vantage point as a former systems' programmer – the more you diddle, the harder it is to upgrade the next release. ... The real responsibility is with the vendors. They need to provide more secure systems. It's hard, because security is always a trade-off with convenience. But they have to stop taking shortcuts in their system architectures.

(Smb: email interview)

Even when technical fixes have been made to fix security flaws, the latest update of the system incorporating the fix is not utilised by an organisation. If organisations use the very latest operating system from a vendor it tends to be relatively secure. However, to avoid the expense of constantly updating, earlier versions of operating systems tend to be used and left untouched and may not have been upgraded for a number of years:

The best example of this is SunOS 3.5. There are many, many holes in that system. And there are many, many sites that still run it, because the upgrade to SunOS 4.0 just wouldn't run on many systems without expensive upgrades. Even on newer systems, finding the resources to do something as simple as pulling over a patched version of a vendor's utility can be difficult to get done.

(Holbrook: email interview)

The ever-present commercial pressure of limited resources leads to *ad hoc* alterations of systems in order to increase their performance, but this may lead to an intrinsic mismatch between a system's nominal and actual security, taking into account the way the system actually functions on a day-to-day basis. In addition, few if any systems have been designed from the bottom up with security as a primary objective. The quality that sells computers (as with cars) is raw power rather than security features. The following quotation highlights how such pressures interact:

Yes, Von Neuman architecture is *inherently insecure*, as concepts of 'security' and 'safety' have not been fully realised (or even reflected) in its basic concepts. Example: while a secure system would deny illegal services *in its innermost kernel*, contemporary security is implemented *on top of today's system*; if you succeed to penetrate the shell, the kernel is open for any action. As the current trend optimizes performance (more storage, faster processing, broader and faster channels and devices), concepts of safe systems are forgotten even where some hardware features (such as: protection bits) are available.

(Brunnstein: email interview)

Rob Nauta offers a Dutch hacker's perspective on the commercial pressures that lead to the continual failure to fix security holes:

> The OS [operating system] is being sold by a company, not the programmers. Hence the company weighs profit and minimising costs (avoid updates) against loss of sales due to bad publicity (the general image of the OS as good, or bug-ridden). Thus patches and updates are only released when necessary. A company like SUN listens much to the customers, which are academic sites and research companies. Most bugs are found for SUN's since they are the most used computers, but all get fixed soon. Companies that sell to business managers deal with the management who don't follow the news and are more influenced by advertisements than by word of mouth. Hence HP-UX (HP-SUX is its nickname), IBM's AIX and DEC's ULTRIX are notorious for the time it takes to fix anything.

(Nauta: email interview)

The exaggerated claims of marketing

The potential for security breaches is exacerbated by the exaggerated claims of marketing. They lead to a lack of co-ordination/symmetry between what a system is promised to do and what it can actually be made to do:

> Marketing, of course, and the way business is run in general, have a lot to answer for. Promise anything, *then* figure out how to (or if you can) deliver. Make the sale. If that involves telling people that all they have to learn to perform an incredibly complex task is to push one button, then tell them that.

(Slade: email interview)[4]

Marketing puts pressure upon technical staff to produce improved systems. These systems may work, but the hurried nature of their construction means that adequate security features are often lacking. Dr Cohen describes these marketing pressures that help to create a 'leaky sieve' effect for computer security:

> So many holes because so few 'experts' know about them. So many holes because making things work right takes more skill than making them barely work at all, which is what the research people do – get things prototyped. Unfortunately, prototypes go into production so fast that we cannot get them fully sorted out, so we leave big holes so we can fix operational features – leaving enormous protection holes in their place ... there are surely many

reasons – but I think the most important is a marketing reason – people won't pay to make themselves safe – they would rather buy the newest upgrade of the word-processor. They can buy insurance from an insurance company.

(Cohen: email interview)

Apathy and hype

Most bugs are found in networking code, since it runs at the system level, yet it is accessible by user programs. Most network protocols were designed without concern for security. NFS has no security at all, but SUN now allows to require [*sic*] a reserved port, which is a first step. NIS (YP) is also a good example. I wrote a program called YPX which could retrieve the password file from any machine, it has caused a SUN patch to be issued. Other vendors haven't announced anything, people are already complaining, I wonder if the other companies will ever bother to fix it.

(Nauta: email interview)

There was, in the view of a broad cross-section of interviewees from both the computer underground and the computer security industry, a general feeling that approaches to computer security were also often apathetic. Tozer used the example of motorway accidents: on the stretch of motorway following the scene of a recent crash drivers only temporarily slow down in response to the safety concern caused by the sight of the crash. Similarly, after a computer security breach has received large coverage in the media, organisations tend to be more concerned about their security, a concern that quickly fades once the short-term memory of the breach has faded. The result tends to be alternating periods of apathy and over-reaction with regard to computer security services. Even when attention is focused upon such holes it may often fail to address the underlying security weakness, due to the exaggerated and misdirected nature of the response.

The converse of the low profile generally enjoyed by efficient security work within organisations is the hyperbole that surrounds those that have made a deliberate decision to make security their business:

Let's try and distinguish between people who look after security in the usual organisation and people in the security service industry selling computer services. The people in fact in the user industry have got to keep a low profile and have their job done well when no one hears about them. When someone hears about them and a breach has been made, then they get a high profile which is destructive to their job. The essence of their success is having a low profile because they've protected the systems they're responsible for. In contrast, the service industry is concerned with publicising, hyping up any breaches of security that have occurred, so that they can sell their various protection devices; anti-virus guns and the like.

(Taylor: Knutsford interview)

The computer security industry has thus been accused of promoting fear about security breaches in the form of hacking and viruses in order to increase its business. Dr Fred Cohen, for example, relates how an article he had written on the subject of the possibility of developing benevolent viruses was altered by the publishers:

> they mangled it to promote the protection business. The main point of the article … was that benevolent viruses are possible and that only the computer security industry wants to claim that they are not – and the reason is so that they can scare you into paying them … there is a tremendous risk in an uncontrolled protection racket that goes by the name of 'computer security'. If I told you your house would burn down unless you paid me $100/year, you would probably report me to the police (and wonder why I charged so little). If someone in the protection racket tells you your computer will crash and you will lose all your data unless you pay them $100/year, how is that any different?

(Cohen: email posting)

The software crisis and refractory reality

While there exists a considerable body of theory documenting the methods of system development and software engineering in various industrial settings – there exists no such theory describing 'hacking' as a method for creating computer artifacts. While there seems to be considerable consensus among hackers about what 'hacking' as a method for software creation is (i.e. like pornography, they can recognise it when they see it), this consensus seems to be rooted in a communal culture, rather than theory).

(Hannemyr 1997: 7)

Within computing, worries about security weaknesses can be seen as part of wider concerns regarding the nature of software production. These concerns are encapsulated in the phrase, *the software crisis*. There are various elements to the software crisis including: the threats posed by computer viruses; the problems caused by the proliferation of different standards; shortages of skilled programmers; etc. Peláez argues that, despite varying interpretations of what actually constitutes the software crisis, it is the 'gap between expectations and demands placed on software, on the one hand, and actual achievements of software, on the other' (Peláez 1988: 178). There are two different explanations for this gap. One explanation emphasises the problem of the relative immaturity of the software industry: 'We build systems like the Wright brothers build airplanes – build the whole thing, push it off the cliff, let it crash; and start all over again' (Peláez 1988: 179). The second explanation of the gap between ambitions and achievements underlines the previous points made about the pressures imposed by the commercial environment: 'users' illusions were actively promoted by the computer industry itself, especially by its marketing people. ... Software was being produced in an environment of unreality, a fetishised even fraudulent environment' (Peláez 1988: 181).

The software crisis gave rise to a debate over how software should be produced and tested. The debate has been characterised as the 'science' versus 'craft' view of software development. The former emphasises how the production of software should emphasise the use of formal design methods to prove that the program will do exactly what it says it will, and so avoid the gap between expectations and performance. The craft approach prefers to emphasise the ways in which programs need to be responsive not only to mathematical proofs but also to the requirements of implementation in the real world. Computing, in an attempt to overcome the software crisis, has increasingly evolved from the craft-like approach to the more scientific reliance upon standardised procedures. The knowledge involved has become increasingly codified, and the process of software production has increasingly concentrated upon what software should do and the internal consistency of those specifications.

The above aspects of the software crisis have relevance to hacking. The movement away from a craft approach has meant that those programmers of a creative but ill-disciplined bent have been increasingly marginalised and this arguably explains the roots of at least some of the antipathy felt towards hackers (broadly defined to include all four generations ranging from first-generation creative programmer hackers to fourth-generation intruders). Weizenbaum, for example, explained to me[5] the grounds for his distaste of first-generation hackers by describing how from his experience at MIT over the years there were many examples of programmers who could produce concise and elegant solutions to programming puzzles, yet the fact that the programs were produced by original, inventive, but sometimes idiosyncratic, methods severely reduced their practical usefulness due to their lack of explanatory documentation. Upon the departure of the original author, the remaining programmers would find it extremely difficult to maintain or adapt his work because they were not privy to his private, undocumented logic. In a similar fashion, fourth-generation hackers may have potentially useful technical knowledge but such knowledge often does not sit comfortably with the academic and commercial world's preference for ethically unproblematic and rigorously researched knowledge.

Those within the computing establishment, such as Professor Herschberg, who are largely sympathetic to the hands-on approach of hackers, argue that computing's increasingly more formal programming environment fails to recognise the real-world limitations of the formally based engineering approach and that hacking knowledge is thus still of potential relevance to security. Whilst the science-based approach enables verification as to whether a program will meet its specifications, the craft approach points out that there is no way of formally proving that they are correct. In other words, it prefers to emphasise the messiness of the real world, which mathematics alone cannot tame. Hence, the security of systems cannot be formally proved in advance because their implementation takes place in a changing, non-theoretical and real environment. It is possible to theoretically assert, for example, that a system is invulnerable to certain types of attack but it is impossible to anticipate all the potential threats a system might face, particularly when human interaction with systems is involved. This inherent inability to guarantee total security is illustrated by the various security weaknesses of which hackers make use.

The software crisis and the origins of hacking

> A hacker ... does not in general work in teams ... his preferred working environment is a communal setting very much like that of an artisan or craftsman engaged in pre-industrial production. Given this setting, it becomes clear why the hacker is not too concerned about how some unknown end user may perceive his or her product. Because the hacker is not alienated from his product, his foremost objective is to create artifacts that are eminently suited to the needs of himself and his community. Like the workers in programming teams, hackers make use of the components of others. But there is a difference. While the industrial ideal is to treat such components as 'black boxes', of which nothing needs to be known except how to interface to it – hackers generally like to have a complete understanding of the systems they work on, including the components contributed by others ... the difference between the hackers' approach and those of the industrial programmer is one of outlook: between having an integrated and holistic attitude towards the creation of artifacts, and having a fragmented and reductionist one.
>
> (Hannemyr 1997: 10–11)

We have already seen how the word 'hack' evolved from originally referring to a quick bit of work that achieves its aim, but is not done particularly well. The word became associated specifically with clever programming techniques. The meaning of the word evolved as it became more and more associated with the ingenuity of programmers forced to modify programs on an *ad hoc* basis until they met the often vaguely expressed requirements of the customer. This led to the originally pejorative dictionary definition of the word, assuming a more positive connotation as programmers' methodologically unstructured, trial and error hacks achieved desirable practical results. Thus the origins of the activity of hacking itself stem from this craft-like quality of programming. The holistic approach adopted by the hacker under this definition of the activity explains not only the origins of the first generation of hackers but also hacking's lasting appeal to subsequent generations:

For the craftsperson, results are achieved through clever tricks, and professional excitement is derived from 'not quite understanding what he is doing'. In this streamline age, one of our most undernourished psychological needs is the craving for Black Magic and apparently the automatic computer can satisfy this need for the professional software engineer, who is secretly enthralled by the gigantic risks he takes in his daring irresponsibility.

(Peláez 1988: 201–2)

This image of programming, and by extension hacking, having elements akin to black magic is encouraged by the seemingly intrinsic baroque complexity of computing in the face of which anyone exhibiting practical knowledge receives the awe of the 'uninitiated':

For thousands of years, man has been captivated by magic. People, gathered around campfires, would be spellbound by sorcerers. Using a wand and some exotic artefacts they would produce startling effects and the innocent would gaze on in amazement ... many of the sorcerers' techniques have been acquired by the mechanically adept. ... Computer communication is still a black art, even to those in the computer world. For those in the know, this can be exploited. ... The communications expert is, in his or her own way, a magician, able to conjure up vast reserves of memory and computing power at the touch of a button.

(Gold 1990: 47–8)

The black-magic quality of hacking is further encouraged by hackers' conceptualisation of themselves. An example of both of these points is provided by a hacker who calls himself *The Dark Adept*:

A wizard is a person who believes everything is interrelated and attempts to find the interrelation and controls his universe by it. One such branch of wizardry is the Computer Underground ... I chose the handle The Dark Adept because I believe that out of darkness comes light. Out of the darkness of lies and oppression comes the light of truth and freedom. One just needs to be Adept enough to catalyse the reaction.

(The Dark Adept 1990: file 7)

Such romantic portrayals of the craft associations of hacking meet with much more critical interpretations:

To hack, is according to the dictionary, 'to cut irregularly, without skill or definite purpose; to mangle by or as if by repeated strokes of a cutting instrument'. I have already said that the compulsive programmer, or hacker as he calls himself, is usually a superb technician. It seems therefore that he is not 'without skill' as the definition will have it. But the definition fits in the deeper sense that the hacker is 'without definite purpose': he cannot set before him a clearly defined long-term goal and a plan for achieving it, for he has only technique, not knowledge. He has nothing he can analyze or synthesize; in short, he has nothing to form theories about. His skill is therefore aimless, even disembodied. It is simply not connected with anything other than the instrument on which it may be exercised. His skill is that of a monastic copyist who, though illiterate, is a first rate calligrapher.

(Weizenbaum 1976; cited in Hannemyr 1997: 7)

This fundamental disagreement over the implications of the craft aspects of hacking is one of the underlying factors in the dispute between the computer underground and the computer security industry, to which we turn to next.

Conclusion

This chapter set out to analyse the following main issues: the extent to which security weaknesses exist; the reasons they are not eliminated; and the potential role of hackers in providing security expertise. The reasons why security flaws are not eliminated are linked to the factors that give rise to their existence in the first place. The two main causes of the existence of security weaknesses and the accompanying gap between programming's achievements and expectations are shown to be computing's relatively immature status as an industry and the pressures to skimp on security caused by the demands of marketing. The former gives rise to a scarcity of theoretical knowledge surrounding computer security with various calls for more hands-on experience of security to supplement more formal theory. The combination of commercial pressures and apathy that exacerbate security weaknesses have also been recounted.

Hawks and doves respond differently to the fact that the nature and motivation of a computer intruder is hidden from those in charge of the system. Whereas such figures as Taylor, Tozer and Jones use the unknown nature of intruders as an argument for having to treat all intruders as if they were criminals, Herschberg emphasises that the ethical desire to castigate should be supplanted by the technical responsibility of system operators to maintain their systems' security. In this, those responsible for security should accept help from whichever quarter it is offered from. This failure to fully address computing's inherent security and operational weaknesses is what leads Professor Herschberg to assert that 'the proof of the pudding is in the hacking'. It is the same failure, however, that also leads hawkish figures to press for the stigmatisation of hackers and their subsequent exclusion from influence within computing.

Hackers' potential to provide useful information about security weaknesses remains, despite criticism from the hawks, due to the fact that there are always likely to be difficulties in attempting to anticipate the possible sources of security breaches. The hackers' approach to testing security is a practical way of providing that information. In addition, it is likely that hacking will survive in some form or another, considering it exhibits aspects of the craft qualities of programming that have not been (and are unlikely to be) totally eliminated as programming develops towards more science-based methods. Finally, the software crisis is a significant concept for the way in which it describes the origins of hackers' declining influence within computing. The pressures within computing to adopt more rigorous methods of software development have contributed to the marginalisation of the more craft-based hacker-type programmers. This has provided the origin of the 'them and us' scenario: the subject of the next chapter.

5 *Them and us*

The hawks and the doves

Introduction

> social groups create deviance by making the rules whose infraction constitutes deviance, and by applying those rules to particular people and labelling them as outsiders. From this point of view, deviance is not a quality of the act the person commits, but rather a consequence of the application by others of rules and sanctions to an 'offender'. The deviant is one to whom that label has successfully been applied; deviant behavior is behavior that people so label.
>
> (Becker 1963: 9)

Culture formation is an ongoing process and the delineation of boundaries between the computer underground and the rest of computing depends upon this active differentiation from others. Previous chapters have explored: hacker culture; the motivations lying behind the act; and the extent to which computing can be said to be vulnerable and insecure. The next stage is to examine how, given this context of the potential widespread vulnerability of computer systems, those in the computer security industry respond to hackers. Significant elements of the computer security industry wholeheartedly oppose hacking and its purported ethic, and we will look at its subsequent attempts to isolate the computer underground as part of the process by which the computer security industry promotes its own identity. This identity, however, like that of the computer underground is not homogenous. Despite the computer security industry inhabiting the institutional worlds of business or academia it shares some of the amorphous qualities of the computer underground. People often gain security expertise, on a somewhat *ad hoc* basis and reputations spread by word of mouth rather than on the basis of formally recognised qualifications.

The term 'computer security industry' is thus used guardedly; there are, for example, various figures that have changed their nominal group status: previous members of the computer underground are now involved in the provision of security services, a phenomenon that can be characterised as 'the poacher-turned-game-keeper' scenario, and some academics may straddle both main groups. Within the computer security industry itself, there are two broadly conflicting strands of opinion regarding hacking. There are arguments for both non-co-operation and co-operation, views I term as belonging to *hawks and doves* respectively. As the two phrases imply, the former strongly oppose hackers whilst the latter advocate listening to their views and in some cases actively co-operating with them in order to improve computer security. These two groups are two extremes of a spectrum of opinion with regard to hackers. This chapter seeks to illuminate the extent of the differences that exist between hackers and their opponents, and the consequences of such differences for the development of computer security.

Potential for co-operation: freedom of information

> I read something somewhere that when the first people that were coming in to the new world inquired of the natives as to the ownership of the land, the natives thought the whites were off their heads. Isn't it obvious that the land belongs to everybody? ... Simply put, I believe that once a person has created something, it belongs to the world. That's the Nature of the product, if it has any worth. Isn't it true, that after creating something, the natural impulse of the author is to show it off to someone, to release his/her 'child' to the world? And isn't it true that the absolute *best* feeling in the world is that 'flowing' creative act, including the 'labor' part of it? (That is, if it's motivated not by some sort of profit, but by the act itself). To my mind, those facts point towards that hacker philosophy that the Nature of information is to be free.
>
> (Mark Jacobs cited in Newton: website)

When looking at the professed motivations of hackers, some of the explanations put forward for their activity focus upon the belief that people should be able to freely access computer systems and the information contained within them. One of the differentiating features of the computer security industry compared to the computer underground is this attitude to the access of information. This 'open-to-all' attitude to information and computing is rarely shared by those who tend to oversee the systems to which hackers desire access:

> young people tend to see access to the computer network as an 'entitlement'. Some of them believe that entitlement to be so fundamental that it should not be subject to control by authority. The administrators of that access believe the access to be contingent upon continued orderly behavior. Since they understand the vulnerability of their systems to disorderly behavior, they generally respond by attempting to isolate any such behaviour, i.e. they suspend the user account or disable the terminal or line of origin. Not surprisingly, the young people see this as painful, arbitrary, punitive (rather than remedial), and excessive. While they refuse to amend their behavior, they argue that the only available and effective remedy, i.e., denying access,

is simply too Draconian to be contemplated by a civilized society. Continued monitoring of what passes for dialog between these two armed camps gives me little hope for early reconciliation of these opposing views.

(Murray 1992: 34)

Despite the antipathy that can be shown towards the computer underground by the computer security industry, there is evidence that there are practical benefits to be gained for both parties if a way could be found for them to share a policy of 'full information disclosure':

> If hackers have found it difficult to market their skills openly, there are less direct ways they can aid in the fight against computer crime. Information security consultants, including King, Stang, and experts at SRI International Inc., admit that they gather most of their information about computer-system weaknesses by frequenting underground bulletin-board systems and talking with hackers. 'All of the good vendors in one way or another absolutely do that', says Stang. 'There are some hackers who believe in "full disclosure,"' notes Richard Feingold, project leader of CSTC's Secure Systems Services division, which helps government and corporate clients evaluate and reduce their risk from hacker attacks. 'As soon as there is a new security vulnerability or technique out there, they will publish it on the Net. That's where a lot of our own techniques come from'.
>
> (Roush 1995: 6...7)

Similarly:

> Hackers, particularly the young, attempt to break security with the same atti-tude as computer game players demonstrate: single-mindedness; enjoyment in the intellectual challenge – but much, much more importantly, a belief (more, a solid *conviction*) that the security hole exists, just like the way to resolve a particular problem in a computer game like Zork actually exists. It is this mental attitude – much more than the technical skill – that is important in a hacker, and which must be understood by those who would seek to stop them. It is also this attitude that security project teams seek to introduce when they include a (hopefully reformed) hacker as part of the team.
>
> (Barrett 1997: 200)

Given this potential for mutually beneficial co-operation, individuals are trying to bridge the gap between the two communities:

> I hope to break down this barrier of resentment by crossing over the lines of the Underground into the 'real' world and providing valuable information about systems, security, interfacing, etc. I hope others will follow suit, and that the private sector will reciprocate by allowing technical information to flow into the Underground. Ultimately, I hope there will be a rapport

between hackers and members of the private sector so that we may learn from each other and make the best use possible of this greatest of inventions, the computer.

(The Dark Adept cited in Rosteck 1994:14)

This heart-felt appeal for more co-operation between the computer underground and the computer security industry for the ultimate greater good of computing has found at least some resonance with the more sympathetic doves of the computer security industry.

The rationale for hackers: the doves

Computer intruders of the 90s aren't stone pocket-protector techies. They're young white suburban males, and look harmless enough, but sneaky. They're much the kind of kid you might find skinny-dipping at 2AM in a backyard suburban swimming pool. The kind of kid who would freeze in the glare of the homeowner's flashlight, then frantically grab his pants and leap over the fence, leaving behind a half-empty bottle of tequila, a Metallica T-shirt, and probably, his wallet.

(Sterling 1991: 2)

The dovish element of the computer security industry adopt a relatively paternalistic and tolerant attitude to the computer underground. It tends to argue that the potential harm of hackers is exaggerated by their opponents. The corollary of this tolerant position is that given adequate ethical encouragement and opportunities co-operation with hackers is a legitimate and potentially beneficial path to follow.

The potential for co-operation: the dove's perspective

The typical skill level of the computer criminal is a topic of controversy. Some claim that skill level is not an indicator of a computer criminal, while others claim that potential computer criminals are bright, eager, highly motivated subjects willing to accept a technological challenge, characteristics that are also highly desirable in an employee in the data-processing field.

(United Nations *International Review of Criminal Policy*: par. 33)

There are various levels at which the arguments for co-operation with hackers are pitched. At one level there is the idealist position of basic agreement with the hacker position that information should be free. From this position, illicit access to other people's systems is not viewed as being inherently wrong. A more pragmatic approach exhibits of a resigned acceptance that, although some hacker activity may be ethically questionable, access (through dialogue) to their knowledge about systems' security is needed in order to find ways in which the single-mindedly destructive computer intruders can be thwarted.

A further facet of the more pragmatic arguments relates to the view put forward by Professor Herschberg in the previous chapter, namely that 'the proof of the pudding is in the hacking' and the commonplace notion of the advantages to be gained from following the adage 'set a thief to catch a thief'. Professor Herschberg's view that security knowledge could be improved by analysing the techniques of hackers draws attention to the issue of the correct degree of responsibility and blame to attach, not just to the perpetrators of security breaches, but also their victims. The ethical issue for Herschberg centres more upon the moral requirement facing those in charge of systems to maintain security, than to blame those that breach security. Hackers are criticised because, without their existence, there would be much less need for security in the first place, and therefore on balance they amount to a waste of resources. The dovish rejoinder to this prefers to emphasise the practical safety issues hackers draw attention to, rather than the waste of resources that may be attributed to them. A successful hack, defined as gaining super-user status in a system, means that the hacker may obtain complete control of a financial or a safety-critical system:

> The fact is that you can't by their actions, at least not easily and not from the outside, tell a hacker from a criminal and you never know at what stage criminals do get interested. Quite apart from the fact, at least all major enterprises, and that includes the entire financial scene, have a vital concern to have no intruders, whatever their origin, or whatever their purposes ... that point that if there were no hackers there would be no need for security, does not follow since there always is a prima-facie suspicion of somebody being out to, let's say, distort the uses you put your system to; you better employ a hacker because your criminal might have designs on you. An ounce of prevention is better than a pound of cure.
>
> (Herschberg: Delft interview)

Thus from this perspective, ethical considerations are subsumed under the instrumental usefulness of the practical security information that hackers can provide. This instrumental usefulness can be subdivided into the psychological insights 'benign' hackers may provide about their malevolent counterparts and technical information about specific security faults. Phillip King, president of Data Integrity Services, a Kansas City-based security consulting firm admits that:

> I make my living trying to stop hackers from breaking into systems, so it sounds kind of funny for me to say this, but most of them are pretty good guys ... [my goal] is not to catch hackers and put them away. It's to understand them and to use that knowledge to stop the truly malicious vandals.
>
> (Roush 1995: 5)

Co-operation may provide both technical and more psychological information:

> the hacker presence constantly pushes forward the limits of computer secu-
> rity techniques. There can be no real test of a security system's reliability,
> many professionals say, until some wily hacker attempts to break it. As
> members of 'tiger teams' hired to test computer security or develop better
> password or encryption systems to keep out unauthorized users, ex-hackers
> are often better grounded in the real-world challenges of keeping informa-
> tion secure than are most of the former law enforcement agents, inventors
> of new security devices, and academics who have traditionally made up the
> information-security profession. 'To understand a hacker certainly requires
> a bit of the hacker's mentality', says Stang [information security consultant].
> 'Those kinds of people make good security officers'.
>
> (Roush 1995: 5)

Faced with the extent of security problems described in the previous chapter,
hackers sometimes make dramatic claims regarding the extent to which their
activity improves standards of security within computing:

> Without hackers, computing would be a boring, drudgerous tool people
> would use because they need to get something done that they don't want to
> do. Hackers are computer enthusiasts more than anything else; it is through
> their enthusiasm for computers that they were able to find security bugs. If
> you consider a 'hacker' someone who unlawfully enters systems, then
> without hackers the nation would be nakedly awaiting serious attack from
> thieves and foreign agents. I have no doubt in my mind that the existence of
> hackers in this country has been a beneficial one except for certain well-
> documented cases; cases which would have been much worse if it had not
> been for hackers before them who have been able to close off the more
> wide-open security flaws/bugs
>
> (Maelstrom: email interview)

This argument can then be further divided into the claims that hacking can
be either a direct or an indirect benefit to computing. Direct benefits would stem
from innovations in programming methods and security, along with hardware
developments. An example of this would be Levy's first generation of hackers.
With regard to the indirect benefits of cracking, it can be claimed that the existence of hacking has led to a general climate of improved security consciousness
and that this has led to 'trickle down', indirectly related improvements in data
security. Thus, for example, potentially crucial data can be lost to a business due
to the usually insured risks of fire, flood or theft, but it can also be lost due to a
system failure that coincides with poor back-up storage procedures for data. An
indirect benefit of hacking, therefore, is that faced with the fear of external
threats to the security of a system and its data from hackers, system operators are
more liable to make regular back-ups than they might usually otherwise make.

These regular back-ups can then provide insurance against accidental losses of data from events other than hacking incidents. The system becomes more secure than it would have been originally, due to awareness of the possibility of being hacked.

An additional argument in favour of increased co-operation with hackers is that greater access to systems tends to make 'hacker types' more responsible computer users, who are then more liable to make productive use of the security knowledge they have gained illicitly. In the case of the former hacker, John Draper (alias *Captain Crunch*), this actually led to him 'punishing' users on the system he was in charge of, in the event that their hacking led to behaviour that adversely affected other users on the system. From his experience as a system manager, he claimed that:

> it is clear that by closely working with potential hackers and students, you can go a long way in cutting down malicious hacking. I took a firm hand in keeping them in check, while at the same time, I tried to direct their energies into useful productive work. One thing I remembered was a HACKING CONTEST (under tight supervision) where I challenged them to break into the library account, and if they succeeded (and told me how they did it), they would get three months free usage. ... Several people broke in, and I had about 2 people dedicated to helping me, and found a security flaw in the system. In this case, BOTH were winners. So yes!! There can be a positive lesson learned here, and that is to adopt a less fascist approach when dealing with hackers, and be less 'Punitive', but firm when dealing with them.
>
> (Draper: email interview)

Mofo, a US hacker, also gave the following detailed account of his experiences of the potential that exists for co-operation between those in charge of security and those who enjoy testing it. His description reinforces the previous discussion of the significance and desirability of direct, hands-on experience of security issues:

> I've gained knowledge on how to make computers and their operating systems more secure. Instead of complain about it and act foolishly (i.e. involving Keystone Kops), I took a proactive role to determine intent and repair the situation as best I could. My preference is to deal with intruders as human beings. In my experience, 'crackers' have been very receptive toward that attitude. Since my systems are always backed up on a regular basis, the few destructive 'cracking' attempts have been relative non-events. The admin community as a whole seems to be quite paranoid about security information and their highbrow attitude leaves experience as the only expert tutor.
>
> (Mofo: email interview)

A more damning indictment than the charge of being highbrow is made by Goggans (ex-Legion of Doom member, who went on to become one of the founding members of ComSec Ltd, a computer security firm staffed by ex-hackers). His claim was:

> The computer security industry is a farce, the key players who hold the majority of clients are the big 6 accounting firms, with Deloitte & Touche and Coopers and Lybrand in the lead. I wouldn't ask a mechanic to perform a triple-bypass on me just because he understands valves, no more than I would want an accountant auditing my computer security just because he does the financial audits of my accounting programs. ... One company we contacted had an audit by one of the accounting firms. An auditor was onsite for 10 hours a day for 8 weeks. The report came back saying that they should put an exit sign in the computer room. This same company had a PBX controlled by computer, a dial-out option on the PBX active with the code 1234, and an AS-400 with poor password management. I noticed this upon initial contact. But the accounting firm had already turned them off to outside security audits, so their problems still exist. $100,000 for a damn exit sign.
>
> (Goggans: email interview)

This feeling that 'legitimate' computer security providers are out of touch with the practicalities of intrusion prevention is an important element of the rationale that hacking should be recognised as a valuable resource to improve computing standards.[1] Efforts akin to those called for above by the Dark Adept are being made to bridge what was referred to in the previous chapter as the seeming *knowledge gap* between the two parties:

> University of Dayton law student Jeff Moss – known to his former hacker compatriots as Dark Tangent – chips away at the wall of suspicion between hackers and security officials by inviting both to the 'Def Con' hacker conventions he organizes annually in Las Vegas. The 300 attendees at 1994's meeting included such luminaries as Phillip Zimmerman, inventor of the Pretty Good Privacy encryption system, and Gail Thackeray, a Phoenix district attorney who helped organize the 1990 hacker crackdown of Arizona's Organized Crime and Racketeering Unit. 'A lot of time was spent in substantive presentations', says Thackeray, including seminars on search-and-seizure laws, hacker ethics, and technical hacking methods.
>
> (Roush 1995: 7)

A failure of the computer security industry to benefit from hacker knowledge has led to substantive criticisms being made of the ability of non-hacker, establishment-type firms to provide an adequate appraisal of the security status of a system:

> In theory, actual hacking would be the best way to 'debug' security proce-
> dures. In practice, only outsiders can look at a system from an unbiased
> viewpoint, so this opens up potential security problems. Part of what we do
> at ComSec we call system penetration testing. This is an audit of external
> security practices currently in effect by subjecting them to a hacking attack.
> I personally think this is THE ONLY WAY to get a snapshot of security
> problems to get a foundation of what needs to be fixed, but only an outsider
> can do it accurately. We go in with only a release form. No passwords, no
> dialups, no information at all. We return a report outlining all dialups, pass-
> words, and information gained. This leads indirectly to an internal audit to
> fix the internal errors that left the systems vulnerable to outside attacks.
>
> (Goggans: email interview)

We have seen how the various generations of hackers have evolved since the
earliest days of computing. Hacking has historically played a major part in the
development of both computer hardware and software. The energies of hackers
helped to revolutionise computing from the cumbersome valve-dominated technology of its early days to the mass proliferation and dispersion of personal
computers by such pioneering hackers as Steve Wozniak of Apple Computers.
The contribution to positive technical developments from the latest generation of
hackers, crackers, is perhaps less easy to identify due to their more underground
status. One example of some of the practical benefits the computer industry can
gain from the fourth generation of hackers, however, is given by Jean-Bernard
Condat of the French Computer Chaos Club who describes how:

> When a hacker works, three months after, the bug that he uses will be
> discovered and/or repaired. In France, it's 75% translation of bugs from
> American programs and 20% of normal password indiscretions. Some of
> my members are building a well-known program ... that help end-users or
> customers of great computers to find easy-to-understand password ... but-
> hard-to-find, too. The dictionary of such a program is terribly important
> and these 5 boys are using all the available time to build this extremely
> useful program ... already sold to two big companies in Paris!
>
> (Condat: email interview)

Potential underestimation of the role of hackers

One reason why this potential may have been under-rated is the fact that hackers
do not generally publicise their findings of security weaknesses in conventional
channels. Those who notice hacking information on their bulletin boards,
however, may then report the faults the hackers have documented, a fix will then
occur, but hackers may not receive recognition for the impact of their activity:

> In general: finding errors in installation (mostly bad file protections), as done
> by a tool like COPS, is useful, since beginning crackers [*sic*] use these. Bug

fixes are hard to do yourself, and just a bug report won't get the bug fixed, enough people must complain about it. That's why publicity about bugs is a good thing. Whether to report them is another thing, I inspired 2 SUN bug fixes with my programs (cover.c, which used a fault in telnet, and ypx which uses YP design oversights), yet I don't get credited, but the people who saw my programs and sent them to SUN do. It's a strange world.

(Nauta: email interview)

Thus the belief that hackers are unoriginal and contribute little to security knowledge may, to some extent at least, result from a failure of such knowledge to be correctly attributed and accredited to a hacking source. A failure that may be exacerbated by a reluctance upon the part of hackers to freely publicise and disseminate their knowledge due to fears of prosecution and general hostility from the computer security industry and legal establishment.

Rationale for non-co-operation: 'the hawks'

Technical arguments against hacking

Goggans has been previously cited as pointing out that some computer systems are safety-critical to the point that human death may be a result of any system failure. In so far as this chapter has shown that hacking offers the potential to provide useful information with which to remedy some security weaknesses, the question remains as to why more use is not made of hackers' expertise. Fuller co-operation is avoided in preference for 'security through obscurity'. This is because although co-operating with hackers may provide security practitioners with useful information with which to fix security holes, it also threatens to increase the knowledge of hackers by offering them more access to potential hacking targets and opportunities for *social engineering*.[2] Unsolicited hacking activity is also problematic because it threatens to damage the delicate nature of many modern, interconnected systems.

> Hacking can provide us (information security, audit, vendors, etc.) with information about vulnerabilities. Yet, the problem today is that the stakes are too high for this type of teaching to continue. Specifically, the interconnected world is too fragile to allow 'volunteers' to test the security of organizations without being invited to do that.
>
> (Sherizen: email interview)

In addition, the *ad hoc* and largely unsolicited testing methods of hackers do not fit well into the professional structure and requirements of the computing industry. The unorthodox aspects of hacking are not conducive to establishing a rapport between those obtaining knowledge about the security of systems, by illicit, unauthorised means, and those in charge of maintaining the systems who could benefit from such knowledge. This is due to two main reasons. First, as described in the previous chapter, the nature of much hacking activity does not sit well with members of the computing industry who tend to inhabit a techno- logical environment where discipline of method and obedience to instructions tend to be valued more than evidence of unstructured and generally undocu- mented technical brilliance. Second, the unsolicited nature of illicit hacking means that systems are being used without the prior permission of the owners. These two factors lead to a situation that gives rise to an immediate lack of affinity between hackers and the computer security industry.

The previously cited attribution of a knowledge gap suffered by the computer security industry is redirected back at the hacker community by its opponents. The criticism made in this case by a Norwegian computer security officer is that the unstructured and idiosyncratic nature of hacking means that it can miss out on the equally practical benefits to be gained from a more structured approach:

> It is true that computer underground hackers sometimes are used commer- cially to check the security of systems. I have myself been approached by a number of clients who want to know whether I can muster a couple of tame hackers for rent. I have always advised against it – not for ethical reasons, but because of expediency. The sysadmin will learn a lot more about the vulnerability of the system if he himself runs SATAN and similar tools ... in one of the two cases I know of in Norway where computer underground hackers were used to QA the security of the installation, the ploy was not effective (not because of the dishonesty of the computer underground hackers, but because their un-systematic 'rattle the doors' approach failed to uncover a disastrous programming flaw in one of the sub-systems – a flaw that was blatant when the sub-system was reviewed using the more orthodox method of structured walk-through).
>
> (Hannemyr: email interview)

An additional criticism of the idea that hackers provide a useful research and development resource is the contention that hackers very seldom make use of any original security weaknesses:

> All that breaking into a system teaches is how to break into systems. It's very similar to testing software with random testing, for instance. If the proce- dure fails, what knowledge has been gained? Does it mean that the system is secure? Does it mean that the cracker didn't try hard enough? In testing, if a set of random tests fail, we cannot conclude the software under test is correct (I can give you scores of references on this). It is only a crude approximation, and is viewed as 'real' testing only by the uninformed.
>
> (Spafford: email interview)

Members of the computer security industry have argued that the educational benefits to be derived from hacking are exaggerated:

I think it's a misconception to believe that most (emphasis: 'most') hackers have expertise that's particularly worthwhile. Many, of course, work from cookbooks, lists of known holes. While such lists are useful to the vendors and to CERT, they're in some sense, uninteresting – few, if any, show any degree of conceptual novelty.

(Holbrook: email interview)

Professor Spafford, in keeping with the formal methods side of the software crisis debate, argues that:

A true computer security specialist learns about more than just weaknesses – she/he should learn about issues in software engineering, formal methods, testing theory, operating systems, language design, human factors, risk assessment, the law, networking, cryptography, and a number of other topics. Breaking into a system teaches NONE of these things – it simply serves to illustrate how poorly configured many systems are, and how poorly tested the software is. But that should be obvious to anyone studying software engineering or security!

(Spafford: email interview)

Dr Fred Cohen also emphasises the point that within computing there is a general awareness of widespread inadequacies and faults in many systems, and so hackers' actions provide little original security information:

I've never seen a 'cracker' who broke into a system in a particularly novel way. Every attack of this sort is one we have known about for 20 years and just not acted on. It's like taking candy from a baby. What we need is fewer computer security babies and more well-educated experts.

(Cohen: email interview)

This tendency for the majority of hackers to make use of unoriginal security weaknesses is recognised by some of the hackers themselves. Thus Nauta agrees that:

Most crackers are beginners at the OS, and use standard tricks, well known bugs, and most of all, bad installation or management. As delivered, the system has some faults and bugs, but when used, the security may weaken due to installation of extra programs, changing file permissions, etc. Finding out new holes is something for 1) luck or 2) an expert. Experts generally know how to crack a system but don't find it challenging, worth the trouble.

(Nauta: email interview)

The criticism of technical justifications for hacking relies on the charge that the knowledge it produces is very seldom, if ever, original. Whilst Cohen's view still allows for some benefits to stem from hacking in the sense that hackers may 'cut their horns' [*sic*] by gaining practical, if not particularly original, knowledge. The thrust of his argument is that such knowledge does not aid the development of computing and could be obtained in more orthodox ways. His criticism, along with Spafford's (who claims that the poor security of systems 'should be obvious to anyone studying software engineering'), returns us to the reasons discussed in the previous chapter of why such holes continue to exist with such prevalence. It also leads us to a consideration that will be pursued more fully later, that the pursuit and punishment of hackers can to some extent at least be a substitute activity for fixing security flaws.

The question of trust: the case of Robert Schifreen

Another important factor mitigating against increased co-operation with hackers is the practical consideration of being able to trust both the integrity and obedience of workers within an industrial/commercial setting. Tozer and Taylor, two British security consultants, for example, were both at pains to emphasise the need for employers to be able to expect their workers to only do the task given to them without allowing their curiosity to divert themselves. A 'vicious circle of trust' can develop, however, whereby the only way to achieve specific knowledge of security issues is to indulge in illicit hacking activity, but the ownership of such knowledge subsequently debars the holder from being legitimately employed in the computer security industry.

One example of the general reluctance of the computer security industry to co-operate with, or to employ, hackers is given by 'Smb', a US security consultant. His reason why hackers' knowledge is not better used by the computing establishment is:

> Because they can't be trusted. I'm perfectly serious – would you hire someone for a sensitive position without good evidence that they weren't going to abuse their position? The hackers are either directly criminal, in which case you'd be a fool to hire them, or they're simply demonstrating a great deal of immaturity. In that case, why do you think they'll grow up if they get a new job? ... I'm not speaking in absolutes, of course. Circa 20 years ago, when I was working for a university computer center, I was faced with two students engaging in questionable activities. A brief investigation showed that both primarily wanted access to computing – but one of them was doing some fairly dubious things with his access. We turned that case over to the dean, and hired the other.
>
> (Smb: email interview)

These examples show that, in previous times, hackers were valued for their technical ability and less concern was shown to such issues as trust or formal education in programming methods. With the more widespread dispersal of computers within the business world there has been a disproportionate increase in antipathy towards hackers, considering the act itself has remained constant.

Dr Taylor gave the following explanation of his particular lack of trust for hackers:

> Well, it's the old, old story, if you employ someone who is close to your system security who is known to have a sort of criminal background or past criminal background, you don't know what they're going to do in terms of passing on information to third parties, because criminals have the wrong sort of information networks ... there's just this fear that they're going to pass to some of their friends, associates and so on, the information to hack into a system or some information they extracted out of it. If you let a hacker look around your system, they're bound to look into all sorts of confidential information like company plans for the next five years, which are on most big computers. It's the fact that they can't be trusted.
>
> (Taylor: Knutsford interview)

Despite the fact that hackers have at least a potentially useful role in the elimination of security holes, the issue of legitimacy mitigates against co-operation between the computer underground and the computer security industry. There are pragmatic considerations of whether or not hackers should be trusted with access to a company's systems, such as the possible litigious ramifications resulting from allowing known hackers access to systems that might subsequently be damaged. Mercury highlights the 'cover your back' type of approach to security, which arguably concentrates more upon fulfilling institutional and legal expectations than it seeks the best possible technical fix to a given security weakness. He describes how:

> I once sent out letters to hospitals offering my services. I included a xerox of an article about lax computer security in hospitals. Having been employed by a local software supplier to these hospitals, I was able to identify a couple of obvious examples. No takers. One system manager told me that it might be true that I knew more about computer security than a Big Eight Accounting Firm. 'But they bring other things to the table', he said. He meant that if he got an expensive audit from a Big Eight Firm and someone died anyway, he would be covered from liability.
>
> (Mercury: email interview)

Apart from the issue of trust, there is also the question of keeping the innate curiosity of a hacker in check. Both Dr Taylor and Tozer emphasised that in a commercial setting one of the most important requirements they demand from their workers is a discipline to strictly follow instructions, and that they did not believe hackers would have such discipline. Thus Tozer stated that:

> If these people aren't layabouts, if they've been looking for jobs, then the industry is desperate for people who have a good discipline and good technical ability. But have they got good discipline? In other words, could you

ever use a hacker to do a proper job or would he want to go off on his own and do what he wants to do … I think it must be a lack of discipline some-where. You tell someone to go away and write a program to do something, not to do part of it and not to do all of it plus a bit more.

(Tozer: Hawarden interview)

Finally, Professor Spafford is noted within the Internet community for his more acerbic articulation of the belief that there should be minimal co-operation between those who are professionally responsible for the security maintenance of systems, and hackers:

Everyone I know in major corporations, when faced with a choice between: a) a student whose resumé brags about all the machines he's broken into over the network; or b) a student whose resumé lists courses in cryptography, law, and software engineering would hire (b) and avoid (a) like the plague. If someone has already demonstrated a contempt for privacy and property rights, why would you want to hire them into a sensitive position working with important company data? It's like hiring a confessed arsonist to install fire alarms, or hiring an admitted paedophile as a teacher.

(Spafford: email interview)

Robert Schifreen

Robert Schifreen was arrested in 1984 for breaking into the Duke of Edinburgh's electronic mail account; the case and its subsequent publicity providing impetus for the subsequent drafting of the Computer Misuse Act of 1990. Acknowledging that computer security industry figures are often hostile to and denigrate the usefulness of hacking knowledge, Schifreen relates how he sometimes finds it difficult to find a receptive audience for his expertise:

which is why I tend to speak at conferences and put things in writing rather than act as a consultant and go and talk to people face-to-face, or go and look at their computer systems and say 'I wouldn't do that if I were you'. Because yes, I can understand their reticence. They'll come and talk to me and ask me questions, general questions, nothing too specific, but there's a lot of knowledge out there that's either wrong or incomplete or non-existent and if I can scratch the surface and try and educate people, then I'll try and do so.

(Schifreen: London interview)

Schifreen's account of his reception within the computer security industry emphasises the willingness of firms to listen to general warnings concerning security weaknesses, yet a lack of trust and reluctance to accept detailed tech-nical help from someone carrying the label *hacker*.

Hostility

Although hackers violate laws and professional codes of ethics in the domain of computing, I would not characterize the hackers I have met as 'morally bankrupt' as some people have called them. I have not seen any data to support allegations that they are in general more prone to lie, cheat, or steal than others. The hackers I have met have seemed to me to be decent people.

(Denning 1992b: 60)

Mostly they seem to be kids with a dramatically underdeveloped sense of community and society.

(Cosell: email interview)

Somewhere near vermin i.e. possibly unavoidable, maybe even necessary pests that can be destructive and disruptive if not monitored.

(Zmudsinki: email interview)

electronic vandalism.

(Warman: email interview)

System crackers take the 'public good' stand to try and justify their actions. I'd wager NOT ONE of them ever said, 'Hey, let's break into xxxx system tonight because I think they're violating the privacy rights of the local town-folk'. Pardon the expression, but that's a lot of bullsh*t. It's a coverup – and a weak one.

(Johnson: email interview)

I am for making the penalties for computer trespass extremely painful to the perpetrator. ... Most administrators who've had to clean up and audit a system of this size probably think that a felony rap is too light a sentence. At times like that, we tend to think in terms of boiling in oil, being drawn and quartered, or maybe burying the intruder up to his neck in an anthill.

(Johnson: email posting)

The above quotations illustrate how people's response to hacking can range from benign tolerance through benign disapproval to open hostility. Concern about the vulnerability of computer systems and the subsequent potential of hacking to cause damage fuels the sense of antipathy that exists between the computer security industry and the computer underground.

Maybe I'm a bit old-fashioned but in my mind once a criminal, always a criminal ... I reject utterly the idea that they browse, I reject utterly and completely that because I don't believe they know. Many installations wouldn't know because they don't keep that type of record ... there's lots of crashes in many systems ... further over in North Wales, they had a system crash, they never found out why that system crashed, I made several suggestions as to why it had crashed, they didn't want to know. I reckon the DP manager knew damn well what had happened, somebody had mucked about with the software.

(Tozer: Hawarden interview)

The language used to express the hostility that stems from such feelings of vulnerability can be non-specific and moralistic, an example being Professor Spafford's argument that using hackers' knowledge on a regular basis within the computer security industry is equivalent to employing a known arsonist as your fire-chief, a fraudster as your accountant, or a paedophile as your child-minder. The technical insights that hackers could provide or that could be derived as a byproduct of their activities become subordinate to the need to express opprobrium against the morality of the actions themselves. The language of blame and morality is consistently used by hawkish members of the computer security industry to refer to hackers in what they would argue is a process of *blame displacement*. The computer security industry is accused of using moral condemnation as a means of deflecting any responsibility and blame for security breaches that might be attached, not just to the perpetrators of intrusions, but also their victims:

The pseudo-moral arguments and the moralistic language certainly cloud the issue in my view. I think it obscures the fact that system owners or system administrators have a moral duty to do at least their level best to stop penetrations. They are very remiss in their duty, they couldn't care less and therefore at least, there is quite an understandable tendency to blame the penetrator rather than blaming themselves for not having taken at least adequate counter measures, in fact in some cases counter measures have not been taken at all ... if it is proved to you that you haven't done your homework, then you almost automatically go into a defensive attitude which in this case, simply amounts to attacking the hacker, blaming him morally, heaping opprobrium on his head ... yes, the fear factor is involved.

(Herschberg: Delft interview)

This undercurrent of moral censure was a recurrent quality of the fieldwork interviews with members of the computer security industry, for example:

I've been in this game ... this is my thirty-sixth year, in the interests of hacking as a whole I think hacking is something which is derogatory; to be played down, to possibly in fact, be treated as a minor form of criminal activity ... the last thing you want to do is to make hackers into public figures; give them publicity. I think it needs to be played down when it occurs, but it shouldn't occur ... I wouldn't have them, no, under any circumstances.

(Taylor: Knutsford interview)

Dr Taylor and other interviewees, involved in the provision of computer security, had had surprisingly little direct contact with hackers. I asked him about this lack of direct contact/interplay and his perceptions of the motivations of hackers:

> Well, there shouldn't be [any interplay] because the industry doesn't want to hear about hackers and certainly doesn't want to see the effects of what they do. ... To me I'm not concerned with what the hacker does, I'm more concerned with keeping him out to start with. ... You've talked to what are called the more ethical members of the hacking community for whom it's an intellectual challenge, but there are in fact people who are psychopaths, and Doctor Popp[3] is one of these, where they just want to level a score with society which they feel has been unfair to them. ... A chap called Whitely has just gone to prison for four years for destroying medical data at Queen Mary's hospital, London. He just destroyed utterly and he wasn't just a hacker that was browsing, he was a psychopath almost certainly.
>
> (Taylor: Knutsford interview)

In contrast, and as an illustration of the negative perceptions each group has of the other, a hacker, Mofo, argues that psychotic tendencies are not the sole preserve of the hacking community:

> my experience has shown me that the actions of 'those in charge' of computer systems and networks have similar 'power trips' which need be fulfilled. Whether this psychotic need is developed or entrenched before one's association with computers is irrelevant. Individuals bearing such faulty mental health are present in all walks of life. I believe it is just a matter of probability that many such individuals are somewhat associated with the management of computers and networks [as well as intrusion into computer systems].
>
> (Mofo: email interview)

Dr Taylor is wary of the damage to computing that greater publicisation of hacking could cause, yet as the above reference to Dr Popp and Nicholas Whitely shows, ironically, he seemed to be dependent upon the most publicised cases of hacking for his perceptions of hackers. A further argument that prevents the computer security industry accepting hackers as potentially useful fault-finders in systems is the simple charge that without the existence of hackers in the first place, there would be very little need for extensive security measures. Even if hackers are of some use in pointing out various bugs in systems, such a benefit is outweighed by the fact that a large amount of computing resources are 'wasted' on what would otherwise be unnecessary security measures. For example, Dr Taylor's view is that:

hacking is a menace that stops people doing constructive work. ... A lot of money gets spent today on providing quite complex solutions to keep ahead of hackers, which in my view should not be spent. ... They're challenging the researchers to produce better technical solutions and they're stimulating the software service industry which provides these solutions and makes money out of it. But you answer the question for me, what's that doing for society?

(Taylor: Knutsford interview)

Thus one reason for the use of moral language is in order to displace blame from those in charge of the systems where security is lax, to those who have broken that lax security. Irrespective of the state of security of systems, there is a project of group formation whereby those who implement computer security wish to isolate and differentiate themselves from the computer underground, in a process that highlights the inherent differences that exist between the two groups. This project is vividly illustrated in the following excerpt from the keynote Turing Award acceptance speech given by Ken Thompson:

I have watched kids testifying before Congress. It is clear that they are completely unaware of the seriousness of their acts. There is obviously a cultural gap. The act of breaking into a computer system has to have the same social stigma as breaking into a neighbor's house. It should not matter that the neighbor's door is unlocked. The press must learn that misguided use of a computer is no more amazing than drunk driving of an automobile.

(Thompson 1984: 763)

This degree of sentiment was consistently expressed amongst some of the most prominent and accomplished of those figures from the computer security industry who were generally opposed to hackers:

Unfortunately ... it is tempting to view the hacker as something of a folk hero – a lone individual who, armed with only his own ingenuity, is able to thwart the system. Not enough attention is paid to the real damage that such people can do ... when somebody tampers with someone else's data or programs, however clever the method, we all need to recognise that such an act is at best irresponsible and very likely criminal. That the offender feels no remorse, or that the virus had unintended consequences does not change the essential lawlessness of the act, which is in effect breaking-and-entering. And asserting that the act had a salutary outcome, since it led to stronger safeguards, has no more validity than if the same argument were advanced in defense of any crime. If after experiencing a burglary I purchase a burglar alarm for my house, does that excuse the burglar? Of course not. Any such act should be vigorously prosecuted.

(Parrish 1989: file 11)

Several of the above quotations are notable for their heavy reliance upon the visual imagery of metaphors comparing the ethical issues arising from computing with real-world situations, a topic that will be looked at shortly.

Fear of anonymity

We have seen previously how hacking's anonymous quality can feed the hyperbole of the media. Its anonymity adversely influences the computer security industry's perception of hackers and this often creates a tendency to assume the worst intentions behind the actions of intruders:

> There is a great difference between trespassing on my property and breaking into my computer. A better analogy might be finding a trespasser in your high-rise office building at 3 AM, and learning that his back-pack contained some tools, some wire, a timer and a couple of detonation caps. He could claim that he wasn't planting a bomb, but how can you be sure?
>
> (Cosell: email interview)

The role anonymity plays in the media hyperbole surrounding hacking is mirrored in some of the more extreme over-reactions of the computer security industry seen in the above instances of the 'them and us scenario'. The general prejudice held by the computer security industry towards the computer underground is heightened by its anonymity. It encourages doubts and paranoia as a result of being unable to assess the motivation of intruders and the likelihood that any harm that has been committed will be difficult to uncover.

A vivid example of this doubt is the comparison below made by Mike Jones of the UK's Department of Trade and Industry's security awareness division. I pointed out that many hackers feel victimised by the establishment because they believe it is more interested in prosecuting them than patching up the holes they are pointing out with their activity. Jones accepted that there was prejudice in the views of the computer security industry towards the computer underground. That prejudice, however, is based upon the *potential* damage that hackers can cause. Even if there is no malicious intention from the hacker, suspicion and doubt as to what harm has been done exists:

> Say you came out to your car and your bonnet was slightly up and you looked under the bonnet and somebody was tampering with the leads or there looked like there were marks on the brake-pipe. Would you just put the bonnet down and say 'oh, they've probably done no harm' and drive off, or would you suspect that they've done something wrong and they've sawn through a brake-pipe or whatever ... say a maintenance crew arrived at a hanger one morning and found that somebody had broken in and there were screw-driver marks on the outside casing of one of the engines, now would they look inside and say 'nothing really wrong here' or would they

say, 'hey, we've got to take this engine apart or at least look at it so closely that we can verify that whatever has been done hasn't harmed the engine'.

(Jones: London interview)

Both Cosell and Jones's quotations proffer an important explanation of the alleged paranoid and knee-jerk reactions to hacking activity from the computing establishment.

Clandestine co-operation

government agencies, as well as firms like American Express, Dun & Bradstreet, and Monsanto, have ... hired tiger teams to probe their systems' vulnerabilities. Former hacker Ian Murphy founded and led the Pennsylvania firm IAM/Secure Data Systems from 1986 to 1993, which performed such services as breaking into the headquarters of banks and insurance companies, logging onto their computer systems, then submitting detailed reports on how the penetration was accomplished. Murphy told Information Week magazine that he and his employees, all convicted computer felons, netted a peak $500,000 per year for their services. Lawrence Livermore National Laboratory's Computer Security Technology Center ... has occasionally called on former hackers to lend their expertise as 'subcontractors', says staff member Allan Van Lehn.

(Roush 1995: 6)

Despite the above contentions against co-operation with hackers, diverse figures from my fieldwork with the computer underground have claimed to have used their hacking ability in the wider computing community. The rhetorical devices used to establish the computer security industry presupposes that there is a section of the putative community that does deal with the computer under- ground and thus needs convincing of the unethical nature of this. Thus evidence is given below of the 'clandestine co-operation' that does in fact take place between the computer security industry and the computer underground. There seems to be a gap between the public pronouncements of the computer security industry and the fact that they may ironically mirror the ways in which hackers privilege access to information, over the ethics of that access, by dealing with the computer underground. In addition, on several occasions members of the computer security industry casually admitted to me that when they have needed quick access to information or a system then they have used hacker techniques to overcome established access procedures. The justification for such acts being that the practicalities of the situation necessitated a quick solution and their inten- tions did not involve damage to the systems or the information they contained.

Despite the fact that the computer security industry uses various rhetorical processes, such as its internal boundary-forming discourses and its external use of media stigmatisation and symbolic legislation, to marginalise the computer underground, it also co-operates with the computer underground out of the public's gaze. Roush describes this growing willingness of the computer security industry to work with the computer underground as a new détente:

> while hackers and their pursuers are coming together based on mutual interests, the two camps have only just begun to explore common ground. 'Co-operation' is therefore not quite the right word for the new relationship emerging between those battering at the Net's electronic fortresses and those still trying to bar the doors. 'Detente', an easing of tensions, is closer. ... Many active or former interlopers, fed up with their criminal cousins for giving all hackers a bad name, are therefore applying their skills as software developers, security consultants, and pamphleteers for responsible hacking. ... The main obstacle to greater co-operation between the two groups, of course, is their mutual suspicion. But cultural changes under way in both camps – including growing recognition of a common enemy – are making room for a cautious truce and even an alliance of sorts.
>
> (Roush 1995: 2, 5)

Whilst the inherent sensitivity of the area of computer crime makes definitive corroborative research impracticable, the claim that clandestine co-operation occurs was made by various computer underground and computer security industry interviewees.

Conclusion

> In 1994 [he] led a three-day training seminar for 13 member nations of NATO at the Allied European Command Center at the Hague, and there are 'financial institutions that want to fly me out at a moment's notice', he says. Other organizations' resistance to working with former hackers, Goggans suggests, stems from fear of the unknown. 'But it takes only a few minutes of earnest dialogue before people realize that those like myself are not of a mindset to do any kind of damage to any company'.
>
> (Roush 1995: 6)

A famous former hacker who attempted to move into the computer security industry, Chris Goggans, has simultaneously had his expertise recognised by inter-governmental agencies, but has also had to routinely overcome the reluctance of businesses to talk to him. His experience seems to summarise the ambivalence with which the computer security industry confronts the computer underground. There seem to be two main opposing pressures when the possibility of the computer underground and the computer security industry working together is raised. On the one hand, the alleged *knowledge gap* means that despite the use of security audits by auditors/business consultants, first-hand hacker knowledge is often likely to be viewed at a premium since it may give a more realistic assessment of vulnerability than could otherwise be gained from more conventional sources. On the other hand, the very 'street-level' quality of the information needed to accurately assess the safety of a system from external intrusions makes it politically difficult to acknowledge the source of the information. Thus it might be difficult to use hacker expertise formally, despite the fact that it may well reveal more weaknesses than a security audit prepared by an established firm of impeccable credentials, whose report is more likely to fulfil the requirements of insurance companies etc. This stigma with which hacking information is viewed is both caused by and contributes to a social process that reflects the increasing professionalisation of the computer security industry and the marginalisation of hackers within society: the subject of the next two chapters.

6 The professionalisation process

Introduction

Wherever rules are created and applied, we should be alive to the possible presence of an enterprising individual or group. Their activities can properly be called moral enterprise, for what they are enterprising about is the creation of a new fragment of the moral constitution of society, its code of right and wrong.

(Becker 1963: 145)

The story of the creation of this 'social menace' is central to the ongoing attempts to rewrite property law in order to contain the effects of the new information technologies that, because of their blindness to the copyrighting of intellectual property, have transformed the way in which modern power is exercised and maintained.

(Ross 1991: 80–1)

The technical evolution of computing and its ubiquitous spread into all areas of life has created a qualitatively new context compared to that encountered by hacking's first generation and its original milieu in the computer labs of MIT. Within this new context fiercely contested ethical judgements are often made as to what constitutes the ethical use of computer resources. The technical objections of the hawks to co-operation with hackers are supplemented by their ethical critique of the computer underground. This chapter examines the purported basis and subsequent maintenance of this hostility as part of a boundary-forming process whereby groups reaffirm their own identities by marginalising others. The purpose of the boundary formation exercise is to exclude hackers from influence within computing, whilst, at the same time, it aims to develop a consistent ethical value system for 'legitimate' security professionals.[1]

Dougan and Gieryn (1988), like Meyer and Thomas (1990), have examined the deviancy aspects of computer crime by comparing its boundary formation processes within computing to the historical examples of witch trials. Witch-hunts tend to occur in periods of social transition where there are significant levels of anxiety, a relatively modern manifestation being the McCarthy hearings conducted during the height of the cold war. The purported IT revolution has created conditions of large-scale social and technical transition, which in the eyes of some commentators have led to hackers being made the scapegoats of the accompanying social unease. Dominant social groups initially mythologise and then stigmatise peripheral groups that do not share their value structure. The initial awe and even respect with which hackers were originally viewed as 'technological wizards' has given way to the more frequent hawkish perception that they are instead 'electronic vandals'. The tendency towards stigmatisation has been exacerbated by the fear and ignorance that flourishes due to hacking's predominantly covert nature.

Creation of the computer security market and professional ethos

> The most prominent hacker crossover success-and-failure was that of Comsec Data Security, a Houston consulting firm founded in 1991 by three former members of the Legion of Doom. Though the firm quickly built a client list that included several Fortune 500 companies, 'media hysteria' and 'blackballing' by competing Establishment firms cost the firm those same commissions and forced it out of business in 1992, says cofounder and former president Christopher Goggans. 'There are a large number of people who would kill to do nothing but get paid to hack legitimately, so everybody in the hacker community was watching Comsec', says Goggans. 'From the treatment we got, you can expect that hackers who want to sell their skills as information security consultants in the future are going to have to hide their backgrounds'.
>
> (Roush 1995: 6)

Given the previously cited hawkish reasons for non-co-operation, it is perhaps unsurprising that hackers who have openly, as opposed to clandestinely, sought to market their knowledge have encountered difficulties. The antagonism caused by the conflict between the hawkish elements of the computer security industry and the anarchistic tendencies of the computer underground gives rise to strongly held and expressed views that fuel boundary formation. The certainties of the resultant rhetorical extremes reflect the radical uncertainty of the day-to-day exigencies of the IT world and its rapidly evolving mores. There is also the widely held belief that, along with legitimate reasons for differentiation between the two groups, there is also an element of manufactured difference. There are allegations from security practitioners themselves, for example, that with the advent of the first computer viruses, 'viral hype' was used to help stimulate the demand for computer security products and this sense of hype remains within the computer security industry:

It's very hard getting facts ... because the media hype is used as a trigger by people who are trying to sell anti-virus devices, programs, scanners, whatever. This is put about very largely by companies who are interested in the market and they try to stimulate the market by putting the fear of God into people in order to sell their products, but selling them on the back of fear rather than constructive benefits, because most of the products in the industry are sold on constructive benefits. You always sell the benefit first, this is selling it on the back of fear which is rather different, 'you'd better use our products or else'.

(Taylor: Knutsford interview)

Similarly, Ross argues:

software vendors are now profiting from the new public distrust of program copies ... the effects of the viruses have been to profitably clamp down on copyright delinquency, and to generate the need for entirely new industrial production of viral suppressors to contain the fallout. In this respect it is hard to see how viruses could hardly, in the long run, have benefited industry producers more.

(Ross 1991: 80)

Hackers, along with viruses, can be portrayed as an external threat to security against which computer security professionals and their products are needed as a safeguard. At the same time, however, there also seems to be an implicit recognition that computer systems are inherently susceptible to bugs and intrusions but that some sort of social solution to such vulnerabilities is more realistic than finding the necessary technical resources to fix the problems. In other words, hackers may provide a useful reminder of the need for improved security, but there is a practical limit to how far this usefulness can be recognised and acted upon outside of a punitive framework.

Like peas in a pod: the need to professionalise

Ironically, these hackers are perhaps driven by the same need to explore, to test technical limits that motivates computer professionals; they decompose problems, develop an understanding of them and then overcome them. But apparently not all hackers recognise the difference between penetrating the technical secrets of their own computer and penetrating a network of computers that belong to others. And therein lies a key distinction between a computer professional and someone who knows a lot about computers.

(Parrish 1989: file 11)

The hacker Craig Neidorf, alias *Knight Lightning*, in his report on a computer security industry conference, underlines the theory that the debate over hacking centres upon a project of professionalisation, with the argument that what mostly distinguishes the two groups is the form, rather than content, of the knowledge they seek to utilise:

> Zenner and Denning[2] alike discussed the nature of Phrack's[3] articles. They found that the articles appearing in Phrack contained the same types of material found publicly in other computer and security magazines, but with one significant difference. The tone of the articles. An article named 'How to Hack Unix' in Phrack usually contained very similar information to an article you might see in Communications of the ACM only to be named 'Securing Unix Systems'.
>
> (Neidorf 1990: file 6)

The implication is that hackers' security knowledge is not sought due to reasons other than its lack of technical value; rather, the computer security industry fails to utilise such knowledge more fully because it interferes with their boundary-forming project that centres upon attempting to define the difference between a hacker and a computer professional.

Another interesting example of the similar traits that the computer security industry and computer underground share is the case of Clifford Stoll's investigation of an intrusion into the Berkeley University computer laboratories, which he subsequently wrote up in the form of a best-selling book, *The Cuckoo's Egg*. Reviewing Stoll's book, Jim Thomas of the *CuD* points out that:

> Any computer undergrounder can identify with and appreciate Stoll's obsession and patience in attempting to trace the hacker through a maze of international gateways and computer systems. But, Stoll apparently misses the obvious affinity he has with those he condemns. He simply dismisses hackers as 'monsters' and displays virtually no recognition of the similarities between his own activity and those of the computer underground. This is what makes Stoll's work so dangerous: His work is an unreflective exercise in self-promotion, a tome that divides the sacred world of technocrats from the profane activities of those who would challenge it; Stoll stigmatises without understanding.
>
> (Thomas 1990: file 4)

What makes Stoll's behaviour even less understandable is that throughout the book he recounts in detail how he himself engages in the same kind of activities that he criticises others for indulging in. The fact that Stoll, for example, labels hackers as 'monsters' despite the fact he shares some of their qualities[4] illustrates the rhetorical qualities of the computer security industry's boundary-forming process. This is called a degradation ritual, which aims at redefining the social acceptability of a group by using assertion and hyperbole in the place of reasoned argument. Thus Stoll refers periodically in his book to hackers as 'rats, monsters, vandals, and bastards' (cited in Thomas 1990: file 4).

Witch-hunts and hackers

> The kinds of practices labelled deviant correspond to those values on which
> the community places its highest premium. Materialist cultures are beset by
> theft (although that crime is meaningless in a utopian commune where all
> property is shared). ... The correspondence between kind of deviance and a
> community's salient values is no accident ... deviants and conformists both
> are shaped by the same cultural pressures – and thus share some, if not all,
> common values – though they may vary in their opportunities to pursue
> valued ends via legitimate means. Deviance ... emerges exactly where it is
> most feared, in part because every community encourages some of its
> members to become Darth Vader, taking 'the force' over to the 'dark side'.
>
> (Dougan and Gieryn 1990: 4)

Theories that seek to relate hacking to wider social and historical trends are
bound to be somewhat tentative and speculative. They do, however, provide an
explanation of the strength of opposition and fear directed at a group that is
labelled as deviant despite the fact that its members share some of the same
characteristics as their computer security industry counterparts (and frequently
cross over into it). Part of the cause of the witch-hunt mentality, as it has
allegedly been applied to hackers, is the increasing tendency within society
towards the privatisation of consumption. John Perry Barlow identifies the
hacker as the latest such scapegoat of modern times in a series including
communism, terrorism, child abductors and AIDS. He sees post-cold-war feelings of vulnerability and the information/generation gap being constitutive
factors in the witch-hunt mentality:

> More and more of our neighbours live in armed compounds. Alarms blare
> continuously. Potentially happy people give their lives over to the corporate
> state as though the world were so dangerous outside its veil of collective
> immunity that they have no choice. ... The perfect bogeyman for modern
> times is the Cyberpunk! He is so smart he makes you feel even more stupid
> than you usually do. He knows this complex country in which you're perpet-
> ually lost. He understands the value of things you can't conceptualize long
> enough to cash in on. He is the one-eyed man in the Country of the Blind.
>
> (Barlow 1990: 56)

The pressures to commodify information can be seen as an extension of the
decline of the public ethos in modern society, which is accompanied by the
search for scapegoats that will justify the retreat from the communitarian spirit.

The hardening of attitudes

Computer crimes have evolved from exotic incidents to a major societal
issue. They have quickly moved from hacks to attacks, from fooling around

to fouling up, and from violations to virucide. In order to fight computer crime, the society, and computer professionals in particular, face some very difficult decisions on some very fundamental issues. This is a serious moment in our society, as we seek to establish an appropriate balance between old law and new technology.

(Sherizen 1992: 39)

From the late 1980s onwards it is possible to trace a hardening of attitudes towards hackers due to both changes within the computer underground and the agendas of groups that began to increasingly set themselves in opposition to it. Landreth, a US member of the hacker group known as the *Inner Circle* talks of a major change occurring in the computer underground in the late 1980s. In addition to the effect of the increased dispersal of personal computers, there was also the effect of the 1989 hacker movie, *Wargames*:

In a matter of months the number of self-proclaimed hackers tripled, then quadrupled. You couldn't get through to any of the old bulletin boards any more – the telephone numbers were busy all night long. Even worse, you could delicately work to gain entrance to a system, only to find dozens of novices blithely tromping around the files.

(Landreth 1985 :18)

These 'wannabe' hackers are portrayed as typically immature and lacking in the original hacker ethic. Chris Goggans from the *Legion of Doom* concurs with this identification of a change in the basic nature of the computer underground environment. He argues that in the early days:

People were friendly, computer users were very social. Information was handed down freely, there was a true feeling of brotherhood in the underground. As the years went on people became more and more anti-social. As it became more and more difficult to blue-box the social feeling of the underground began to vanish. People began to hoard information and turn people in for revenge. The underground today is not fun. It is very power hungry, almost feral in its actions. People are grouped off: you like me or you like him, you cannot like both. ... The subculture I grew up with, learned in, and contributed to, has decayed into something gross and twisted that I shamefully admit connection with. Everything changes and everything dies, and I am certain that within ten years there will be no such thing as a computer underground. I'm glad I saw it in its prime.

(Goggans: email interview)

One reason for the changing nature of the computer underground was thus simply the fact that more wannabes arrived. 'Elite' hackers such as Goggans felt that this cheapened in some way the ethos and atmosphere of camaraderie that had previously existed. Sheer numbers alone would mean the demise of the previous emphasis hackers placed upon sharing knowledge and the importance of educating young newcomers. The idiosyncratic actions of the first-generation hackers, within the isolated academic context of MIT, were often praised for their inventiveness. Similar actions in the wider modern computing community tend to be automatically more disruptive and liable to censure. Once the proto-type days of a technology are over, society's investment in the technology makes cavalier attitudes, by figures such as hackers, increasingly unacceptable. Sanford Sherizen compares the situation within computing to that of the early aviation industry and its maverick pilots:

> historical change shows how certain individual behaviours become changed by societal restructuring. ... These barnstormers were wild, didn't respect property, and were constantly challenging authority. When they crashed their system, it really went down. They were a unique breed of individuals, who tested the limits of the world of aviation, sometimes literally by walking on the wings and performing amazing and often dangerous stunts. They were necessary for the early stages of aviation because they tested the limits of the technology. ... What finally led to the end of the barnstorming pilots was that the business interests of airlines got precedence over the aviation interests. ... After the industry reached a certain level of develop-ment, these 'pilot hackers' could have quite literally killed the industry ... certain deviant behaviors get resolved, often without changing the behavior but by creating an institutionalized patterning, accepting certain activities and sidetracking other behaviors. There will be a process that will challenge the computer crime problem. It will not necessarily be the same as with airline pilots but it will be a process whereby at least a temporary resolution will be reached.
>
> (Sherizen 1992: 43)

The risks of taking physical metaphors too far when analysing computer security is treated in detail in the next chapter; at this point it is worth pointing out that, whereas the earliest pilots were a relatively easily identifiable group that could be either marginalised or co-opted into mainstream flying, once again the anonymous qualities of their chosen environment means that hackers provide a potentially much more problematic group to marginalise completely. Nevertheless, continuing with the aviation metaphor, there is a perceived need to subject hackers who were previously tolerated to new social strictures:

> When the first 'airplane hackers' began working on their devices, they were free to do essentially as they pleased. If they crashed and killed themselves well, that was too bad. If their planes worked – so much the better. After it became possible to build working airplanes, there followed a period in which anyone could build one and fly where he liked. But in the long run that

became untenable. ... If you want to fly today, you must get a license. You must work within a whole set of regulations.

(Leichter 1992: file 1)

Thus perceptions of people's interactions with technology evolve over time, even if the activities themselves remain unchanged in essence. They begin to be viewed differently as society's mores adapt to the evolving technology. An example of this is the changing role of system crashes. In the earliest days of computing, the computers functioned by means of large glass valves, which after relatively short periods of use were liable to over-heat, thus causing a system crash.[5] Even if hackers were responsible for some of the system crashes that occurred, the fact that they were equally liable to be caused by non-hackers led to a climate whereby hacker-induced crashes were accepted as a minor inconvenience even when they were extremely disruptive by today's standards.

Pressures to criminalise

The law-makers have endorsed that schizophrenia pressed by the electro-cognoscenti, and they have endorsed it out of fear, ignorance and misunderstanding. How else to react to the omniscient, omnipotent power of cyberspace? Well, take its unruly tenants at their word [they seem to know what they are talking about], and treat cyberspace as a competing reality: regulate it, and break it up into chunks called property. But alternative universes provide a very bad model: Neither law nor technology benefits. The law founders and sinks in the clear blue fungible sea of the network. And the electronic community is on the verge of being legislated to death, ruled out of fear and loathing, chained by broad and detailed laws that can make anything – the movement of an electron – illegal.

(Karnow 1994: website)

One of the major side-effects of the professionalisation process has been the pressure to criminalise the computer underground with specific anti-hacking legislation. The computer underground argues that the legislation is precipitate and inappropriate. Legislation is seen as a short-cut to reducing hacking whilst simultaneously avoiding having to fix the faults it highlights:

We should not be surprised by computer crime, but we seem to be. In *The Great Train Robbery* Michael Crichton suggested that society is often offended by this new technology crime to the point of outrage. Likewise, it should come as little surprise, that, like the railroad, the automobile, and the telephone before it, the computer has been the subject of premature, if not pre-emptive, legislation. The politicians are certain, that, somewhere in any dung heap, there must be a pony.

(Murray 1992: 31)

The message of Ken Thompson[6] in his 1984 Turing Award Lecture unwittingly adds weight to this charge by the way in which it conflates the ethical, legal and technical issues of hacking. The basis of the speech was a description of the ease with which undetectable bugs can be introduced into programs, and the subsequent implication that error-free software is easier to obtain from a trusted source. This lack of assurance about technical security leads to the search for a non-technical solution. Thompson thus argued for a sharper legislative response to hacking:

> I would like to criticise the press in its handling of the 'hackers', the 414 gang, the Dalton gang etc. The acts performed by these kids are vandalism at best and probably trespass and theft at worst. It is only the inadequacy of the criminal code that saves the hackers from very serious prosecution. The companies that are vulnerable to this activity (and most large companies are very vulnerable), are pressing hard to update the criminal code.
>
> (Thompson 1984: 763)

The computer security industry shows a marked reluctance to differentiate between 'responsible hackers' and vandals. Instead, it tends to emphasise the more malicious and destructive elements of hacking, and distinctions between malevolent and harmless browsing are played down. There are thus strong pressures to treat all hacking activities as criminal, which the computer underground argues results in Draconian legislation that fails to deal with the computer security weaknesses that still remain.

Legislation

> Through legislation we can turn what the hackers do into a crime and there just might be a slim chance that we can stop them. But that won't fix poorly designed systems whose very existence is a violation of our privacy.
>
> (Goldstein 1993: file 1)

> We now face the task of adapting our legal institutions and societal expectations to the cultural phenomena that even now are springing up from communications technology.
>
> (Kapor 1991: 1)

> The law only has sledgehammers, when what we need are parking tickets and speeding tickets.
>
> (Mitch Kapor cited in Sterling 1991: 6)

Society's attempts to reconcile competing views about informational property rights are reflected in the debate as to whether or not non-malicious system cracking/browsing should be treated as a criminal act. Anti-hacking legislation is the logical extension of the stigmatisation process. Moral language is used in both legislative debates and in the law enforcement techniques adopted, exacerbating the 'them and us' feelings of polarisation. This section explores the specific case of the 1990 United Kingdom Computer Misuse Act. Material is taken from the parliamentary debates and committee readings of the Act, which was brought to the House of Commons as a Private Member's Bill, by Michael Colvin MP. This was after a previous attempt by Emma Nicholson MP to pass a similar bill had been thwarted due to a lack of parliamentary time.

There are three main types of argument put forward against a legislative response to hacking: it will not succeed in eliminating hacking and as such can be described as 'symbolic legislation';[7] it will increase the likelihood that existing security weaknesses will shelter behind the law and remain unrectified; and a potential problem associated with even successfully implemented legislation is the danger of driving hacking knowledge into the hands of the criminal fraternity. Legislators face the further problem of trying to draft laws that will keep pace with a constantly evolving technological environment and the unprecedented situations it may throw up. The challenge to the legal profession and the rest of society resides in the fact that information has an ambivalent status as a commodity and is something to which property rights cannot easily be assigned, as Dr David England, of Glasgow University, describes:

> I think it stems from the cultural (in a sociological sense) basis which we use to attach financial values to things. Cars and houses have a financial and personal value which most people can negotiate and agree on. If we suffer loss or damage to this kind of object we can usually gauge that loss and society can work out some recompense for that loss (insurance, punishing offenders etc.) I think information, especially electronic information is different. We don't have the necessary agreed mechanisms on which to establish its financial and personal value. By its very nature it is very easy to move ('steal'). Thus given the lack of effort in 'stealing' it and the lack of any perceived damage (on behalf of the thief) it is not seen (by them) as a real crime.
>
> (England: email interview)

In this context, hackers fail to perceive much of their activity as a crime. They see the new emphasis being deliberately placed upon ethics in the professional worlds of business and science as part of an attempt to develop a coherent response to the contradictions associated with information's evolving nature:

> For all the trumpeting about excesses of power and disrespect for the law of the land, the revival of ethics, in the business and science disciplines in the Ivy League and on Capitol Hill ... is little more than a weak liberal response to working flaws or adaptational lapses in the social logic of technocracy.
>
> (Ross 1991: 22)

The 'weak liberal response' has produced, in the eyes of some commentators, an ill-thought out response:

> Lobbying by computer users for the criminalisation of cruelty to (their) computers has been extensive and vociferous. The imposition of criminal sanctions is seen as some sort of magic talisman ... the law takes the computer too seriously. All sorts of magical qualities are ascribed to the machine. The debates on the Computer Misuse Act are replete with demonic images of hacking and its consequences. The computer is the ultimate bogeyman and has produced a knee jerk reaction from Parliament.
> (Ian Lloyd, Strathclyde University Law Department, 9 June 1993: Edinburgh University AI Dept. Seminar)

Additional subsidiary factors are likely to limit the efficacy of legislation designed to prevent hacking: law-makers encounter the problem of adequately gauging the level of intent lying behind a hack; many conventional legal concepts fail to transpose literally into the world of cyberspace, for example, when computer intrusion is compared to 'breaking and entering' the analogy begs the question of what is actually 'broken' (or for that matter 'stolen' if a copy is taken and the original remains); and, finally, legislators are faced with a dearth of reliable statistics – in the context of this information gap there seems to be a tendency for spurious computer crime estimates to gain legitimacy if for no other reason than they are repeated often enough.

Symbolic legislation

> While the Computer Fraud and Abuse Act has been amended several times, it still does not cover every conceivable computer crime. Therefore it is imperative that legislators continue to amend the Act, as well as pass other criminal statutes, as the technology and scope of computer crime expands. Without such statutes, law enforcement agencies and prosecutors will be handcuffed in their efforts to combat this new generation of computer criminals. As one commentator points out, 'The revolution has only just begun, but already it's starting to overwhelm us. It's outstripping our capacity to cope, antiquating our laws, transforming our mores, reshuffling our economy, reordering our priorities, redefining our workplaces, and putting our Constitution to the fire'.
> (Scalione 1996: 6)

Hollinger and Lanza-Kaduce (1988), along with Michalowski and Pfuhl (1990), use computer crime as a specific example of the process whereby legislation is produced and then passed as a largely symbolic act with little chance of practical success. The former describe how, in their view, computer crime provided a useful opportunity for legislators 'to maximise their individual media exposure without offending any major constituency' (Hollinger and Lanza-Kaduce 1988: 113), and 'this opportunity for positive political exposure resulted in the passage of what is sometimes termed symbolic legislation, i.e. legislation whose purpose is more ideological than instrumental' (Michalowski and Pfuhl 1990: 261). Michalowski and Pfuhl conclude that computer crime legislation resulted from:

> the unexpressed understanding [of legislators] that unless computer-resident information was extended the ideological and practical protection of the law, established relations of property and hegemonic authority relations could be deroutinised by 'information thieves'. ... It was within this ideological framework that the dangers of computer crime proclaimed by computer security experts and the press *made sense*. And in the final analysis, it was this ideological framework that made the passage of computer crime laws a low-risk, high visibility opportunity for law-makers.
>
> (Michalowski and Pfuhl 1990: 271)

Vinten's analysis of hacking legislation concludes that:

> Legislation will at least raise the profile of computer security. Enforcement will be another question. ... Nobody can deny the potential and actual threat of hacking. The Law can serve as one plank in its prevention and deterrence. Increasingly the law is giving out clear signals. It is too early to judge the impact of this ... [but] one cannot but wonder if hacking will prove as intractable as the drugs and Aids issues, and whether the legal response will be as effective as King Canute trying to beat back the waves.
>
> (Vinten 1990: 15)

Thus there is a perception that computer crime legislation has been used as a 'bandwagon' upon which legislators and technical experts could jump in order to further their own career-orientated goals. In support of this hypothesis is the noticeable lack of public pressure for computer crime legislation. Not only was there no apparent public pressure, there are also various qualities of computer crime that may evoke particularly tolerant, even admiring, attitudes from the public. There is a range of reasons why the public may be reluctant to censure computer criminals: computer crime is comparatively rare; people are more interested than bothered by it; people tend to admire the daring often associated with hacking exploits; most of the victims of computer crime are faceless institutions that do not appeal strongly to people's sympathies; elementary precautions are often omitted in the systems that are attacked that can lead to a displacement of blame from the attacker to the victim; and, finally, the game element of much computer crime such as system cracking means that it is often viewed as being outside of 'real-world' moral bounds.

Instrumental legislation

> the computer industry will welcome the Bill because it cannot build into its technology the necessary safeguards to prevent hacking or other offences. At the moment such safeguards are technically impossible and, therefore, the law must fill the gap.
>
> (Hogg, Hansard 1990a: 1143)

In contrast to the symbolic interpretation of legislation, the parliamentary debate that accompanied the 1990 United Kingdom Computer Misuse Act arguably illustrates how hawkish computer security industry values were incorporated into the statute book for instrumental rather than merely ideological reasons. Hackers have claimed that they are victims of blame displacement from those responsible for the security of systems that have suffered a security breach. The notion of the *a priori* responsibility of a computer crime victim to secure his system to the best of his ability was raised by Mr Cohen MP:

> In my view, a computer system that is not properly secure can potentially cause more damage than a Rambo maniac who gets hold of guns, horrific though that is. Logic surely dictates that computer owners should be legally responsible for the security of their computers just as gun owners are responsible for their guns.
>
> (Cohen, Hansard 1990b: 88)

The subsequent parliamentary responses to this point encapsulate the instrumental rationale lying behind the criminalisation of hacking. They express the view that, since purely technical solutions to systems weaknesses are too expensive, hacking should be prevented by the use of legislative rather than technical fixes. Legislation was introduced in the context of an apparent unwillingness of companies to invest sufficiently in security measures: 'It could be argued that perhaps one fifth of investment in a computer software system should be allocated to security. Very few companies adopt that principle' (Nicholson, Hansard 1990b: 88). Legislation was thus a cost-effective countermeasure with which to confront an otherwise expensive problem:

> In much the same way as we lock our doors to deter burglars, it is possible to protect computers, and many people do. ... However, there is no complete form of protection for computers. High levels of security can be achieved but they are horrifically expensive, in terms of money, inconvenience or both. Security systems tend to slow up the computer. When speed is the essence, that can be extremely costly. We do not expect householders to turn their homes into Fort Knox. We expect them to take sensible precautions and we add to that the support of sound laws against burglary. That is precisely my approach in the Bill.
>
> (Colvin, Hansard 1990a: 1139)

The consensus of opinion during the parliamentary debate emphasised the fact that although hackers might possess potentially useful technical knowledge, legislation should aim at their removal so that they cannot exacerbate the security weaknesses that are acknowledged to exist:

> A study of 20 European companies carried out by Coopers and Lybrand showed that 19 had inadequate standards of security which were a real threat to the economic development of those companies. The report said: 'The catastrophic effects of poor security are likely to discourage organisations from becoming any more dependent on their network systems'. *That suggests that there may be a level of complexity in our society beyond which, because of safety interests, we may be frightened to go.* If hacking increases our fears, there will be damage to the cohesion and organisation of our society. That is a perfectly good and sufficient justification for the Bill.
>
> (Arbuthnot, Hansard 1990a: 1179 [emphasis mine])

The use of the word 'fears' is significant because it draws attention to an aspect of the parliamentary pressure to criminalise hacking: the fact that legislation is used as a conduit to formally express and codify elements of the 'them and us' scenario, whilst the reference to the 'level of complexity' beyond which society may be frightened to go due to safety fears, implicitly admits that a legislative solution is being sought for ultimately technical problems. Dr Taylor's model of computer security measures cost against the security provided by that expenditure. At the lower level of the model there are basic precautions such as paper shredders, and the rotation of staff between jobs if they might be likely to collude. More complicated (and therefore expensive) technical precautions are measures to introduce more secure operating systems. Encrypted passwords (which may even be programmed to move about the operating system ahead of any potentially curious intruder) are just one example of more sophisticated access control that protects against browsing from someone who has gained access to the password file. The basic underlying factor of all these measures is the direct linear relationship between the level of security obtained and the expense incurred. Secure, technically sophisticated operating systems may involve man-years of effort.

Dr Taylor described his view of what role, given this direct cost–security relationship, legislation has to play:

> If there is no law in place to protect information, then according to the value of your information's sensitivity, you have to install appropriate technical measures which cost more and more money as they become more and more sophisticated to protect your information ... then you don't need these higher levels of sophistication, because you know that in fact as a private sector user, if anyone starts trying to get into your system and get at things like passwords and your log of events ... you prosecute. So my view of the Computer Misuse Act is that it's trying to provide a legal procedure, which

will provide quite a lot of protection to quite sophisticated systems which then require less technical protection, so there's a trade-off ... legal measures cost quite a lot of money whatever level of security you want, because you have to put things like the Computer Misuse Act in place, provide the methods to prosecute the people that have breached it ... police time and so on. ... What this means is that provided the legal protection is in place and working, it makes unnecessary the more complex levels of protection.

(Taylor: Knutsford interview)

He seemed to recognise, however, that legislation may not be an unequivocally good thing:

I suppose that is really going the wrong way because to get quite a good level of security by providing legal protection, you've still got to spend a lot of money ... whatever the breach of security. If it's a very simple one like pinching certain copies of paper, or it's a breach of an operating system, the cost of processing that particular breach is pretty constant, because you've got to invest in police time, in court time, and so on.

(Taylor: Knutsford interview)

A further factor limiting the effectiveness of legislation is its lack of feasibility for certain publicity-sensitive organisations such as banks. The adverse publicity that may result from taking a security breach case to the courts is likely to result in a marked reluctance to take recourse to legal solutions; affected companies are more likely to take internal disciplinary measures than resort to prosecution under the Act. Yet a general over-reliance in the rest of the economy and society upon legal recourse will mean that such sensitive organisations will remain vulnerable to security breaches.

Symbolic deterrence

The above instrumental view of legislation relies upon such laws as the 1990 United Kingdom Computer Misuse Act to deter would-be hackers. Doubt remains, however, regarding the value of legislation as a deterrent and further doubt has been expressed as to whether or not such a desire to deter was the main motivating force behind the legislation in the first place. This adds weight to the symbolic view of computer misuse statutes. A specific charge relates to the scant resources available if the Act is likely to be enforced:

I hope that the Minister will deal with the problem of enforcement. We are reminded that out of 150,000 police officers in England and Wales only five are mainly concerned with computer crime. ... Fewer than 100 have received even the minimum four weeks basic training and the Serious Fraud Office has one computer-knowledgeable official.

(Leigh, Hansard 1990a: 1172)

Claims that the Computer Misuse Act is largely a symbolic measure are also inadvertently supported by some of its own proponents who question the likely efficacy of the Bill whilst affirming the sentiment behind it. This is a characteristic of symbolic legislation (and to a lesser extent most legislation): that it should espouse a particular social message irrespective of the law's likely ability to enforce that message. An example of this characteristic is the MP, Dr Moonie's questioning of whether or not the Bill would provide adequate deterrence:

It may deter the occasional recreational hacker, but the seriously disturbed person who perpetrates serious offences may not be adequately deterred by it. People will not be deterred if there seems little chance of being caught. … Will inventive minds find some way of circumventing the Bill? I hope that its drafting is secure enough to prevent that. I support the Bill in principle. Its internal structure is sound, but it is a matter of conjecture whether it will do what it is purported to do.

(Moonie, Hansard 1990a: 1160)

The charge that the Act is more symbolic than a real deterrent is also strengthened by the belief that the timing of the Bill's introduction had more to do with a desire to be seen to be doing something about the problem, rather than a sudden realisation that there was a problem in the first place:

Arguably, any need to deter abuse existed long before the enactment of computer crime statutes. In fact, the available data suggest that serious economic losses linked to computer abuse have been and continue to be attributed to current and former employees of the victimised organisation rather than to interloping hackers with modems. The temporal lag in the criminalisation of computer abuse (not observed with the introduction of other technological changes), seriously challenges the extent to which the computer crime laws can be understood purely as instruments of classical deterrence.

(Hollinger and Lanza-Kaduce 1988: 116)

The classical deterrence view, however, still seems to hold sway in the mind of the legal establishment. In the same case as the eventually acquitted Paul Bedworth, two of his co-defendants were sentenced to prison terms. The judge explicitly stated that his sentencing rationale was based on the desire to deter other hackers. In his summing-up he said:

'If your passion had been cars rather than computers we would have called your conduct delinquent, and I don't shrink from the analogy of describing what you were doing as intellectual joy-riding. ... There may be people out there who consider hacking to be harmless, but hacking is not harmless. Computers now form a central role in our lives. ... Some, providing emergency services, depend on their computers to deliver those services. It is essential that the integrity of those systems should be protected and hacking puts that integrity into jeopardy'. He said that hackers need to be given a 'clear signal' by the court that their activities 'will not and cannot be tolerated'.

(*Independent* Saturday 22 May 1993: 4)

The parliamentary debate as degradation ritual

The prototype of the rule creator ... is the crusading reformer. He is interested in the content of rules. The existing rules do not satisfy him because there is some evil which profoundly disturbs him. He feels that nothing can be right in the world until rules are made to correct it. He operates with an absolute ethic; what he sees is truly and totally evil with no qualification. Any means is justified to do away with it. The crusader is fervent and righteous, often self-righteous.

(Becker 1963: 148)

Previously, the process whereby stigmatisation is enacted has been referred to as a *degradation ritual*. The following is evidence that, at least to some extent, such a process has occurred in the parliamentary debate. Parliamentary stigmatisation can be seen as taking two closely related forms. In the first, the motivations of hackers are impugned, and, in the second, the dubious nature of hackers' motives are highlighted by a group-bonding process that emphasises the 'them and us' scenario.

The following is an example of the first form; it is Dr Lewis Moonie MP's portrayal of the motivations of hackers:

The motive ... is simple to understand – human greed. Although we do not condone theft, we can possibly understand the need or personal circumstances which may drive someone to commit that act. That is not the case with the kind of computer misuse that we are discussing. Very often the people involved are educated professional people and they have the wherewithal to afford to carry out such behaviour. ... Although we may not accept greed, we can understand it. The motive for malice is more difficult to comprehend. ... There are many kinds of people involved and most, although not exclusively all, are men. Although I have never professed to have espoused the cause of Freud in my psychiatric work, I believe that a profound sexual inadequacy is often related to such behaviour.

(Moonie, Hansard 1990a: 1156)

The second aspect of the stigmatisation process: the construction of the *them and us* scenario takes the form of, first, reinforcing group identity by underlining those qualities that produce the *us* and, second, contributing to perceptions of the alien nature of *them*. An example of the former is the way in which Powell 'proves' the potential menace of hacking by referring to the social position of a figure calling for legislation to deal with hacking:

> Yesterday I received a letter from a constituent who is a leading official in one of the world's leading banks. He asked me to support the Bill, and I am happy to assure him that I do so with enthusiasm. ... When such an important official troubles to write to a Member of Parliament about a specific piece of legislation, knowing the background of his career I have not the slightest doubt that the menace of hacking and its consequences is widespread.
>
> (Powell, Hansard 1990a: 1147)

The difference between such a constituent and those of the culture against whom anti-hacking legislation is aimed is starkly apparent:

> To show the sort of twisted culture that the Bill is trying to stamp out, I have an extract from a bulletin board ... stating: 'who's seen the news in the "Sunday Times" ... page A5 ... about hacking ... and phreaking Mercury ... they also want restrictions on BBS's ... it's that stupid cow ... the Devon MP "computer expert" [Nicholson] ... don't make me laff ... could be bad news tho ... maybe someone should assassinate her?' Did somebody suggest that hacking is a harmless culture? All that I can say is that it is a privilege and I am honoured to join my hon. Friend on the hackers' hit list.
>
> (Colvin, Hansard 1990a: 1137)

Once the sense of the *us* has reinforced a sense of group identity, the process to establish unequivocally who we are not begins. Colvin continues by relating how he hoped 'that the debate will dispel any lingering belief that the computer hacker is some sort of Raffles of the microchip' (Hansard 1990a: 1142). Nicholson describes in detail various salacious and potentially destabilising aspects of hacking activity ranging from proliferation of pornography on bulletin boards to interest being shown by political groups such as the Greens, Anarchists and those behind the *Electronics and Computing for Peace Newsletter*. She seeks to distance herself from 'people who believe that they have a right of access to all knowledge and that everything should be out in the open – and should specifically be open to them'. Nicholson proceeds to relate reported incidents of hackers who have allegedly 'tried to kill patients in hospital by accessing their drug records and altering their prescriptions on computer' (Hansard 1990a: 1151, 1153). Finally, Nicholson advocates legislation against hackers because:

It is no good saying that people must increase their protection, because hackers are very clever. They will find a way around every form of protection that one buys or creates. That is what they are there for. They make a great deal of money out of it and the German hackers, at any rate, support a drug-based lifestyle on their activities. I was about to say, 'enjoy', but I should certainly not enjoy a lifestyle based on drugs. Because drugs are expensive, hackers need to make a great deal of money to support their lifestyle.

(Hansard 1990a: 1154)

Nicholson fails to give any corroborating evidence for many of these assertions. Her association of German hackers and drugs is possibly a reference to the case of Pengo, the hacker Stoll tracked down in *The Cuckoo's Egg*, but that individual case does not seem to warrant the status of being generally applicable to the whole German hacking scene. This example of lack of specific evidence underlines the information gap surrounding computer crime that policy makers are faced with. Nicholson exemplified the degradation ritual's tendency for reliance upon rumour rather than empirical facts by referring to the unsubstantiated case of Scottish poll tax computers having had details of those eligible to pay the tax substituted with information of dead people, whilst Waller demonstrated the role 'guestimates' played with his observation that 80 per cent of the computers in Hong Kong have been infected with at least one kind of virus. The disproportionate reliance upon the 'casual empiricism' of rumour and 'guestimates' ironically increases pressure to legislate against hacking because of the increased levels of fear the lack of statistics may produce: 'while we are aware of the tip of the iceberg, we do not know how much lies beneath the surface' (Waller, Hansard 1990a: 1161).

The problems with legislation

The criminal law has no business here. For the network has no borders, and the autonomous space of hyperperfect illusion and flawlessly recombinant culture is too slippery for any statute.

(Karnow 1994: 8)

Despite temptations to use the legislative process to facilitate the process of professionalisation within computer security, various anomalies tend to result from the attempted literal transposition of real-world criteria on to cyberspace. The introduction of inappropriate legislation is rooted in the ultimate non-transferability of virtual-world concepts to the real world. 'Disembodied' is the phrase Michalowski and Pfuhl (1990) use to refer to computer-based crime in relation to the growing immateriality of information. An obvious implication of such disembodiment is that the act of attempting to illicitly access and use such information does not fall neatly into existing laws that are designed to deal with traditional notions of theft:

In one ... lament, Business Week claimed that even if information thieves are caught 'it is not always easy to prosecute them. Larceny means depriving someone of their possessions permanently. Can a person be tried for stealing a copy of information when the supposedly stolen information remains in the computer?' Similarly, Mano complained, that one 'might as well play billiards with a sash weight' as try to control computer abuse by applying existing laws to this new threat.

(Michalowski and Pfuhl 1990: 268)

Society thus finds it increasingly difficult to protect traditional property rights in the realm of computing due to the qualitatively different features of electronic data storage. In the face of these problems, Gongrijp contends that the establishment response to computer crime has been of disproportionate and unjustified strength when compared to similar real-world crimes. For instance, he argues that whereas normally within the justice system the intentions of the defendant are an important part of the alleged crime, the same allowance for motives is not made with incidents involving computers:

you can steal a document in a company, photocopy it and take it home, and they could do nothing, maybe within the company, but there would be no criminal offence, within the company they could fire you. And then if you do the same thing with a computer it should be a criminal offence, why? In all the rest of the justice system it depends on what you do with them [documents or whatever], it depends on your intentions, and as soon as you use a computer, your intentions are no longer important, it's just that you use a computer, it's a magic area that we don't understand and that we can't control so that we must take you one step before you do harm and we must not care about your intentions: it's bullshit!

(Gongrijp: Amsterdam interview)

From the viewpoint of some hackers, the problems encountered in legislative approaches are indicative of a wider misguided societal tendency to equate the real and informational worlds:

If we succeed in convincing people that copying a file is the same as physically stealing something, we can hardly be surprised when the broad-based definition results in more overall crime. Blurring the distinction between a virtual infraction and a real-life crime is a mistake.

(Goldstein 1993: CuD 5.43)

The need to develop legal concepts better suited to an information society was voiced in the UK parliamentary debate on computer misuse. Mr Cohen MP warned that with the criminalisation of such activities, such as non-malicious browsing:

The Bill's net is being cast far too wide, and it will lead to many people, some vulnerable, committing a crime where none now exists ... In years to come, the Bill could apply to a washing machine, controlled by a chip ... That is nonsense.

(Cohen, Hansard 1990a: 1166, 1167)

Another MP asked the rhetorical question:

Are we really saying that members of staff who make unauthorised use of a firm's personal computer to produce their own CV or every perpetrator of a childish prank that their misdemeanour is worthy of a criminal record they will keep for the rest of their life?

(Leigh, Hansard 1990a: 1173)

In addition to concerns that the legislation is too broad there is the worry that legal measures cannot hope to keep up effectively with the rapidly changing technologies it confronts. In the United Kingdom Computer Misuse Act, for example, nowhere is the term 'computer' actually defined. In the words of Mr Colvin, the MP who brought the Bill before the House:

The problem is that it was six weeks ago when I first defined the word 'computer' to my satisfaction. That definition is already out of date. The passage of time and the pace of development within the computer industry mean that any definition of a computer or a computer system would soon be out of date.

(Hansard 1990a: 1159)

Conclusion

This chapter has illustrated aspects of the social process whereby hackers are marginalised and stigmatised, whilst, simultaneously, the computer security industry and establishment figures reinforce their own group identities. A basic difference between hackers and their adversaries was shown to be their conflicting interpretations of the compatibility between real-world and informational conceptions of property. These interpretational differences were seen to reach a head over each group's assessment of the applicability of such conceptions in the legislative process. There is a hard-line mentality within sections of the computer underground that fails to accept any negative ethical aspects of phone-phreaking or hacking. This is forcefully opposed by factions of the computer security industry, whose typical sentiment is that hackers have forgotten 'that sometimes they must leave the playpen and accept the notion that computing is more than just a game' (Bloombecker 1990: 41). Given these sharply divergent stances, the next chapter examines in detail the roots of the ethical differences between the computer underground and their opponents, and the rhetorical strategies with which these differences are constructed and then maintained.

7 The construction of computer ethics

Introduction: ethical differences between the computer security industry and the computer underground

> teenage hacking has come to be defined increasingly as a potential threat to normative educational ethics and national security alike. ... Consequently, a deviant social class or group has been defined and categorized as 'enemies of the state' in order to help rationalize a general law-and-order clampdown on free and open information exchange.
>
> (Ross 1991: 80, 81)

In the face of the ethical complexities of hacking, there is perhaps a temptation to adopt the moral certainties contained within the polarised positions of the *them and us* scenario. Such certainties reflect the technical environment within which they are formed:

> computer software is itself a markedly binary discourse. The binary logic of computer technology is vivid in its contrasts between 'working' and 'not working': on/off; zero/one; right/wrong. As one of the partners of a management consultancy with responsibility for computer reliability put it: Things are either right or wrong. It is a world which grey does not easily inhabit. And a small error doesn't make it just a little bit wrong.
>
> (Woolgar and Russell 1990: 34)

Elements of the computer security industry vehemently oppose both the 'playpen attitude' advocated by elements of the computer underground and also their apparent unwillingness to equate computer crime with real-world illegality. The different perceptions the two groups have of hacking is illustrated in the two quotations below.

> Hackers are like kids putting a ten-pence piece on a railway line to see if the train can bend it, not realising that they risk de-railing the whole train.
>
> (Jones: London interview)

Technically, I didn't commit a crime. All I did was destroy data. I didn't steal anything.

(Bank of America employee caught after planting a logic bomb in the company's computer system)[1]

Presupposing that no destructive harm is done, hackers tend to believe that it is not wrong to explore systems without prior permission, whilst those concerned with the security of those systems would characterise such a belief as offensive:

Just because YOU have such a totally bankrupt sense of ethics and propriety, that shouldn't put a burden on *me* to have to waste my time dealing with it. Life is short enough to not have it gratuitously wasted on self-righteous, immature fools. ... If you want to 'play' on my system, you can ASK me, try to convince me *a priori* of the innocence of your intent, and if I say 'no' you should just go away. And playing without asking is, and should be criminal; I have no obligation, nor any interest, in being compelled to provide a playpen for bozos who are so jaded that they cannot amuse themselves in some non-offensive way.

(Cosell 1991: file 2)

Bob Johnson, a Senior Systems Analyst and Unix System Administrator at a US military installation criticises the justifications used by hackers as an example of the modern tendency to indulge in 'positional ethics'. Referring to the Internet Worm case he states:

The majority of people refuse to judge on the basis of 'right and wrong'. Instead, they judge the actions in terms of result, or based on actual damages, or incidental damages or their own personal ideas. In my mind, Morris was WRONG in what he did, regardless of damages, and should therefore be prepared to pay for his deeds. Many others do not suffer from this 'narrow frame of mind'. By the way, positional ethics is the same line of reasoning which asks, 'When would it be right to steal a loaf of bread?' I believe that the answer is 'It may someday be necessary, but it's never right'

(Johnson: email interview)

The hawkish elements of the computer security industry are unequivocal in their condemnation of hacking. Some argue that the lack of ethics shown by hackers is indicative of a wider societal decline. Smb, for instance, characterises the alleged degeneration of the average person's ethics, not as a breakdown in morality, but rather as a spread of amorality: 'I'm far from convinced that the lack of ethics is unique to hackers. I think it's a societal problem, which in this business we see manifested as hacking. Amorality rather than immorality is the problem' (Smb: email interview). With very similar language, Bob Johnson argues that:

In a larger sense, I view them [hacking and viruses] as part of the same problem, which is a degeneration of the average persons ethics – i.e. integrity and honesty. There's a popular saying in America – 'You're not really breaking the speed limit unless you get caught.' I believe an ethical person would neither break into systems, nor write viruses.

(Johnson: email interview)

Cosell takes this argument further, the 'degeneration of the average person's ethics' is applied to a loss of respect by hackers for property rights:

The issue here is one of ethics, not damages. I'll avoid the 'today's children are terrors' argument, but some parts of that cannot be avoided: the hackers take the point of view that the world at large OWES them amusement, and that anything they can manage to break into is fair game [an astonishing step beyond an already reprehensible position, that anything not completely nailed down is fair game].

(Cosell: email interview)

Vinten's study of business ethics (1990) points out that ethical judgements tend to be harsher, the older the person making the judgements. Members of the computer security industry tend to be older than hackers and view computers as a tool of their normal working life. Hackers, in contrast, tend to see computers as more of a hobby and may hack in order to gain access to systems that their youth precludes them from accessing by legitimate means. This age difference is perhaps one obvious reason why there are such fundamental differences in the ethical outlook of members of the computer security industry and the computer underground.

Blurred ethics

Despite their various shared values there is often a lack of agreement even amongst computer professionals as to what constitutes the correct procedures with which to confront certain research and educational issues within computing. A specific example of this lack of agreement is the debate caused by the publication of an article by Dr Fred Cohen, entitled 'Friendly contagion: Harnessing the subtle power of computer viruses' (cited in Spafford 1991). In the article, Dr Cohen suggests that the vendor of a computer virus prevention product should sponsor a contest encouraging the development of new viruses, with the provisos that the spreading ability of the viruses should be inherently limited, and that they should only be tested on systems with the informed consent of the systems' owners. Professor Spafford responded with the charge that:

For someone of Dr Cohen's reputation within the field to actually *promote* the uncontrolled writing of any virus, even with his stated stipulations, is to act irresponsibly and immorally. To act in such a manner is likely to encourage the development of yet more viruses 'in the wild' by muddling the ethics and dangers involved.

(Spafford 1991: 3)

Furthermore, even the publication of 'fixes' can be viewed in certain instances as an unethical act, leading to what has been previously described as the phenomenon of 'security through obscurity'. Professor Spafford argues that:

> We should realize that widespread publication of details will imperil sites where users are unwilling or unable to install updates and fixes. Publication should serve a useful purpose; endangering the security of other people's machines or attempting to force them into making changes they are unable to make or afford is not ethical.

(Spafford 1990: 12)

Robert Morris jr. and the Internet Worm

The complexity of the ethical issues surrounding computer security is further illustrated by the aftermath of the Internet Worm when a debate raged amongst computer professionals as to both the moral and technical implications of the event. The nature of the ensuing discussion reinforces Vinten's observation that ethical subgroup variation and a general lack of clear-cut moral boundaries is typical of the modern ethical environment. This is especially true when there are strongly contrasting opinions as to the originating motivations behind specific acts. Such a debate was reflected in the 'Communications of the Association of Computing Machinery (ACM)' Forum of Letters, where even the ACM's president received quite strident criticism for his position, indicated in the title of his letter: 'A hygiene lesson', that the Internet Worm could be viewed as beneficial in so far as it increased awareness of security problems. The president's view was described by one contributor to the forum as, 'a massive error in judgement which sends the wrong message to the world on the matters of individual responsibility and ethical behaviour ... [it] is inexcusable and an exercise in moral relativism' (P.J. Denning 1990: 523). In contrast, another writer illustrates the disparate nature of the feelings produced by the Internet Worm incident when he pointedly remarks:

> while Spafford praises the efficacy of the 'UNIX "old boy" network' in fighting the worm, he does not explain how these self-appointed fire marshals allowed such known hazards to exist for so long. ... If people like Morris and people like him are the greatest threat to the proper working of the Internet then we face no threat at all. If, on the other hand, our preoccupation with moralizing over this incident blinds us to serious security threats and lowers the standards of civility in our community, then we will have lost a great deal indeed.

(P.J. Denning 1990: 526, 527)

Dougan and Gieryn (1990), sum up the boundary-forming aspects of responses to the Internet Worm in their analysis of the email debate that occurred shortly after the incident. The response of the computer community to the event is characterised as falling into one of two categories. The first is described as belonging to a group organised around a principle of *mechanic solidarity*; the second, one of *organic solidarity*. The mechanic solidarity group's binding principle is the emphasis they place upon the ethical aspect of the Morris case; his actions are seen as unequivocally wrong and the lesson to be learnt in order to prevent future possible incidents is that a professional code of ethics needs to be promulgated. These viewpoints have been illustrated in this study's depiction of the hawkish response to hacking. The organic solidarity group advocates a policy more consistent with the dovish element of the computer security industry and those hackers that argue their expertise could be more effectively utilised. They criticise the first group for failing to prevent 'an accident waiting to happen' and expecting that the teaching of computing ethics will solve what they perceive as an essentially technical problem. The likelihood of eliminating the problem with the propagation of a suitable code of professional ethics seems to the organic group remote; in the words of one security professional:

> I would like to remind everyone that the real bad guys do not share our ethics and are thus not bound by them. We should make it as difficult as possible – (while preserving an environment conducive to research) for this to happen again. The worm opened some eyes. Let's not close them again by saying 'Gentlemen don't release worms.'
>
> (Dougan and Gieryn 1990: 12)

Cornell University itself conducted its own official enquiry into the Internet Worm. One of the most interesting aspects of the report is the way in which it implicitly recognises and accepts the widespread existence of security weaknesses and proceeds to imply that in order to avoid the full consequences of such weaknesses more ethical training of users is needed. The problem is thus redefined from the technical to the social. The report concluded that one of the main causes of the act was Morris's lack of ethical awareness. The report censures the ambivalent ethical atmosphere of Harvard, Morris's Alma Mater, where, in the context of computer usage, he failed to receive a clear ethical sense of right and wrong. However, it is interesting to note that the social/ethical and the technical are conflated in the report's analysis. The unclear ethical environment facing Morris reflects a somewhat confused technical environment. There is no consensus, for example, as to whether it is better to adopt a *full disclosure* approach to computer security information with the hope of thereby shoring up security holes more comprehensively, or, alternatively, given the vagaries of the ways such repairs are carried out in the real world, an equally tenable position is to keep one's knowledge private. The report cites this confusion as one of the factors influencing Morris's subsequent behaviour:

Many members of the UNIX community are ambivalent about reporting security flaws in UNIX out of concern that knowledge of such flaws could be exploited before the flaws are fixed in all affected versions of UNIX. There is no clear security policy among UNIX developers, including in the commercial sector. Morris explored UNIX security issues in such an ambivalent atmosphere and received no clear guidance about reporting security flaws from his peers or mentors at Harvard or elsewhere.

(P.J. Denning 1990: 256)

Ross rather dismissively interprets the conclusions of the Cornell report:

Generally speaking, the report affirms the genteel liberal idea that professionals should not need laws, rules, procedural guidelines, or fixed guarantees of safe and responsible conduct. Apprentice professionals ought to have acquired a good conscience by osmosis from a liberal education, rather than from some specially prescribed course in ethics and technology.

(Ross 1991: 86)

Elsewhere, however, Ross interprets more proactive legislative responses to computer crime as being infused with the paranoid climate of the age of Aids and general cultural 'viral hysteria'. This implies that authorities may often be caught between a rock and a hard place when it comes to gauging their response to hacking. In defence of the Cornell Report, it at least identified one of the key issues surrounding the computer underground, namely the problematic relationship between new technological situations and the ethical lessons to be drawn from them. Whereas Ross imputes a desire for genteel ethics from the Cornell report, one can equally argue that the Cornell authors recognised that Morris received no clear guidance from his Harvard peers because there was no unproblematically clear guidance to be given.

The Cornell report itself can be seen as one of the initial steps in the construction of the clearer guidance being sought. It exhibited some sensitivity to the potential pitfalls of an overly hawkish response to computer crime:

Sentiment among the computer science professional community appears to favor strong disciplinary measures for the perpetrators of acts of this kind. Such disciplinary measures, however, should not be so stern as to damage permanently the perpetrator's career.

(P.J. Denning 1990: 257)

In the light of the ensuing heated debates and conflicts within computing it also showed some prescience with its recognition of the disparate values and constituencies that exist within the general term, 'computing':

Prevailing ethical beliefs of students towards acts of this kind vary considerably from admiration to tolerance to condemnation. The computer science profession as a whole seems far less tolerant, but the attitudes of the profession may not be well communicated to students.

(P.J. Denning 1990: 257)

The report is additionally quite open about the vestigial nature of clear guidelines for computer behaviour stating that they are required on Cornell's own doorstep. Whilst it had some guidelines for its central facilities it was acknowledged that guidelines need to be rolled out into the wider University community:

> In view of the pervasive use of computers throughout the campus, there is a need for *university-wide* policy on computer abuse ... there is also a need for a university-wide committee to provide advice and appropriate standards on security matters to departmental computer and network facility managers.
>
> (P.J. Denning 1990: 257 [emphasis in original])

The report's argument for more ethical guidance in the area of computing is borne out by subsequent large-scale Government-sponsored research:

> Education can play a pivotal role in the development of ethical standards in the computer service and user communities. Exposure to computers occurs at a very early age in many countries, often at the primary school level. This presents a valuable opportunity to introduce ethical standards that can be broadened as children progress through school and enter the workforce. Universities and institutes of higher learning should include computer ethics in the curriculum since ethical issues arise and have consequences in all areas of the computer environment.
>
> (United Nations *International Review of Criminal Policy*: par. 231)

Experience and practice at the 'screen-face' also seems to reinforce the call for more ethical content to computing education:

> I teach computer science at the local state university, and one of my concerns has been the ethical use of computers. When I've polled my classes, I've found that the consensus attitude towards crackers is very negative, especially after my lectures on computer risks and security. These kids have a strong attachment to their privacy and their money – threaten those and they get angry. There's always a minority who are interested in hacking and cracking, and my war stories entrance them. What I've tried to do with them is develop their moral sense, showing them how their actions affect others and themselves – 'What goes around, comes around.' It seems to work. The carrot is that I'm willing to write a recommendation for them if they pass my course. The stick is that cracking that hurts others is a fast way to get on my wrong side ... BTW, I'm also qualified as an instructor for

soccer referees. I find the best raw talent is often a good, dirty, young player who I've thrown out of a couple of games for retaliating.

(Computer security officer [anonymity requested]: email interview)

The report's recommendation that punishment should not be so severe as to permanently damage the offender's future career is underscored by this teacher's implicit recognition that illicit behaviour may disguise misdirected but ultimately socially useful energy.

Computer ethics

Underlying some of these ethical problems has been the tendency identified by Professor Spafford (1990) to 'view computers simply as machines and algorithms, and ... not perceive the serious ethical questions inherent in their use' (Spafford 1990: 12). He points to the failure to address the end result of computing decisions upon people's lives, and, as a result, he argues that there is a subsequent general failure to teach the proper ethical use of computers:

Computing has historically been divorced from social values, from human values, computing has been viewed as something numeric and that there is no ethical concern with numbers, that we simply calculate values of 0 and 1, and that there are no grey areas, no impact areas, and that leads to more problems than simply theft of information, it also leads to problems of producing software that is also responsible for loss and damage and hurt because we fail to understand that computers are tools whose products ... involve human beings and that humans are affected at the other end.

(Spafford: US interview)[2]

Professor Spafford argues that often the staff of computer faculties are uncomfortable with the subject, or don't believe it's important. Their backgrounds are predominantly in mathematics or scientific theory and hence they don't adequately understand how practical issues of use may apply to computing. He suggests that engineering provides a more appropriate model of computing than science in so far as it addresses the human as well as the scientific dimensions.

Computer science is really, in large part an engineering discipline and that some of the difficulties that arise in defining the field are because the people who are involved in computing believe it's a science and don't understand the engineering aspects of it. Engineers, for a very long time, have been taught issues of appropriateness and ethics and legality and it's very often a required part of engineering curricula ... computing is more than just dealing with numbers and abstractions, it does in fact have very strong applications behind it, a very strong real-world component.

(Spafford: US interview)

Despite the real-world component of computing, the largely immaterial nature of the way in which people interface with it means that the construction of widely recognised ethics for cyberspace has lagged behind its physical world's counterpart:

> People seem naturally predisposed to depersonalise complex systems. Remote and in some cases un-attributable computer access intensifies this predisposition. General ambivalence and a resulting sublimation of ethics, values, and personal roles ... seem to encourage in some people a rationalization that unethical behaviour is the norm and somehow or other justifiable. Furthermore, encroachments on the rights of other individuals somehow seem less heinous to those who do not realise that they may also be affected.
>
> (Neumann 1992: 3–4)

The extent to which computing has a non-material dimension, however, constantly mitigates against Professor Spafford's desire for computing to be approached in a similar ethical manner to that of an engineering discipline. I would contend that there is a fundamental difference between the environments of real and virtual worlds, and this difference makes the literal transposing of ethical judgements from the former to the latter, difficult, if not untenable. The correct balance with which to transpose ethical judgements from one realm to another is essentially contestable and this debate is usually carried out with recourse to physical analogies.

Hacking and analogies

> clearing into cyberspace is ... an excessive activity that takes analogy to a breaking point. In the break, cyberspace is felt as a wanting space, a space of default. Cyberspace is a site of disjunction, where analogical production comes to find the limits of analogy.
>
> (Moreiras 1993: 198)

> if we begin to mistake rhetorical for material description, we can forget how they are not.
>
> (Rosenthal 1991: 95)

The fact that the real world and cyberspace are such different realms has led to a need to explain and make ethical judgements about hacking from a more conventional frame of reference, that is, using analogies based upon the physical world. In an attempt to redefine in a grounded manner the immaterial concept of informational property rights, physically based analogies and metaphors are used not only as explanatory tools but also in the production and maintenance of the value systems that separate the two groups. Analogies and metaphors allow what would otherwise be potentially complicated technical and ethical questions to be approached in a more manageable and everyday manner, yet they also contribute directly to the formation of ethical boundaries due to their frequently high emotional content:

> As far as the raison d'être for attackers, it is no more a valid justification to attack systems because they are vulnerable than it is valid to beat up babies because they can't defend themselves. If you are going to demonstrate a weakness, you must do it with the permission of the systems administrators and with a great deal of care.
>
> (Cohen: email interview)

Hacking is defined in terms of 'theft', 'trespass' and even 'rape', and employing a hacker has been compared to making 'an arsonist your fire chief' or 'a paedophile a school teacher'.

With such rhetoric the actions of hackers are taken out of the realms of cyberspace and reintroduced into the concrete realm of threatening real-world situations. Once the physical analogy is accepted, then the danger and harm to be suffered from such actions are more readily understood and feared, and hackers are more effectively turned into moral pariahs.[3] The computer security industry emphasises the transgressive 'breaking and entering' qualities of hacking,[4] whilst, in contrast, the computer underground rejects such dramatic analogies and prefers to emphasise hacking's intellectual and pioneering qualities. They prefer to compare hacking to such pastimes as chess and appeal to its perceived frontier ethos with repeated images taken from the Wild West.

Property issues

> The battle of the metaphor always erupts in the face of new and powerful technologies. Our imagination is fired, but our stability is threatened; and we always seek precedent for understanding. So we use the property analogy; the metaphor of invaded homes and goods when systems are attacked, the allusion to space and universes. But this is a category mistake. Computer mediated 'space' is no more space than DNA is a person, no more than digital signals are a picture or a novel. Bits and bytes are not the equivalent to their manifestations; the genotype is not the phenotype.
>
> (Karnow 1994: 8)

In relation to informational ethics, members of the computer security industry emphasise authorisation and rights of access issues. Such criteria are held to be fundamental because they stem from the basic belief that information and computer systems are the sole property of their owners, in the same way that property rights exist in material objects. Physical analogies thus become a means to restrict the computer security debate:

to questions about privacy, property, possessive individualism, and at best, the excesses of state surveillance, while it closes off any examination of the activities of the corporate owners and institutional sponsors of information technology (the most prized 'target' of most hackers).

(Ross 1991: 83)

The problem with physically based analogies, which seek to emphasise the way in which hacking tends to transgress property rights, is that they inevitably fail to map exactly on to the increasingly immaterial aspects of information, for example:

> copyability is INHERENT in electronic media. You can xerox a book but not very well and you don't get a nice binding and cover. Electronic media, video tape, computer discs etc., do not have this limitation. Since the ability to copy is within the nature of the media, it seems silly to try to prevent it inherently more easy than with physical commodities: copyability is intrinsic to the medium itself.
>
> (Mercury: email interview)

Maelstrom contends that he 'can't remember a single analogy that works. Theft is taking something else that belongs to someone without his/her permission. When you pirate you don't steal, you copy' (Maelstrom: email interview). Similarly, in the case of cracking:

> In absolutely no case can the physical analogies of 'theft' and 'trespassing' be applied in the matter of computer system 'cracking'. Computers are a reservoir for information expressed in bits of zeroes and ones. Homes and property have things far more intrinsically valuable to harbour. Information protected properly whilst residing on a system is not at issue for 'theft'. Encryption should have been a standard feature to begin with and truly confidential information should not be accessible in any manner via a remote means.
>
> (Tester: email interview)

Analogies: breaking and entering

Of course, there are computer intruders who take nothing from a penetrated system. They break security, peruse a system, perhaps leaving a mystery for the sysop to puzzle over. Would any computer intruders be as pleased to have a physical intruder enter their house, and rearrange their belongings as he toured the residence? The distinctions on the intruders' part are basically physical ones: location, movement, physical content, manner of penetration, for example. The victims' perspectives are more similar: privacy and security violated, unrest regarding future intrusions, and a feeling of outrage. Just as a person can assume the law protects his physical possession of a computer, whether he secures it or not, why can he not assume the same for its contents. What after all is the intent of the intruder in each situation? To be where he should not be and alter the property that is there without the approval of its owner. Each case disregards approved behavior and flaunts the power to do so.

(Citarella 1992: 57)

The above quotation provides a clear illustration of how the choice of an analogy is used to set up the subsequent 'proof' of the hypothetical hacker's malicious intentions. In order to emphasise the potential harm threatened to systems by anonymous intruders the physical analogies used often concentrate upon the fear and sense of violation that tend to accompany burglaries. The dispute between the computer security industry and the computer underground as to whether or not it is ethical to break into systems is most often conducted with reference to the analogy of breaking and entering into a building. Because of the divergence between the real world and cyberspace, however, even such a simple analogy is open to varying interpretations: 'My analogy is walking into an office building, asking a secretary which way it is to the records room, and making some Xerox copies of them. Far different than breaking and entering someone's home' (Cohen: email interview).

One of the best illustrations of the differences in approaches to the question of if hacking should be viewed as a criminal act is the marked contrast in the perceived applicability of this breaking and entering analogy. Hackers prefer to compare computer intrusion to being tempted to walk into somebody's house when the door has been left open. In the case of such negligence, and assuming that no damage is done (such an intrusion will be inevitably non-violent because of its non-physical nature), hackers argue that even if the morality of such an intrusion is questionable, there are insufficient grounds to make it a criminal offence.

> In common sense as in criminal law there exists the notion that the victim of a crime is partly or fully responsible if the crime was made possible by negligence on the victim's part ... if I don't lock my car and it is stolen, my insurance company won't reimburse me and the perpetrator of the crime will get away with a lenient sentence, as he was led into temptation by me and it is partly my fault that the car was so easy to steal. ... Common sense tells most people that 'breaking' into a wide-open computer system is not a crime – if there was sensitive information in the computer, it wouldn't be wide open, would it? Sadly enough that kind of reasoning doesn't hold. Security on many government and research facilities is appalling.
>
> (Freiss: email interview)

Despite the hackers' argument that breaking into a system that is wide open should not be labelled a crime, the legislation that has been passed regarding hacking treats computer intrusion more harshly than it would its physical counterpart. The 1990 United Kingdom Computer Misuse Act, for example, holds it as an offence to intentionally obtain unauthorised access to a program or data held on any computer, whereas the act of physical trespass, unaccompanied by any aggravating conduct, is not criminal, but rather a civil offence. Hackers argue that this discrepancy between the real and virtual worlds is being systematically used against them. There have been, for example, various instances in the US where hackers have claimed that their First and Second Amendment rights have been infringed in a manner that would not have been allowed if the situation had arisen with a paper-based medium.[5] In a similar way, the application of a punitive legislative response to hacking in excess of that applicable to a physical intrusion is seen as inherently unjust.

Cosell presents the following scenario with which he attempts to frame the ethical issues surrounding hacking:

> Consider: it is the middle of summer and you happen to be climbing in the mountains and see a pack of teenagers roaming around an abandoned-until-snow ski resort. There is no question of physical harm to a person, since there will be no people around for months. They are methodically searching EVERY truck, building, outbuilding, shed etc., trying EVERY window, trying to pick EVERY lock. When they find something they can open, they wander into it, and emerge a while later. From your vantage point, you can see no actual evidence of any theft or vandalism, but then you can't actually see what they're doing while they're inside whatever-it-is.
>
> (Cosell 1991: file 2)

From this scenario, various questions arise, such as: do you call the Police? What would the intruders be charged with? Is the behaviour of the 'intruders' comparable to a real-world situation?:

> Of course you should call the cops. Unless they are authorised to be on the property (by the owner), they are trespassing, and in the case of picking locks, breaking and entering. However, you're trying to equate breaking into a ski resort with breaking into a computer system. The difference being: 99 times out of 100, the people breaking into a computer system only want to learn, have forgotten a password, etc. ... 99 times out of 100, the people breaking into the ski resort are out for free shit.
>
> (Rob Heins: *CuD* 3(13))

The computer underground accuse the computer security industry of preferring to use physical analogies in order to marginalise a group, rather than make use of their information for improving the security of systems:

> When you refer to hacking as 'burglary and theft' ... it becomes easy to think of these people as hardened criminals. But it's just not the case. I don't know any burglars or thieves, yet I hang out with an awful lot of hackers. It

serves a definite purpose to blur the distinction, just as pro-democracy demonstrators are referred to as rioters by nervous political leaders. Those who have staked a claim in the industry fear that the hackers will reveal vulnerabilities in their systems that they would just as soon forget about.

(Goldstein 1990: file 1)

This is one explanation of why, if physical analogies are inevitably only crude analytical approximations and rhetorical devices with which to conceptualise computing issues, they are frequently used by the computer security industry in their discourse. However, Johnson argues in response that:

> If a policeman walks down the street testing doors to see if they are locked, that's within his 'charter' – both ethically and legally. If one is open, he is within the same 'charter' to investigate – to see if someone else is trespassing. However, it's not in his 'charter' to go inside and snoop through my personal belongings, nor to hunt for illegal materials such as firearms or drugs. ... If I come home and find the policeman in my house, I can pretty well assume he's doing me a favour because he found my door unlocked. However, if a self-appointed 'neighbourhood watch' monitor decides to walk down the street checking doorknobs, he's probably overstepped his 'charter'. If he finds my door unlocked and enters the house, he's trespassing. ... Life is complicated enough without self-appointed watchdogs and messiahs trying to 'make my life safe'.
>
> (Johnson: email interview)

Thus, hackers are seen to have no 'charter' that justifies their incursions into other people's systems, such incursions being labelled as trespass. Even comparisons to trespass, however, tend to be too limited for those wishing to identify and label hacking as an immoral act. The computer crime detective, Harry Onderwater, makes this distinction with his particular use of analogies: 'Trespassing means in Holland if somebody leaves the door open and the guy goes in, stands in the living room, crosses his arms and doesn't do anything'. In contrast, hacking involves the active overcoming of any security measures put before hackers; Detective Onderwater sees it as more analagous to the situation whereby:

> you find somebody in your house and he is looking through your clothes in your sleeping room, and you say 'what are you doing?' and he says 'well, I was walking at the back of the garden and I saw that if I could get on to the shed of your neighbour, there was a possibility to get on to the gutter, and could get to your bathroom window, get it open, that was a mistake from you, so I'd like to warn you. ... You wouldn't see that as trespassing, you would see that as breaking and entering, which it is and I think it's the same with hacking.
>
> (Onderwater: Hague interview)

Parliament's use of breaking and entering analogies

> The story of the creation of this 'social menace' is central to the ongoing attempts to rewrite property law in order to contain the effects of the new information technologies that, because of their blindness to the copyrighting of intellectual property, have transformed the way in which modern power is exercised and maintained.
>
> (Ross 1991: 80–1)

The debate over the Computer Misuse Bill provides numerous examples of the tendency in discussions of hacking to make use of physical analogies with which to transpose real-world criteria to the virtual reality of computing. The analogies used in the debate over the Bill compare hacking to burglary and acts of violence, and the promulgation of this concept prepares the ground for further stigmatising statements. Nicholson illustrates the use of analogies with the following rhetorical rebuttal:

> Mr Cohen spoke of a new power to make a computer owner liable if a criminal commits an offence against his computer. ... If a madman with a knife attacks another person in a street and then stabs himself, would the victim be liable for compensation for not taking reasonable care to prevent the man from stabbing himself?
>
> (Nicholson, Hansard 1990a: 88)

Similarly, Mr Powell MP contends that:

> Computer hacking has many parallels with burglary. Burglary takes many shapes or forms. It can be with intent ... or it can be aggravated burglary, as it appears in aggravated offences. Computer hacking remains astonishingly akin to the offence of burglary.
>
> (Powell, Hansard 1990a: 1147)

> The hacker who says that he is performing a public service is doing exactly the same as the burglar who advances by way of mitigation the argument that he is performing a public service.
>
> (Powell, Hansard 1990b: 89)

In contrast, Cohen responds: 'Stabbing and burglary, are not relevant examples. If a person has been negligent, left his doors open and been burgled, I bet a lot of insurance companies have a get-out clause to avoid payment' (Hansard 1990b: 89). Cohen's response questions Powell's belief that conventional criminal concepts can be successfully transposed into virtual reality. We see here how the use of analogies tends to encourage a continual redefining of the particular question at issue. Small changes in the analogy are used in order to question the suitability of the original premise the analogy sought to illustrate. Despite doubts such as those expressed by Cohen, the parliamentary debates leading up to the Bill explicitly sought to criminalise hacking and stigmatise hackers:

> We must think of hacking as a form of burglary. We must stigmatise such criminal activities for what they are. Because computer buffs use a different vocabulary and have a method of thought different from the conventional method that we all use does not alter the fact that the principles of criminal law are just as clearly at stake.
>
> (Powell, Hansard 1990a: 1148)

Hackers' rejection of breaking and entering analogies

> Cyberspace is not real! ... Hacking takes place on a screen. Words aren't physical, numbers ... aren't physical. ... Computers simulate reality, such as computer games that simulate tank battles or dogfights or spaceships. Simulations are just make-believe, and the stuff in computers is not real. Consider this: If 'hacking' is supposed to be so serious and real-life and dangerous, then how come nine-year-old kids have computers and modems? You wouldn't give a nine-year-old his own car, or his own rifle, or his chainsaw – those things are 'real'.
>
> (Sterling 1992: 84)

Hackers' descriptions of their motives emphasise the intellectual stimulation it affords as opposed to its breaking and entering connotations. Gongrijp, for example, emphasised the chess-like qualities of computer security, and was at pains to reject any analogies that might compare hacking to physical breaking and entering:

> Computer security is like a chess game, and all these people that say breaking into my computer systems is like breaking into my house: bullshit, because securing your house is a very simple thing, you just put locks on the doors and bars on the windows and then only brute force can get into your house, like smashing a window. But a computer has a hundred-thousand intricate ways to get in, and it's a chess game with the people that secure a computer ... it's their job to make the new release of their Unix system more secure, and it's the job of the hackers to break in.
>
> (Gongrijp: Amsterdam interview)

Goggans turns the burglar analogy on its head when he argues that:

> People just can't seem to grasp the fact that a group of 20 year old kids just might know a little more than they do, and rather than make good use of us, they would rather just lock us away and keep on letting things pass them by ... you can't stop burglars from robbing you when you leave the doors open,

but lock up the people who can close them for you, another burglar will just walk right in.

(Goggans: email interview)

The implication of these combined views is that the analogy comparing hacking with burglary fails because the real-world barriers employed to deter burglars are not used in the virtual world of computing. Such preventative measures are either not used at all, or are of a qualitatively different kind to the 'doors' and 'locks' that can be used in computing. Such barriers can be overcome by technologically knowledgeable young people, without violence or physical force of any kind. The overcoming of such barriers has a non-violent and intellectual quality that is not apparent in more conventional forms of burglary, and which therefore throws into question the whole suitability of such analogies.

Bodily analogies

At the most basic level, physical metaphors have slipped into the language of computing, giving rise to the use of terms such as 'computer viruses' and 'computer worms'. The whole process of enforcing and furthering the proprietary attitude to information outlined in Chapter 3 is further strengthened by a new language of physicality resulting from the advent of computer viruses.[6] Computer viruses are described in terms similar to those employed in discussions of the dangers of promiscuous sex. Prophylactic safety measures are seen to be necessary to protect the moral majority from 'unprotected contact' with the degeneracy of a minority group. In this way the language of physicality can be used to facilitate the process of stigmatisation. Bodily analogies are often used by the computer security industry to describe computer attacks, and a security breach of the academic network with the acronym JANET was referred to as the 'rape of JANET'. Spafford admitted to having one of his systems hacked into at least three times; he argued that he 'didn't learn anything in particular that I didn't know before. I felt quite **violated** by the whole thing, and did not view anything positive from it' (Spafford: US interview [emphasis mine]). Ross argues that the use of bodily analogies reflect fears of technological vulnerability that can be related to the wider post-cold-war political climate:

> The form and content of more lurid articles like Time's infamous story, *Invasion of the Data Snatchers* (September 1988), fully displayed the continuity of the media scare with those historical fears about bodily invasion, individual and national, that are endemic to the paranoid style of American political culture. Indeed, the rhetoric of computer culture, in common with the medical discourse of AIDS research, has fallen in line with the paranoid, strategic mode of Defense Department rhetoric established during the Cold War. Each language repertoire is obsessed with hostile threats to bodily and technological immune systems; every event is a ballistic manoeuvre in the

game of microbiological war, where the governing metaphors are indiscriminately drawn from cellular genetics and cybernetics alike.

(Ross 1991: 76–7)

We have already seen how physical analogies are often chosen for their provocative value, even corpses are used for rhetorical effect:

> If the challenge of penetrating a system you do not belong on is an essential way of developing computer skills, as some people contend, then let computer curricula include such tests on systems specifically designed for that. Surgeons develop their skills on cadavers, not on the unsuspecting. Pilots use simulators. Why should computer specialists practice on someone else's property at someone else's expense?
>
> (Citarella 1992: 58)

In conjunction with use of provocative analogies is the more insidious presence of physical terms. In addition to direct comparisons with rape and burglary, stigmatisation also occurs with more subtle references whereby hacking is impugned 'by association':

> Whenever law enforcement follows criminal activity into a new arena, problems arise. It is as true with computer crime as it was with rape and child abuse cases. The answers lie in understanding the common forest of all criminal behavior not in staring at the trees of computer crime.
>
> (Citarella 1992: 58)

This general ease with which physical analogies are used and the strength of feeling behind them is vividly illustrated by Jerry Carlin's response to the question, 'Have system breakers become the "whipping boys" for general commercial irresponsibility with regard to data security?' He replied, 'It's fashionable to blame the victim for the crime but if someone is raped it is not OK to blame that person for not doing a better job in fending off the attack!' (Carlin: email interview).

Problems of using analogies as explanatory tools

> Usually, arguing by analogy is a very weak argument. When it comes to discussing the law, non-lawyers often try to approach arguments this way. I don't think that we can go very far to determine appropriate behaviours if we rely upon analogies. What we need to develop are some social definitions of acceptable behaviour and then to structure 'old law for new technologies'. The physical analogies may help to score points in a debate but they are not helpful here at all.
>
> (Sherizen: email interview)

In addition to the issue of the specific suitability of various metaphors there is the more general inherent problems of using the physical to describe the immaterial. Given the previously analysed conceptual and ethical differences between the computer security industry and computer underground, it is perhaps not surprising that the two groups have widely different interpretations of the suitability of various analogies that compare physical and informational property:

> I am skeptical that we can convey the consequences of hacking entirely through analogies, for example, by comparing breaking into a system with breaking into a house, and downloading information and using computer and telecommunications services with stealing tangible goods. Hackers recognize that the situations are not the same. They can appreciate why someone would not want them to break into their house and browse around, while failing to appreciate why someone would seriously object to their browsing on their computer.
>
> (Denning 1992b: 63)

The grey and indeterminate ethical quality of computing makes it difficult to establish the code of 'appropriate behaviour', which Sherizen seeks and it is in an attempt to do so that physical analogies are used. Emmanuel Goldstein (editor of hacking magazine, *2600*) explores the ethical implications of hacking by questioning the use of an analogy that likens hacking to trespass:

> Some will say … 'accessing a computer is far more sensitive than walking into an unlocked office building'. If that is the case, why is it still so easy to do? If it's possible for somebody to easily gain unauthorised access to a computer that has information about me, I would like to know about it. But somehow I don't think the company or agency running the system would tell me that they have gaping security holes. Hackers, on the other hand, are very open about what they discover which is why large corporations hate them so much.
>
> (Goldstein 1993: file 1)

Similarly, equally inappropriate comparisons are arguably made between hacking and drug addiction. The following excerpt is a newspaper editorial response to the acquittal of Paul Bedworth. It compares computer addiction to a physical addiction for drugs:

> This must surely be a perverse verdict. … Far from being unusual in staying up half the night, Mr Bedworth was just doing what his fellows have done for years. Scores of universities and private companies could each produce a dozen software nerds as dedicated as he. … Few juries in drug cases look so indulgently on the mixture of youth and addiction.
>
> (*Independent* 18 March 1993: 25)

This editorial emphasises how such analogies are utilised in an attempt to formulate ethical responses to an activity of ambiguous ethical content. As Goldstein pointed out, it becomes easier to attribute malign intent if using such analogies succeeds in making a convincing comparison between hacking and an activity the public are more readily inclined to construe as a malicious activity. The promiscuity of this technique is shown by the way the editorial continues to utilise a physical analogy in order to elicit critical responses, this time against the victims of the previously maligned hacker: 'Leaving those passwords unchanged is like leaving the chief executive's filing cabinet unlocked. Organisations that do so can expect little public sympathy when their innermost secrets are brought into public view' (*Independent* 18 March 1993: 25).

One reason why physical analogies may struggle to succeed in any attempted project of stigmatisation/'ethicalisation' of hacking events is the difficulty of convincing people that events that transpire in virtual reality are in fact comparable and equivalent to criminal acts in the physical world. Comparisons flounder upon the fact that hacking intrusions do not contain the same threats of transgression of personal physical space and therefore a direct and actual physical threat to an individual. With the complete absence of such a threat, hacking activity will primarily remain viewed as an intellectual exercise and show of bravado rather than a criminal act, even if, on occasion, direct physical harm may be an indirect result of the technical interference caused by hacking. Both hackers and establishment figures have rejected the implicit assumptions of the 'breaking and entering' analogy of hacking. The Cornell Commission into the Robert Morris Internet Worm, for example, illustrated the complicated nuances that the use of physical analogies can give rise to with their expressive summary of the incident:

> This was not a simple act of trespass analogous to wandering through someone's unlocked house without permission but with no intention to cause damage. A more apt analogy would be the driving of a golf cart on a rainy day through most houses in a neighborhood. The driver may have navigated carefully and broken no china, but it should have been obvious to the driver that the mud on the tires would soil the carpets and that the owners would later have to clean up the mess.
>
> (P.J. Denning 1990: 258)

Hence the use of analogies is fraught with problems of equivalence. Whilst they may be useful as a rough comparison between the real and virtual worlds, the innate but sometimes subtle differences between the two worlds mean that analogies cannot be relied upon as a complete explanatory tool in seeking to understand the practical and ethical implications of hacking:

> They simply don't map well and can create models which are subtly and profoundly misleading. For example, when we think of theft in the physical world, we are thinking of an act in which I might achieve possession of an

object only by removing it from yours. If I steal your horse, you can't ride. With information, I can copy your software or data and leave the copy in your possession entirely unaltered.

(Barlow: email interview)

Information processed by computers is such that previous concepts of scarcity break down when correspondence is sought between the real and virtual worlds. It is not just conceptions of scarcity that are affected, however, and the extent to which information correlates with the real world is questionable at the most fundamental levels:

Physical (and biological) analogies often are misleading as they appeal to an understanding from an area in which different laws hold. Informatics has often mislead naive people by choosing terms such as 'intelligent' or 'virus' though IT systems may not be compared to the human brain. … Many users (and even 'experts') think of a password as a 'key' despite the fact that you can easily 'guess' the password while it is difficult to do the equivalent for a key.

(Brunnstein: email interview)

The Wild West

Becoming computer literate, comments Paul Kalaghan, dean of computer science at Northeastern University, 'is a chance to spend your life working with devices smarter than you are, and yet have control over them. It's like carrying a six-gun on the old frontier'.

(Roszak 1986: 67)

Cyberspace in its present condition has a lot in common with the 19th Century West. It is vast, unmapped, culturally and legally ambiguous, verbally tense (unless you happen to be a court stenographer), hard to get around in, and up for grabs. Large institutions already claim to own the place, but most of the actual natives are solitary and independent, sometimes to the point of sociopathy. It is of course, a perfect breeding ground for both outlaws and new ideas about liberty. … In this silent world, all conversation is typed. To enter it one forsakes both body and place and becomes a thing of words alone.

(Barlow 1990: 45)

The tendency to resort to cowboy imagery to describe hackers provides a useful example of both the suitability and limitations of analogies in discussions of hacking. Commentators tend to 'customise' common metaphors used in the computer security debate in order to derive from the metaphor the particular emphasis desired to further the point being argued:

Much of what we 'know' about cowboys is a mixture of myth, unsubstantiated glorification of 'independent he-men', Hollywood creations, and story elements that contain many racist and sexist perspectives. I doubt that cracker/hackers are either like the mythic cowboy or the 'true' cowboy. ... I think we should move away from the easy-but-inadequate analogy of the cowboy to other, more experienced-based discussions.

(Sherizen: email interview)

The tendency to use the 'easy-but-inadequate analogy' applies significantly to the originator of the cowboy metaphor himself. Thus, when I asked John Perry Barlow his views as to the accuracy of the metaphor, he replied:

Given that I was the first person to use that metaphor, you're probably asking the wrong guy. Or maybe not, inasmuch as I'm now more inclined to view crackers as aboriginal natives rather than cowboys. Certainly, they have an Indian view of property.

(Barlow: email interview)

More negative responses to the comparison of hackers with cowboys came from the hackers themselves:

WHO is the electronic cowboy ... the electronic farmer, the electronic saloon keeper? ... I am not sold. I offer no alternative, either. I wait for hacking to evolve its own culture, its own stereotypes. There was a T.V. show long ago, 'Have Gun Will Travel' about a gunslinger called 'Paladin'. The knightly metaphor ... but not one that was widely accepted. Cowboys acted like cowboys, not knights, or Greeks, or cavemen. Hackers are hackers not cowboys.

(Marotta: email interview)

Laura Miller critiques the use of the Wild West metaphor further by arguing that its widespread largely uncritical adoption makes unnecessary online regulation more likely:

However revolutionary the technologized interactions of on-line communities may seem, we understand them by deploying a set of very familiar metaphors from the rich figurative soup of American culture. Would different metaphors have allowed the Net a different, better historical trajectory? Perhaps not, but the way we choose to describe the Net now encourages us to see regulation as its inevitable fate.

(Miller 1995: 50)

Miller argues that the continued use of the Wild West metaphor is not only unjustified by the peculiarities of cyberspace but that this inappropriateness may have significant negative consequences:

Once made, the choice to see the Net as a frontier feels unavoidable, but it's actually quite problematic. The word 'frontier' has traditionally described a place, if not land then the limitless 'final frontier' of space. The Net on the other hand, occupies no physical space ... it is a completely bodiless, symbolic thing with no discernible boundaries or location. The land of the American frontier did not become a 'frontier' until Europeans determined to conquer it, but the continent existed before the intention to settle it. Unlike land, the Net was created by its pioneers. Most peculiar, then, is the choice of the word 'frontier' to describe an artifact so humanly constructed that it only exists as ideas or information ... the freedom the frontier promises is a liberation from the demands of society, while the Net ... has nothing but society to offer. ... Just as the ideal of chastity makes virginity sexually provocative, so does the unclaimed territory invite settlers, irresistibly so. Americans regard the lost geographical frontier with a melancholy, voluptuous fatalism – we had no choice but to advance upon it and it had no alternative but to submit. When an EFF[7] member compares the Clipper chip to barbed wire encroaching on the prairie, doesn't he realise the surrender implied in his metaphor?

(Miller 1995: 51)

The subtitle of John Seabrook's book, *Deeper*, is *A Two-Year Odyssey in Cyberspace*, and the author structures this account of his experiences on the Net around the metaphor of the pioneering West, underlining it with references to his great-grandfather who had made the trek from the east coast to the west coast of the US. In the last section of the final chapter, however, Seabrook is led to question the relevance of the Wild West metaphor:

During my two years of sitting here in front of my screen, I have sometimes wondered whether destiny has, in its joshing-around way, brought me back to within a few miles of the street in Brooklyn where my great-grandfather started out on his grand adventure, plunked me down here in front of my screen, and somehow compelled me to repeat his experience, in metaphor, in cyberspace. It was as though my ancestor's story was a meme that had propagated itself in me. Just as D.J. Toomey probably did, I had heard colorful accounts of the frontier, depicting it to be a place of action and charm and vast opportunity, and I was restless and eager to better my own circumstances, and if possible to build up the kingdom of God, too, so I left home. But in my case I only had to ride my bike down to the local computer store and buy a modem, then come back here and figure out how to make it work. I didn't need physical courage to get around the frontier, and this strikes me as sort of sad. To find the frontier these days, you have to look inside your own mind, and while that is interesting, and certainly more convenient, it isn't the same thing.

(Seabrook 1997: 263)

8   Conclusion

Introduction

The phrase, *information revolution*, is commonly used to describe the rapid technical advances in computer technology of recent decades. Given that we have as a previous reference point the historical experience of the *industrial revolution*, one would suspect that present-day commentators and theorists would be sensitive to the parallels: the social, historical and cultural aspects of the profound technical changes the information revolution brings. I believe that such sensitivity is largely lacking and where it does exist is frequently misdirected towards extreme hyperbole. This final chapter attempts to rectify such neglect and seeks to provide a range of different perspectives upon hacking in an attempt to place the phenomenon in a wider theoretical and cultural context.

Hackers and cultural lag

> What we have today, instead of a social consciousness electrically ordered, however, is a private sub-consciousness or individual 'point of view' rigorously imposed by older mechanical technology. This is the perfectly natural result of 'culture lag' or conflict, in a world suspended between two technologies.
>
> (McLuhan 1964: 108)

Within a theoretical perspective hacking can be usefully viewed as a recent example of Marshall McLuhan's concept of *cultural lag*. Contemporary society is in this notion 'a world suspended between two technologies': the mechanical and the electronic. The conflicting views and practices recounted in the preceding chapters are emblematic of our general attempts to acculturate to the newer of these two worlds. The ever-present conflict between the computer underground and the computer security industry can ultimately be reduced to the clash between an order established in a physical, mechanical era and the radically new implications of computing technologies. A general and widespread societal unease has accompanied the information revolution:

fear and loathing have clearly fed into the paranoid climate of privatization that increasingly defines social identities in the new post-Fordist order. The result – a psycho-social closing of the ranks around fortified private spheres – runs directly counter to the ethic that we might think of as residing at the architectural heart of information technology. In its basic assembly structure, information technology is a technology of processing, copying, replication, and simulation, and therefore does not recognise the concept of private information property.

(Ross 1991: 80)

Hackers are arguably an intriguing example of a group seeking to overcome cultural lag and inhabit the interstice of the suspended space between the mechanical and electronic forms of technology. To the extent that hackers have pioneered new attitudes to information and its computer systems, they are potentially prototypical exponents of McLuhan's 'social consciousness electrically ordered'. His observation that the mechanical mindset is 'rigorously imposed', however, helps to explain how, despite the initially enthusiastic portrayal of hackers as prototypical pioneers of the information revolution, this status would come to be hotly contested by those still working predominantly within the conceptual paradigms of the mechanical age.

The generation and culture gaps

Familiarity with electronic complexity is slowly spreading among the general population. It is a time when young people are comfortable with a new technology that intimidates their elders. Parents, investigators, lawyers and judges often feel a comparative level of incompetence in relation to 'complicated' computer technology.

(United Nations *International Review of Criminal Policy*: par. 211)

The perennial complaints from adults regarding adolescents' uncommunicative and asocial behavioural patterns are reinforced by a culture gap when the rapid pace of technological change is added to the equation:

For some young people, the computer and the Internet are the only things with which they seem able to truly communicate. Executives have just the opposite view: They love probing and manipulating the complex uncertainties of people and hate computers because they insult them with brusque error messages and make them feel like fools.

(Martin 1996: 1)

This stark difference in outlook and subsequent lack of communication between technologically savvy youngsters and their more powerful elders gives rise to a simultaneous dependency and aversion:

In one Canadian corporation, top management refers to their computer people as Martians ... in the same corporation, the computer people told stories about how if you give top management a computer they try to use the mouse as a foot pedal. ... Top management may regard the long-haired hackers as lunatics, but the lunatics can put the business in a straitjacket. ... The personality of the typical corporate president could not be more different from the personality of the typical computer hacker. ... One president referred to the programmers as 'vampire stenographers,' but they are becoming increasingly critical in the cybercorp jungle. Bewildered users of computers often become dependent on hackers, and the Byzantine tools of their profession, to make their systems work.

(Martin 1996: 1, 2)

A vivid example of the generation gap is provided by Robert Morris sr., who at the time of the following statement was chief scientist for the National Computer Security Centre:

The notion that we are raising a generation of children so technically sophisticated that they can outwit the best efforts of the security specialists of America's largest corporations and the military is utter nonsense. I wish it were true. That would bode well for the technological future of the country.

(Lundell 1989:11)

In a rather ironic twist of fate, Morris found his assertion to illustrate more than he originally intended. His statement was uttered five years before his own son caused widespread disruption of the Internet when he released in November 1988 a self-replicating program that came to be known as the Internet Worm. The ironic example provided by Morris father and son neatly illustrates the gap that seems to exist between both different generations and also official bureaucracies and their computer underground opponents. When once, in Bruce Sterling's words, the authorities had a comfortable margin of control, subsequently Robert Morris sr., a key figure of the computer security establishment, was not even aware of the technical ability of his own son.

Ironically, the concept of the generation gap can also be applied to the computer underground itself. Boundary formation within it takes on a generational aspect that mirrors the perceived gap between the computer security industry and computer underground. Key members of the fourth generation of hackers have criticised the advent of hacker 'wannabes'. Rop Gongrijp complained of the irresponsibility and greed of the Amiga Kids and Chris Goggans gave the following summary of developments within the computer underground:

Today we are faced with a new breed of vandal. ... I have seen the emergence of real computer thugs. These people are from low-class areas who have immersed themselves into the computer networks and look at hacking as a means to control their environment. Hacking to them is more than intellectual fulfillment, it's an ego trip. Where people like myself learned and moved on, these people learn and abuse for their own gain ... I think that the computer underground as I know it will be gone very quickly. It will be replaced with a TRUE criminal underground. The technology is slowly reaching the baser elements of society who are using it for their own benefit. Hackers as we know them will be gone, washed out with the implementation of laws, and technological advances to prevent casual break-ins. The only people who will be intruding into computer systems will be doing so with ulterior motives.

(Goggans: email interview)

Technology and ethics

Cracking, virus writing, and all the rest, fall into the realm of possibility when dealing with intelligent, curious minds. The ethics of such things come later. Until then, users of computers remain in this infancy of cracking, etc.

(Kerchen: email interview)

Alas, there is no hacker's code of ethics other than, perhaps, 'We hack because we can' or 'Hack him before he can hack you. ... It becomes clear, finally, that ethics don't exist in this community because hackers never know what they will stumble across next and once something is perceived as possible there will always be those with the urge to accomplish it.

(Gilboa 1996: 108, 110)

The ethical edges demarcating legal and illicit acts have a higher tendency to be blurred whenever a new technology has a significant presence in the context of the act. The two quotations above illustrate the 'Mount Everest climber' mentality associated with hacking, the justification being in both cases: because it's there and possible. This mentality clashes sharply with the computer security industry view encountered in the previous chapter, namely that 'moral bankruptcy' in the face of new technologies is not excusable:

The criminal obtains that which is not his, violating one of the lessons we all should have learned in childhood. The computer intruder ignores that lesson and substitutes a separate moral imperative: I can, therefore, I may; or, might makes right. The arguments about exposing system weaknesses, or encouraging the development of youthful computer experts, amount to little more than endorsing these behavioural norms. These norms, of course, we reject in all other aspects of society. The majority may not suppress the minority just because they have the numbers to do so. The mob cannot operate a protection racket just because it has the muscle to do so. The healthy young man may not remove an infirm one from a train seat just because he can. Instead, we have laws against discrimination, police to fight organized crime, and seats reserved for the handicapped.

(Citarella 1992: 55)

A study into social and business ethical questions was carried out by Johnston and Wood (1985, cited by Vinten 1990) for the British Social Attitudes Survey. Apart from their major conclusion that the single most important factor influencing the strength of people's ethical judgements was age, they argued that in many of the situations that arise in the modern world (especially in the realm of business), there generally seems to be a lack of clear ethical boundaries and behavioural guidelines. Thus in his summary of the report Vinten describes how:

In situations ranging widely from illegitimate tipping of dustmen to serious corruption, no clear-cut boundaries emerged as between 'right' and 'wrong'. ... Sub-group variation was greatest where situations were complicated by motivation questions, and by being remote from everyday experience.

(Vinten 1990: 3)

Hacking fulfils both of these criteria. The advent of cyberspace tends to divorce computing from 'everyday experience' and exacerbates its ethical ambiguity.

The muddy ethical waters of computing means that acts of hacking have been received with a mix of responses ranging from general uncertainty to the polar opposite positions of admiration and condemnation. This ethical uncertainty extends to the views of hackers themselves. The computer underground has provided a range of ethical justifications for their activities:

Some hackers ... argue that it is the responsibility of the system mangers to prevent break-ins, and that they are the scapegoats of poor security practices. Some hackers go further and argue that most systems should be accessible for the purpose of learning. They say that the real crime is information hoarding. Many hackers acknowledge that break-ins are wrong – just not *that* wrong.

(Denning 1992b: 61)

The blurred nature of computer ethics is further illustrated by the description of a teacher's reaction to the behaviour of small school children and how this reaction may illustrate in microcosm society's ambivalent response to the ingenuity exhibited in hacking. It shows how in certain technologically mediated situations definitive ethical judgements can prove difficult to make:

Think of the dilemma expressed unknowingly by the mathematics teacher who spoke of the enthusiasm her 9 and 10-year-old students exhibited when she allowed them to use the school's computers. 'They are so excited' she said, 'that they fight to get onto the system. Some of them even erase others' names from the sign-up lists altogether'. The idea that this was not good preparation for the students' moral lives seemed never to have occurred to her. ... Unfortunately, both for society and for those that need the guidance, there is no standard within the computer community to define precisely when the playing has got out of hand. If a student uses an hour of computer time without permission, one university computer department may consider it criminal theft of service, while another views it as an exercise of commendable ingenuity.

(Bloombecker 1990: 42)

This ambiguous ethical status of some computing activities relates to what we have previously seen described as society's vacillating responses to the maverick qualities that seem to be at a premium in the hard-to-adapt-to hi-tech world of constant change. The ethical complexities associated with this societal state of flux are further complicated by the potentially pragmatic benefits to be gained from the hacking mentality: 'Indeed, if we were to devise a personality test designed to spot the computer criminal, the first and most difficult task would be to create a task that did not also eliminate most of the best minds who have made computing what it is' (Bloombecker 1990: 39).

Pragmatism and intellectual capital

A corollary to the fear of potential harm from foreign cyberterrorists/ Government secret services is the tacit pride felt in one's own electronic *cognoscenti*. A vivid example of this is that of the Israeli hacker, Ehud Tenebaum (a.k.a. *the Analyser*), who was accused of being responsible for the 'most systematic and organised attempt ever to penetrate the Pentagon's computer systems' (*Guardian* 26 March 1998 [*On-line* section]: 2). Whilst Tenebaum was under house arrest in the Israeli town of Hod Hasharon, the US authorities were seeking to use his apprehension as a deterrent to other hackers: 'This arrest should send a message to would-be hackers all over the world that the United States will treat computer intrusions as serious crimes', said US attorney general, Janet Reno. 'We will work around the world and in the depths of cyberspace to investigate and prosecute those who attack computer networks' (*Guardian* 26 March 1998 [*On-line* section]: 2). Meanwhile, however, Israeli public figures have taken a much more conciliatory attitude to Tenebaum's activities and their implications:

If there is a whiff of witch-hunt swirling around Washington, then in Israel Tenebaum's popularity seems to rise by the day. Prime minister Netanyahu's first comment on the affair was that the Analyser is 'damn good', before quickly adding that he could be 'very dangerous too'.

(*Guardian* 26 March 1998 [*On-line* section]: 2)

Tenebaum's lawyer actively sought publicity to bolster his client's public image using what I have previously labelled the industry benefit argument: ' "It appears to me he brought benefit to the Pentagon ... in essence he came and discovered the Pentagon's coding weaknesses," ... says Zichroni, adding sardonically that the US authorities should maybe pay Tenebaum for his services' (*Guardian* 26 March 1998 [*On-line* section]: 3). Such comments can be dismissed as a lawyer's tongue-in-cheek defence of his client. However, the deeper significance of the way in which the unethical aspects of Tenebaum's actions are blurred by their potential pragmatic uses to industry and national security is illustrated by the fact he was subsequently asked to appear before the Knesset's committee for science and technology research and development. Its chairwoman, Dalia Itzik, argued that Tenebaum had no criminal case to answer:

> From all the reports I'm hearing this is a young man who did what he did not from criminal intent, but for a challenge. He didn't cause damage, but rather exposed flaws in terms of the protection of important computer information ... his huge amount of knowledge should be used to help the state, but this time in accord with accepted rules and standards.
>
> (*Guardian* 26 March 1998 [*On-line* section]: 3)

Despite Dalia Itzik's call for Tenebaum to adopt the 'accepted rules and standards', the case arguably indicates the fact that in relation to hacking we have still to reach a set of readily agreed-upon computing mores:

> Unlike most rude behaviour, this behaviour is not subject to common cultural or political controls. The computer is so novel that we have not arrived at any consensus about what behavior is to be tolerated. We have no songs, stories, or games designed to tell people how to use it.
>
> (Murray 1992: 33)

In stark contrast to the dovish response of the Israeli authorities, and to underline the ethical *them and us* situation described previously, the director of one of the Internet service providers adversely affected by Tenebaum's activities argued pointedly that: 'This isn't a game or a joke but rather a phenomenon which causes real damage. In my view the Analyser is a vandal, not a hero' (*Guardian* 26 March 1998 [*On-line* section]: 3).

Double standards in the computer security industry?

Although the computer security industry has been vocal in its condemnation of hackers who interfere with other people's privacy rights, there are several instances of the computer security industry using the same techniques that they have criticised in others. For example, system managers argue against hacking activity on the grounds that it is an invasion of the privacy of other users, whilst they retain the right to read other people's electronic mail, or tap their phones. That such instances occur may be partly due to what we have seen is the blurring effect technology can have on ethical judgements. Robert Schifreen, the 'Prestel hacker', describes the extent to which his activities were monitored:

> It's pretty certain that my phone was being tapped. Once or twice I picked up the phone when it was tinkling and there were people talking on the other end saying things like 'shall I record this John?' ... I heard it tinkling on a Sunday afternoon and it said 'oh, sod it, I've got the wires in the wrong order'. I also had an account on Telecom Gold, one of the commercial services run by BT, and there is a little known command on Gold known as stats or fstat, that tells you what files you've got open and I typed that once and it told me that I had a file open such that everything I typed was being copied to a mail-box called 'security', and basically the security manager was logging my entire sessions and I phoned him up and he said 'yes, well as part of my contract with you, BT is entitled to monitor selective lines, to guarantee quality of service' which the interception of communication act, specifically allows, and it then turned out that Steve Gold, my partner in crime was also having his box monitored so make of that what you will.
>
> (Schifreen: London interview)

Morally ambiguous activities are thus on occasion sanctioned in certain instances, yet hacking is argued to be unequivocally wrong. Gongrijp points out that:

> no boss can open up your private mail, no university can steam open your mail if it has your name on it, not without being in serious legal trouble if you find out, and yet every employer thinks he has the right to look at email.
>
> (Gongrijp: Amsterdam interview)

Although recourse is made to arguments based on the premise that computer-stored data, and remotely accessed computer systems, should be treated as if they are physical property, system operators are accused of dropping such criteria in their own computing activity. Thus, Cosell, a commercial systems manager, who was one of the most vociferous of the computer security industry opponents to hackers encountered during the study, compared hacking to the joy-riding of cars: 'Assuming you come out to the parking lot and your car is JUST where it was left, except maybe the engine feels a bit warm. How is this different than discovering that someone had logged into your computer?' (Cosell: email interview). Despite the force of his moral view he also admitted that he:

> had to do this sort of thing once or twice over the years. I recall one incident where I was working over the weekend and the master source hierarchy was left read-protected, and I REALLY needed to look at it to finish what I was doing, and this on a system where I was NOT a privileged user [although I was an authorized ordinary user], so I 'broke into' the system enough to give myself enough privileges to be able to override the file protections and get

done what I needed [at which point I put it all back, and told the sysadmin about the security hole].

(Cosell: email interview)

This experience is particularly interesting because of the way in which Cosell proceeds to imply (by his use of inverted commas) a breakdown of the applicability of a physical analogy when it is applied to his own action. The ease with which ethical quandaries can arise with the question of information is further illustrated by Bruce Sterling's account of his time spent 'trashing' whilst having been temporarily excluded from a particular session of a Federal Computer Investigations Committee (FCIC) security conference he was attending. Sterling proceeds his description of his act of trashing by commenting: 'The legality of trashing is somewhat dubious, but it is not in fact flagrantly illegal'. Backed by this 'lack of illegality' he proceeded to empty one of the trash baskets in one of the office-rooms opposite the security conference. Apart from finding a telephone-card bill from which he found out a woman's home telephone number and a list of acquaintances' numbers that she had phoned, he also sellotaped together fragments of various drafts of a love letter she had written. At this stage in the account Sterling is aware that he was 'Driven by motives that were completely unethical and prurient', yet this did not stop him from examining in detail the handwritten notes (Sterling 1992: 198).

Hacking as postmodern play?

By Postmodernism we mean a reaction against 'cultural modernity' and a destruction of the constraints of the present 'maximum security society' (Marx, 1988) that reflect an attempt to gain control of an alternative future. In the computer underground world, this constitutes a conscious resistance to the domination but not the fact of technological encroachment into all realms of our social existence. The computer underground represents a reaction against modernism by offering an ironic response to the primacy of technocratic language, the incursion of computers into realms once considered private, the politics of the techno-society, and the sanctity of established civil and state authority. ... It is this style of playful rebellion, irreverent subversion, and juxtaposition of fantasy with high-tech reality that impels us to interpret the computer underground as a postmodernist culture.

(Meyer and Thomas 1989: 3, 4)

The ambivalent qualities of hacking continue to flourish when it is placed in a broad philosophical context. Cultural theorists have emphasised the ironic and playful nature of hacking. The fact that hackers do not accept institutionally imposed ways of thinking about technology makes them suitable candidates for the role of living out the postmodern precepts of enjoyment in the death of meta-narratives and postmodernity's general concentration upon the imaginative use of diverse cultural resources (bricolage).[1] In a less positive light, however, any elevated postmodern status we can afford to hackers is perhaps predicated upon a general social malaise that they are not so much immune to as simply better able to cope with than the rest of society:

> The tie between information and action has been severed ... we are glutted with information, drowning in information, we have no control over it, don't know what to do with it ... we no longer have a coherent conception of ourselves, and our universe, and our relation to one another and our world. We no longer know, as the Middle Ages did, where we come from, and where we are going, or why. That is, we don't know what information is relevant, and what information is irrelevant to our lives ... our defenses against information glut have broken down; our information immune system is inoperable. We don't know how to reduce it; we don't know how to use it. We suffer from a kind of cultural AIDS.
>
> (Postman 1990: 6)

Furthermore, set against postmodern interpretations of hacking that emphasise its playfulness can be placed those analyses that see hacking in terms of a modern manifestation of the long historical Western tradition of instrumental reason. Hackers from this perspective are an extreme computer-based version of Marcuse's (1964) accusation that Western man can only find his soul in such consumer durables as his hi-fi. Within cyberpunk literature, for example, the close identification with computers, which sets the hacker community apart as obsessive geeks in the eyes of critical outsiders, raises fundamental questions concerning the relationship between the natural and technological worlds and even if the two worlds can any longer be meaningfully conceptualised independently of each other.

Cyberpunk: hackers and opposition

> We're still not sure what happened to the pirate flag that once flew over Apple Computer's headquarters but we do know that what was once a nerd phenomenon backed by an idealistic belief in the freedom of information became the powerful aphrodisiac behind sexy initial public offerings. Che Guevara with stock options.
>
> (Hawn 1996: 2)

Closely related to the issue of human/machine symbiosis in cyberpunk literature is the further perennial concern over humankind's ability to control technology rather than being controlled by it and here too there is some resonance between the experience of cyberpunks and their real-world hacker counterparts. The sense of powerlessness that accompanies cyberpunk narratives raises doubts as to the potential of cyberpunks (and by implication their real-world representatives, hackers) to be a meaningful focus for cultural opposition to the establishment's control of technology; indeed cyberpunk has been dismissed for 'its re-sexing of the "neutered" hacker in the form of the high-tech hipster rebel' (Ross 1991: 145). Cyberpunk is accused of being rooted in the fears of the white male middle classes rather than being based on a realistic cultural force. It is criticised as feeding off:

> the phantasmatic street diet of Hobbesian lawlessness and the aesthetic of detritus that is assumed to pervade the hollowed-out core of the great metropolitan centers. This urban fantasy, however counter-cultural its claims and potential effects, shared the dominant, white middle-class conception of inner-city life. In this respect, the suburban romance of punk, and subsequently, cyberpunk, fashioned a culture of alienation out of their parents' worst fears about life on the mean streets.
>
> (Ross 1991:146)

Some writers, however, do find within cyberpunk a prototypical description of hacking culture's potential as an oppositional force within an increasingly tech-nological society. Cyberpunk portrays the amalgamation of the technological knowledge of hackers with the anti-establishment ethos of the punk rocker. The potential for this amalgamation to produce a source of opposition to the domi-nant social constituencies is aided by the fact that technology is now more readily accessible and potentially manipulable than ever before. A complicating aspect of this potential for rebellion, however, is the degree to which hackers oppose dominant social forces within computing whilst at the same time containing their very traits. For example, whilst generally opposing trends towards the increasing commodification of information and by extension the ethics of the free market, some hackers at least almost personify market values, leading to the claim that they are not an alternative culture at all:

> the hacker cyberculture is not a dropout culture; its disaffiliation from a domestic parent culture is often manifest in activities that answer, directly or indirectly, to the legitimate needs of industrial R and D. For example, this hacker culture celebrates high productivity, maverick forms of creative work energy, and an obsessive identification with on-line endurance (and endor-phin highs) – all qualities that are valorised by the entrepreneurial codes of silicon futurism. ... The values of the white male outlaw are often those of the creative maverick universally prized by entrepreneurial or libertarian individualism ... teenage hackers resemble an alienated shopping culture deprived of purchasing opportunities more than a terrorist network.
>
> (Ross 1991: 90)

Hackers' ambivalent status as an oppositional force is perhaps an inevitable result of their closeness to the very technological artefacts used to consolidate the power of conventional social authorities. What is less ambiguous about hackers, however, is the way in which they turn on its head the usually negative counter-cultural response to technological progress: instead of demonising artefacts, they prefer to use them to their fullest advantage.

Hackers as mavericks

> Technical culture has gotten out of hand. The advances of science are so deeply radical, so disturbing, upsetting, and revolutionary, that they can no longer be contained. They are surging into culture at large; they are invasive; they are everywhere. The traditional power structure, the traditional institutions have lost control of the pace of change. ... And now that technology has reached fever pitch, its influence has slipped control and reached street level ... times have changed since. ... Science was safely enshrined – and confined – in an ivory tower. The careless technophilia of those days belongs to a vanished sluggish era, when authority still had a comfortable margin of control.
>
> (Sterling 1988: x, xi)

Western society has an ambivalent relationship with rapid technological change. On the one hand Western society has a vested interest in believing that maverick tendencies distinguish it from the more regimented and unimaginative Oriental culture, yet, on the other hand, it seeks to control and punish such creativity when it is perceived to have overstepped its boundaries and gone beyond its control. Leary (1994) provides a somewhat exuberant celebration of the maverick, creative tendency that thrives amidst rapid change.[2] He compares the technologically adept and adventurous cyberpunks of the information revolution to the freelancing samurai known as *Ronin*.

Hackers represent a group that contain Leary's *Ronin* qualities in abundance and who profess to revel in constant change. They epitomise the enjoyment to be had from surfing a technological wave, but part of their enjoyment seems to be had (as with physical wave surfers) from the intrinsic danger to be derived from, and the lack of control they can exert over, the activity they are involved in. One such example is 'Chip Tango' a 'midnight irregular' and archetypal hacker who:

> looks at the future with enthusiasm. His trust in humanity is inexhaustible. He takes for granted that computer technology is out of control, and he wants to ride it like a surfer rides a wave. The opportunities for fouling up the world through computer power are unlimited, but he thinks that people like him are useful agents in establishing a balance, a sense of humaneness and humor ... when presented with a scenario of a world which increasingly uses information in an oppressive Orwellian manner, [he] replied, 'I'm

not worried for a minute about the future. If the world you describe is going to happen, man, I can fuck it up a lot faster than the world we live in now!'

(Vallee 1984: 150–1)

This rebellious aspect of hacking culture does not fit easily with the demands of conventional society; yet, society perceives a need to encourage such attitudes. This conflict of purpose is the basis behind the various ethical quandaries that result from attempting to establish new social mores in an environment of rapid technological change.

MIT to Alcatraz?

As the proliferation of hackers' anarchist tendencies suggests, this culture desperately needs some understanding, as well as a sympathetic ear. We have seen that corporate industry rejects the knowledge and technical expertise of hackers; could not a higher level of technology be realised if these two factions were to work together? The answer to this will be found in the future. As the possibility of a global Information Society draws closer, people must be willing to take their technical education into their own hands. We could all learn a valuable lesson from hackers: that intellectual hunger and the quest for knowledge should be central in our society.

(Rosteck 1994: 15)

Hacking has evolved since its earliest days as mischievous ingenuity at MIT to an activity that increasingly lands its practitioners in prison. Both punitive legislation and open-armed co-operation seem to have their drawbacks. Hackers themselves recognise the vandalistic qualities within their own community and yet they describe anti-hacking legislation at worst like attempting to use a sledgehammer to crack a walnut and at best as largely symbolic and ineffective. Legislators face a seemingly intractable bind. They can be accused of attempting to shoe-horn computer security cases into existing but allegedly unsuitable laws, or, alternatively, they can be accused of producing new laws that misapply traditional concepts such as theft and privacy to the qualitatively different world of computing. Because of the relatively recent appreciation of the problem of computer security and its implications for computing and society, many of the complex legal issues remain to be resolved through the usual processes of legal debate and precedence yet due to cultural lag law-makers risk playing continual catch-up with constantly and rapidly evolving computer technologies.

We have seen in the preceding chapters how security weaknesses will always result from the inevitable fallibility of human-designed systems, and that, given sufficient perseverance and technical knowledge on the part of hackers, bugs and software faults can be used for purposes other than those intended by the original designer. The basic problem facing legislators, therefore, is how to design a legal structure that will deter the illicit use of computing facilities whilst avoiding the potential risk of marginalising 'benign' hackers so that their knowledge and perseverance is herded towards more conventional criminal groups. The doves argue that, rather than seeking to legislate, the computer security industry should be more concerned with the 'access' and 'thirst for knowledge' causes of hacking. Targeting resources in these directions is arguably more productive in the long run than the risk of provoking militant computer underground acts of vandalism with hawkish, unsympathetic responses. This argument gains some credence when one looks at the existence of so-called virus factories in the former Eastern Bloc countries, which existed largely as a result of a lack of productive legitimate outlets for programmers' computing skills.

The fear that by placing hackers in prison such knowledge will be directed into the criminal community is also expressed by Mofo who also uses the example of the Internet Worm. He contends:

> There were individuals who would have Mr. Morris be quartered in an actual prison. Such puerile reaction! I myself was in a position to demand that Mr. Morris receive capital punishment AND a fine, but reason seems to have eventually prevailed in my muddled mind. I present this observation: an intelligent person sent to prison for such an act would certainly come to the conclusion that society demands his/her subsequent interaction with the denizens of such an institution. Thus, I believe that society as a whole would be far better off if the intellect of a person like Mr. Morris was not shared and information not disseminated among hardened criminals with truly malevolent intent.
>
> (Mofo: email interview).

In keeping with this scenario, there is the example of Nicholas Whitley known as the 'mad hacker':

> The only times Nick Whitley was ever approached to do something he thought was illegal was when he was already in jail. The first attempt was made in the exercise yard in London's Brixton prison: Whitely was a hacker, wasn't he? He could break into computers, right? Well couldn't he break into the Police National Computer and change a few files? It would be worth £10,000 to some people to have their police records deleted. Nick declined.
>
> (Clough and Mungo 1992: 42)

The personal experience of hackers, such as John Draper, who have served prison sentences for hacking further illustrates some of the problematic implications of imprisoning hackers:

> In most cases, criminals hackers might meet in jail or prison are too stupid to understand the ramifications of hackers' information. Lately, however, a lot of newer prisoners have been added to the usual murderers, drug

dealers, thieves, etc. These are embezzlers, fraud artists, scam artists, and other 'sharks' that wouldn't hesitate for a moment to capitalise on hacker technology to enhance their scams. ... Your academia experts may know a LOT of things, but until they actually EXPERIENCE inmate life in jail, they will NEVER EVER know what really goes on in prisons. ... In MY experience, when I was released, almost everyone I had contact with in prison has since contacted me after they also got released. Some have even offered me large sums of money to hire me as a consultant. ... In most cases, those hackers approached by ex-cons will be offered huge sums of money as an incentive to 'spill the beans' and teach hacker technology, so a hacker will be most patient, even though they are talking with a moron. Eventually, even the dumbest moron will catch on to the automated techniques of breaking into systems.

(Draper: email interview)

There is thus on the one hand a need to deter troublesome hacking activity, yet to criminalise such activity has potentially dangerous and counter-productive consequences. Understanding the motivation behind hacking activity and the differences between 'responsible' and 'vandal' hackers is seen by the computer underground in particular as necessary in order to target resources to the real causes of hacking without alienating those responsible hackers who may prove to be a useful resource for limiting the destruction of the vandals. The predisposition of the computer security industry to group non-intentional and intentional damage together would seem to increase the tendency towards the criminalisation of hacking whatever its underlying motivation. To borrow a phrase from contemporary politics there would seem to be a need to identify a *third way* in order to steer between the drawbacks of both the hawkish and dovish responses.

The need to find a workable *third way* in the confusing and rapidly changing world of technology will inevitably be difficult but a failure to do so threatens severe implications for the way in which our society fosters and rewards technological curiosity and ingenuity:

We can either treat it as healthy and provide a venue for it, or turn our children into criminals by criminalizing their normal behaviour. ... When I was younger, I knew many 'hackers' who went after systems, and none of them were malicious. Now I know some malicious ones, but they are generally malicious because of family or financial problems, not because they are 'criminals'. In every case I have seen, these people need friends and legitimate ways to explore. They need guidance and moral interpretation from someone they respect, not jail time with rapists and thieves in some stinking cell. ... As the group ages ... people begin to cross the line between explorer and pirate. Unfortunately, many of these latter day Fagans corrupt young people who, in their quest to explore, are not given legitimate venues, and are thus drawn into illegitimate activities ... the reason most of these people are drawn into the 'dark side' is because they are abandoned by the 'good guys'. I for one, will not abandon our youth to criminal activities.

(Cohen: email interview)

The evolution in attitudes

Some people pointed out to Levy that the original Hackers were not so different after all. Many of them came up with equally elaborate schemes to steal time from the university mainframe – they were the 'computer intruders' too, who also found ways to swipe stuff from the coke machines and the pay phones. Many cyberpunks suggest that the dichotomy (of cracker = secretive, malicious, dangerous, destructive, etc. versus hacker = open, socially minded, constructive, honest etc.) is a false one, and that Levy is guilty of a good deal of romanticism. After all, didn't Wozniak and Jobs sell out when Apple patented its system architecture, making it an effective monopoly? Hackers exceed limitations; crackers simply manipulate what's already there. Or so we're told. ... In any case, it's apparently clear that the names 'cyberpunk' and 'hacker' are contested domain; and, to a certain extent, 'computer underground' is, too.

(Mizrach undated: website)

There has been an evolution in the ethical judgements passed upon hackers by society at large. Whereas the idiosyncratic behaviour of the early hackers of MIT was benignly tolerated, hacking is now subject to legal prosecution. Whilst the motivations and lack of regard for property rights associated with hacking have remained relatively constant over time, society has become less tolerant of the activity. Examples of computing's previously *ad hoc* morality abound: what are now condemned as unethical computing practices were routinely practised without moral censure by the first generation of MIT hackers. They engaged in such illicit activity as using equipment without authorisation (Levy 1984: 20), phone-phreaking (1984: 92), unauthorised modification of equipment (1984: 96) and the circumvention of password controls (1984: 417).[3] The challenge faced by society is to co-opt hackers' knowledge, enthusiasm and ingenuity whilst, at the same time, maintaining a wider computing community that is not hamstrung by the need to continually counter the actions of those seeking to test systems' security.

The evolution in attitudes that has taken place towards hacking has been compared by one contributor cited earlier to the early days of the aviation industry: there came a time when the original maverick pilots had to subordinate their high jinks activities to the more mundane requirements of the burgeoning commercial passenger industry. This comparison does apply in some ways to the phenomenon of hacking. It seems (given the difficulties in assessing an inherently underground phenomenon) that in recent years there has been something of a downturn in hacking activity and those with hacking mentalities have found openings in the commercial sector where their network skills are put to good use. However, the comparison arguably breaks down in so far as the aviation industry has managed to discipline its workforce whilst maintaining high safety standards. The worrying aspect of computing that seems to be acknowledged by both the computer underground and the computer security industry in contrast is that even if all hacking ended tomorrow many of the computer systems modern society relies upon would continue to be insecure. This leads me to observe that perhaps we should pay more attention to the implications of hacking rather than the activity itself.

The rear-view mirror and the moon

Marshall McLuhan (1964) compares our attempts to steer ourselves through constant technological change as being akin to driving a car by only looking in the rear-view mirror: we are going forward but we can only see (and by extension understand) what has already passed. It is with resigned acknowledgement of the difficulties implied by the rear-view mirror analogy that I have tried to make sense of the significance of the phenomenon of computer hacking. It is extremely unlikely that there will ever be a tranquil position from which to coolly view technological change, but in an era when it is increasingly difficult to keep pace with its constant waves, hackers, as they enthusiastically and playfully seek out the fastest and biggest surf, are emblematic figures who provide a potentially fruitful source of insights into the way in which society comes to terms with information technology. The wider social significance of hacking tends to be lost in the temptation of writers to pore over either the technical or biographical minutiae of hackers and their activity. An old Chinese proverb states that 'When a finger points at the moon, the idiot looks at the finger.' In a field where there has been much pointing in recent years, I hope I have managed to divert my glance (at least occasionally) from the finger to the moon.

Appendix
Additional examples of media hype

Hacker non-fictional literature

> They [hackers] seem to have a couple of characteristics in common as a group: many have absent fathers or, at least, parents who don't notice what they are doing; a few have been placed in mental institutions or sent in for counselling; some suffer from severe depression or hyperactivity and may take medication for it; and most have explosive tempers and/or egos that need to be continuously fed. They are the classroom bullies who come home to turn on their computers and become even more powerful by virtue of their anonymity. Or if they aren't bullies by day, they become bullies when they go on the net.
>
> (Gilboa 1996: 112)

There are inherent problems in attempting to generalise about a culture such as hacking, which by its very nature is largely immaterial and anonymous. These difficulties have created a tendency to substitute overly speculative psychologising, trivia and hyperbole for substantive discussion of the broader social significance of hacking.

Amateur psychology

The cod psychology used to explain hackers' motivations is evident in Gilboa's statement quoted above, and in *Cyberpunk* poorly founded conjectures are continually made as to the state of mind of various hackers. This somewhat arbitrary assignation of motivation leads the authors to label Kevin Mitnick as the *dark-side* hacker, whereas their analysis of Robert Morris, author of the Internet Worm, is much less condemning despite the fact the latter was arguably responsible for much more damage and man-hours of data-recovery time.[1] The authors write about Kevin Mitnick that:

> When Kevin was three, his parents separated. His mother, Shelly got a job as a waitress at a local delicatessen and embarked upon a series of new rela-

tionships. Every time Kevin started to get close to a new father, the man disappeared. Kevin's real father was seldom in touch; he remarried and had another son, athletic and good-looking. During Kevin's high school years, just as he was getting settled into a new school, the family moved. It wasn't surprising that Kevin looked to the telephone for solace.

(Hafner and Markoff 1991: 26)

Press and television

Faced with the problem of how to report computer security issues in a both accurate and entertaining manner the media have tended to report those stories that contain the highest degree of 'electronic lethality' and (as seen with the above example of Kevin Mitnick) it has exaggerated the 'darkness' of hacking motives. For example, a United Kingdom Channel 4 television documentary, *Dispatches* (1989), entitled its investigation of hacking 'The day of the technopath', whilst the February 1991 edition of *GQ* magazine concerned the growth of virus writers in Bulgaria and was called *Satanic Viruses*. The television portrayals of the problem of computer security seem to be the most superficial and dependent upon sensationalising techniques. Newspaper and magazine articles tend to give relatively thorough and accurate technical descriptions of what it is to hack/write viruses but still make disproportionate use of 'dark-side' imagery.[2] Specific examples of the two media can be seen in an article from the now defunct UK newspaper, *The Sunday Correspondent*, of 17 December 1989 entitled 'A bug in the machine' and part of the transcript of an episode of the US current affairs/chat-show programme, *Geraldo*.

'A bug in the machine'

This article is an example of the tendency of the press to concentrate upon the 'sexy' elements of computer security stories. It contains a cynical description of the UK Member of Parliament, Emma Nicholson, and her unsubstantiated claims that hacking techniques are used for terrorist purposes by the European Green movement amongst others and her emotive description of hackers as: 'malevolent, nasty evil-doers who fill the screens of amateur users with pornography' (Matthews 1989: 39). Yet whilst dispelling in this way some of the alarmist tendencies of such claims, the example of a hacker chosen by the journalists is that of the 'computer anarchist Mack Plug'. Apart from making their own unsubstantiated claim that 'Nearly all hackers are loners' (a contention that is at least made debatable by my interviews with groups of Dutch hackers and the evidence of regular, thriving hacker conferences both in the US and across Europe),[3] their description of his hacking activity seems to deliberately over-emphasise the more 'glamorous' type of hacking at the expense of describing the more mundane realities and implications of everyday hacking:

At the moment he is hacking electronic leg tags. 'I've got it down to 27 seconds' he says, 'All you have to do is put a microset recorder next to the tag and when the police call to check you're there, you tape the tones transmitted by the tag and feed them on to your answering machine. When the cops call back again, my machine will play back those tones. I'll have a fail-safe alibi and I can get back to hacking into MI5'.

(Matthews 1989: 39)

Geraldo *programme*[4]

On 30 September 1991, the Geraldo chat-show focused on hacking. It involved a presentation of various hacking cameo shots, one of which showed Dutch hackers accessing US Department of Defense computers with super-user status. The studio section of the show involved an interview with Craig Neidorf (alias *Knight Lightning*), who underwent a court case in the US for having allegedly received the source code of the emergency services telephone computer programs. Also interviewed was the prosecuting attorney in Neidorf's case. Below I include excerpts from the dialogue that ensued as an example of the extent to which hacking is presented in the media in a superficial, trivialised and hyperbolic manner. In the introductory part of the show, excerpts from the film 'Die Hard II' are shown, in which terrorists take over the computers of an airport. The general tone of the show was sensationalistic with one of the guest hackers, Craig Neidorf, being repeatedly called the 'Mad Hacker' by Geraldo and the prosecutor consistently choosing emotive and alarmist language as shown in the following examples:

> *Geraldo:* Don, how do you respond to the feeling common among so many hackers that what they're doing is a public service; they're exposing the flaws in our security systems?
>
> *Prosecutor:* Right, and just like the people who rape a co-ed on campus are exposing the flaws in our nation's higher education security. It's absolute nonsense. They are doing nothing more than showing off to each other, and satisfying their own appetite to know something that is not theirs to know.

And on the question of the punishment of hackers:

> I don't think they're being punished very much at all. We're having trouble even taking away their gear. I don't know one of them has done hard time in a prison. The book, Hafner's book on Cyberpunk, points out that even Mitnick who is a real electronic Hannibal Lecter ... did not get near any of the punishment that what he was doing entitled him to.

Finally, at the very end of the show, Geraldo asks the attorney to give, in thirty seconds, a worst-case scenario of what could result from the activities of hackers. To which he replies: 'They wipe out our communications system. Rather easily done. Nobody talks to anyone else, nothing moves, patients don't get their medicine. We're on our knees.'

Dispatches – *'The day of the technopath'*[5]

Emma Nicholson MP, interviewed in the United Kingdom Channel 4's *Dispatches* programme (1989), states, 'A really good hacker could beat the Lockerbie bomber any day, hands down' and 'Perhaps only a small fraction of the population dislikes the human race, but they do, and some of them are highly computer-skilled'. This alarmist tone is repeated in the following example taken from the programme's voiced-over commentary:

> Until now the computer hacker has been seen affectionately as a skilled technocrat, beavering away obsessively in his den, a harmless crank exploring the international computer networks for fun. But today it's clear that any computer, anywhere, can be broken into and interfered with for ulterior motives. The technocrat has mutated to the technopath … Government and business are reluctant to admit that they're fragile and vulnerable to such threats, frightened of either the loss of public confidence or of setting themselves up as targets for the technopaths who stalk their electronic alleyways.

Notes

Preface

1 *The Two Cultures and the Scientific Revolution* (1959 Rede lecture).
2 This observation above originally referred to the phenomenon of computer viruses but I contend that its sentiments are directly applicable to the act of hacking.
3 Nicolas Chantler's comprehensive 1995 study is entitled 'Risk: The profile of the computer hacker' (Ph.D. thesis, Curtin University of Technology, Perth, Western Australia; conferred March 1996).
4 Despite this more general connotation the phrase hacking will be used throughout this book as shorthand for computer hacking.
5 This quotation is taken from the short story, 'Burning chrome', in Gibson's collection of the same name (1986a: 215), and originally referred to the protagonist's penchant for mixing prescription drugs with alcohol in order to achieve a desired 'high'.
6 Throughout this book the 'commonly accepted sense' of hacking is used as a working definition, but it is in the nature of the beast that the term is ultimately inadequate as a catch-all phrase to cover a collection of activities the exact social status of which are hotly contested. For example, in addition to the phrase, *hacker*, which for some people has connotations of non-malicious exploration there is also the more specific term, *cracker*, which is more consistently and pejoratively used to describe someone who breaks into systems, often causing deliberate damage. Whilst acknowledging such terminological distinctions, this study will use *hacker* as an umbrella term for the various shades of meaning associated with the phrase rather than labelling a subset of hackers as crackers. The rationale for this is that by leaving the term initially rather loose, the analysis can then focus upon the ways in which various groups seek to solidify the definition of hacking to accord with their own views. From this perspective it would be inappropriate to use contested terms in an unproblematically precise manner since one of the major purposes of this work is to seek to uncover the very processes by which such terms have become used in highly specific ways.
7 Roszak (1986) associates the start of this shift with the Benthamite penchant for politically inspired data-gathering.

Introduction

1 These two elements are evident in an article taken from *Omni* entitled 'Crime bytes back'. The article's by-line emphasises the crime element: 'In tomorrow's world of high-tech crime, the cops will stake out computers, and the robbers will wear electronic masks.' Whilst further into the article under the subtitle, 'electronic hijacks', the wizardry of the hackers' sublime technological skills is highlighted with the observation: 'Computer virtuosos can make electronic walls melt with the stroke of a key' (Marda and Ray 1990: 34, 98).

2 Cf. Sterling (1992) for full details of the E911 case.
3 Kevin Poulsen was the first US hacker to be charged with espionage; part of his exploits involved winning numerous large prizes by rigging radio phone-in competitions so that his was always the first call to be received by the station. Cf. Jonathan Littman's *The Watchman* (1997) for a full account.
4 Julius Rosenberg was a US cold-war spy.
5 Cf. Chapter 7 for a full account of the rhetorical use of physical analogies.
6 Sterling (1992): 95.
7 Readers of this book are likely to have their own examples of some of the worst excesses of the media's tendency to sensationalise hacking. Specific examples of such portrayals are provided in the Appendix in order to illustrate the above-mentioned ambivalence of fear and fascination that is inextricably linked to the issue of hacking and to which the main body of this book seeks to act as a corrective and explanatory counterweight.
8 Cf. the Appendix for more detailed analysis including descriptions of the press and TV accounts.
9 The press reinforces this tendency with repeated references to the similarities between real-life hackers and their movie counterparts. For example:

> Scotland Yard spent £250,000 investigating the 'Datastream Cowboy' a real-life version of the Hollywood movie War Games in which a teenager nearly starts a third world war by hacking into the U.S. defence system.
>
> (*Daily Mail* 22 March 1997: 1)

> Bevan likens his team of half a dozen 'friends and acquaintances' to the fictional group of eccentric technophiles portrayed in the 1992 movie, Sneakers, starring Robert Redford.
>
> (*Guardian* 26 February 1998 [*On-line* section])

> In events reminiscent of Sneakers – a Hollywood film in which a hacker played by Robert Redford steals a code-cracking device that can break into any computer in the world – the Pentagon said last week it was taking 'very seriously' claims by a group calling itself Masters of Downloading that it had successfully penetrated defence department computers to steal software controlling military communications.
>
> (*Sunday Times* 17 May 1998: 26)

> Settle … has since founded his own consultancy, which, in a real-life equivalent of Robert Redford's team of expert hackers in the Hollywood film Sneakers, conducts 'licensed penetrations' to test corporate computer security.
>
> (*Sunday Times* 8 February 1998: 26)

1 *Them and us*: the hack

1 MIT hacker Phil Agre cited in Jargon's 'The meaning of "hack"' (n.d.): 1. Available at: http://beast.cc.emory.edu/Jargon30/APPEND_A/MEANHACK.HTML.
2 *Phone-phreakers* is the phrase used to describe people who used various electronic devices to hack into the telephone networks to explore the system and/or obtain free phone calls.
3 (Alias John Draper – who received this moniker by accessing phone systems using the tone of the toy whistle found in *Captain Crunch* cereal boxes.)

4 Cf. Levy's *Hackers* (1984).

5 Rop Gongrijp was the head of the now-defunct group of Dutch hackers known as *Hack-Tic*.

6 I refer to this hacker simply as M. to protect him from potential incrimination given the legally dubious nature of some of his activities.

7 This example of gene-hacking has arguably been superseded by the advent of Dolly the cloned sheep, developed at the Roslin Institute in Scotland in July 1997.

2 Hacking culture

1 For further information see my article entitled 'Hackers: Cyberpunks or microserfs', *Information Communication and Society* autumn 1998.

2 One of the best examples of this would be Tracy Kidder's *The Soul of a New Machine* (1982).

3 For a full account of hacker jargon see the online version of the hacker dictionary, 'The meaning of 'hack', available at: http://beast.cc.emory.edu/Jargon30/APPEND_A/MEANHACK.HTML.

4 A thorough description of the social organisation of hackers has, nevertheless, been attempted by Gordon Meyer (1989) 'The social organisation of the computer underground', unpublished Master's thesis.

5 Robert Schifreen, a UK hacker, was caught 'breaking into' the Duke of Edinburgh's email account with his accomplice, Steve Gold. They were charged and convicted under the 1981 Forgery and Counterfeiting Act in 1986 at Southwark Crown Court. Their subsequent appeal was upheld and led to the establishment of a Royal Commission to examine the need for new specific legislation against computer crime.

6 The Internet Worm was a worm program written by Robert Morris jr., ironically the son of the National Computer Security Centre's chief scientist. It hit the Internet network of computers on 2 November 1988; estimates of affected machines range from 2,000 to 6,200.

7 Cf. *The Hacker Crackdown* by Bruce Sterling (1992), in which he documents and comments upon the spate of US Secret Service investigations into computer underground activity in the early 1990s.

8 For example, to compensate for the inability of computer communication to convey certain gestures and emotions, users have developed various computer substitutes. During my research I came across the following examples: [; -)] to express a winking face, that is, irony or sarcasm; [: - 0] to express shock; [: -)] happiness; and so on.

9 Cf. De Lacy, Justine 'The Sexy Computer' (1989). It describes, on the basis of the Minitel experience how people seem to have a somewhat surprisingly ready predisposition to swap intimate details of each other's lives, more specifically, their sex lives and accompanying fantasies, a phenomenon that seems to be exacerbated by the fact, peculiar to email correspondence, that those communicating have no visual or aural clues as to the identity of their correspondent.

10 It is arguably therefore the immateriality of the hacker terrain that is at the root of the subsequent ethical debates and cultural lag issues that we will explore in subsequent chapters.

11 Ed Schwartz Show on WGN Radio, 27–8 September 1988. Transcript published in *Phrack* 2(21).

12 Cf. Spertus (1991).

13 In this myth a sculptor falls in love with his sculpted figure of a woman, which eventually is brought to life.

14 It is worth noting in this regard that, according to Claudia Springer, William Gibson (the author of *Neuromancer*) 'wanted to title his first novel *Jacked In*, but the publisher refused on the grounds that it sounded too much like "Jacked Off" '. Springer (1996): 72.

15 Alluquere Rosanne Stone cited in Benedikt (1991): 108.
16 Stone (1991): 109.

3 The motivations of hackers

1 Hacking, therefore, does not have to have predominantly negative effects upon its practitioners, and it is perhaps unfair to attribute to computers qualities of addiction, whilst similar behaviour would not be so described in relation to other activities. In so far as computer/hacking addiction would imply a reduced ability to socially interact, and to concur with Shotton's analysis, at least those hackers interviewed seemed to belie the stereotype of the hacker as the computer geek. Several of the hackers interviewed had started their own computer security businesses with an entrepreneurial zeal that sits uncomfortably with the image of reclusive computer geeks.
2 Howard Rheingold cited in Seabrook (1997): 180.
3 A Computer Science Lecturer at Hull University, formerly of Edinburgh University.
4 A good example of this is the Japanese phenomenon of the Otaku. Cf. Karl Taro Greenfeld, 'WIRED 1.1: The incredibly strange mutant creatures who rule the universe of alienated Japanese zombie computer nerds (Otaku to you)' (1993), available at: http://www.eff.org/pub/Net_culture/Cyberpunk/otaku.article.
5 Cf., for example, the NSA encryption debate covered in John Perry Barlow's *Decrypting the Puzzle Palace*, Communications of the ACM, June 1992.
6 Dr Peter Ross, Deputy Head of Edinburgh University's Artificial Intelligence Department, *Student*, Thursday 25 February 1991, p. 1.

4 State of the industry

1 I refer those readers interested in the incidence of computer hacking to various statistical studies that have been made into computer crime, for example the War Room report (1996) and John D. Howard's Ph.D. thesis, 'Information Security' (1997).
2 The Internet Worm was a self-dispersing computer program introduced into the Internet in November 1988 by Robert Morris jr. Although estimates of the exact damage done vary widely, it caused widespread disruption across the US computing community.
3 Cf. Vinten (1990): 8.
4 Cf. Peláez's (1988) description of the marketing of IBM's 360 family of computers.
5 Prof. Weizenbaum took part in an informal workshop session at a UK academic conference in the summer of 1990, and the sentiments I am attributing to him came from comments he made both during the session and over coffee afterwards.

5 *Them and us*: the hawks and the doves

1 It forms part of what I refer to later as the *knowledge gap*.
2 Defined as tricking legitimate personnel into aiding illicit intrusions, for example, by deceiving a telephone operator into giving security information by pretending to be a telephone company engineer.
3 Joseph Lewis Popp: he was charged in January 1990 with using a Trojan Horse hidden within a diskette to extort money from recipients whose systems had subsequently become infected. The trial did not come to court, however, because his defence argued that he was mentally unfit to stand trial. They described how he had taken to putting hair curlers in his beard and wearing a cardboard box on his head in an apparent attempt to protect himself from radiation.

6 The professionalisation process

1 It should perhaps be noted that the previously identified problem of obtaining information in this inherently sensitive area has implications for the professionalisation process under examination in this chapter. Whilst all manner of social interactions necessarily take discursive forms it can be argued that the opinions put forward in the following pages by the computer security industry are specific examples of rhetorical strategies designed to achieve particular ends. It is therefore likely that the 'party line' contained in some of the following evidence from the computer security industry does not in fact give due emphasis to the true extent of the computer security industry's day-to-day dealings with the computer underground. In short: some hawks may be closet doves.

2 The former was the defence lawyer for Craig Neidorf in the E911 trial of 1990; Dorothy Denning is a computer scientist from Georgetown University, Washington, with an academic interest in computer underground issues.

3 Computer underground electronic magazine.

4 Stoll's activities included borrowing other people's computers without permission and monitoring other people's electronic communications without authorisation.

5 The phrase 'bug in the machine/program' stems from this phase when insects flying through windows (kept open to cool the valves) became trapped within the machines and blew the relatively delicate valves, causing the computers to crash.

6 A programmer, and winner of the 1984 Turing Award.

7 A phrase first used in relation to computer misuse legislation by Hollinger and Lanza-Kaduce (1988).

7 The construction of computer ethics

1 Martin Sprouse (ed.) (1992) *Sabotage in the American Workplace: Anecdotes of Dissatisfaction, Mischief and Revenge.* Cited in Karnow (1994).

2 Professor Spafford kindly provided an audio tape of extended recorded answers to a set of questions that I had previously emailed to him.

3 Hence the comparisons of the debate surrounding Robert Morris jr.'s intrusion into the Internet system with the language and attitudes displayed during the Salem witch trials; see Dougan and Gieryn (1988).

4 Fear of boundary transgression is vividly portrayed in such urban legends as 'the Mexican Dog' and 'the Choking Doberman'; see Woolgar and Russell (1990).

5 Cf. Sterling's (1992) coverage of the Steve Jackson's Game incident (pp. 138–46).

6 Cf. Woolgar and Russell (1990).

7 EFF – the Electronic Frontier Foundation, which is an organisation founded by Mitch Kapor and John Perry Barlow to promote access to as unregulated as possible online communication.

8 Conclusion

1 Jean Baudrillard describes the postmodern concept of playfulness that could be productively applied to hacking:

> neither reality nor pretense is as simple as it has once seemed … in modernity, our experience of the real is primarily playful. Whether we wish to acknowledge it, we are now immersed in play throughout our daily lives … in modernity is play indeed only a mirror, somewhat inferior, derivative, and secondary, of the real, or has play become reality's successor, a virtual phantom invested with its own continuity and essential being?
>
> (Virtual Play: Baudrillard Online [n.d.]: 1, 3)

2 Both examples of Leary's celebration of maverick tendencies and rather more ambivalent fears are present in cyberpunk. Besher's *Rim* (1994), for example, depicts the saturation of Western business culture with Oriental practices and Gibson's protagonists are frequently depicted battling against Japanese gangsters/corporations referred to as *yakuzas/zaibatsus*.

3 References taken from *CuD* 4(11).

Appendix

1 The alleged double standards applied to the Robert Morris jr. case are documented in P.J. Denning [ed.] (1990) and Ross (1991).

2 As shown with the title of Paul Mungo's article, 'Satanic viruses'.

3 Cf. also the discussion of peer recognition in Chapter 3.

4 Cf. *CuD* 3(37).

5 Channel 4 Television documentary on hacking, November 1989.

Bibliography

Baker, Steve (1995) 'Digital life no. 6', available at:
http://www.taponline.com/tap/tech/net-tools/digital/digital.html.

Baricco, A. (1997) *Silk*, trans. Guido Waldman, London: Harvill Press.

Barlow, J.P. (1990) 'Crime and puzzlement', *Whole Earth Review*, fall 1990: 44–57.

Barrett, Neil (1997) *Digital Crime: Policing the Cybernation*, London: Kogan Page.

Becker, Howard S. (1963) *Outsiders: Studies in the Sociology of Deviance*, New York: Free Press.

Benedikt, Michael (1991) *Cyberspace: First Steps*, Cambridge, MA: MIT Press.

Bequai, A. (1987) *Technocrimes*, Lexington, MA: Lexington Books.

Besher, A. (1994) *Rim*, London: Orbit.

Bijker, W.E. (1993) 'Do not despair: There is life after constructivism', *Science, Technology, & Human Values* 18(1), winter 1993: 113–38.

Bijker, W.E., Hughes, T. and Pinch, T. (eds) (1987) *The Social Construction of Technological Systems*, Cambridge, MA: MIT Press.

Bijker, W.E. and Law, J. (eds) (1992), *Shaping Technology/Building Society: Studies in Sociotechnical Change*, Cambridge, MA: MIT Press.

Bloombecker, B. (1990) *Spectacular Computer Crimes*, Illinois: Dow Jones-Irwin.

Bowcott, O. (1993) 'Hacking and the Bedworth Syndrome', *Guardian* Thursday 1 April 1993, review section: 19 .

Bowcott, O. and Hamilton, S. (1990) *Beating the System*, London: Bloomsbury.

Brady, T. (1988) 'Crisis what crisis?', Paper prepared for the PICT Software Workshop, UMIST, 18–19 July 1988.

Brunner, J. (1969) *The Shockwave Rider*, New York: Ballantine.

Callon M. and Latour B. (1981) 'Unscrewing the big leviathan: How actors macro-structure reality and how sociologists help them do it', in K. Knorr-Cetina and A. Cicourel (eds) *Advances in Social Theory and Methodology: Towards an Integration of Micro and Macro Sociologies*, London: Routledge.

Carr, E. (1990) 'Elemental issues', *Micro Decision* June 1990: 30–1.

Chantler, Nicholas (1995) 'Risk: The profile of the computer hacker', Ph.D. thesis, Curtin University of Technology, Perth, Western Australia; conferred March 1996.

Cherny, L. and Weise, E.R. (eds) (1996) *Wired Women: Gender and New Realities in Cyberspace*, Seattle: Seal Press.

Citarella, K. (1992) 'Computer crime, computer security and human values', in NCCV (1992), pp. 55–8.

Clough, B. and Mungo, P. (1992) *Approaching Zero: Data Crime and the Computer Underworld*, London: Faber & Faber.

Colligan, D. (1982) 'The intruder – A biography of Cheshire Catalyst', *Technology Illustrated* October/November 1982, available at: http://www.dsl.org/m/doc/arc/nws/cheshire.phk.

Conley, V. (ed.) (1993) *Rethinking Technologies*, Ohio: Miami University Press.

Cosell, Bernie (1991) 'Is hacking the same as breaking and entering?', *Computer Underground Digest* 3(12): file 2.

Coupland, D. (1995) *Microserfs*, London: Flamingo.

Dann, J. and Dozois, G. (1996) 'Introduction', in *Hackers*, New York: Ace Books.

Dark Adept (1990) 'The hermetic underground', *Computer Underground Digest* 2(15): file 7.

Davis, J. (undated) 'Psychological warfare primer for online activists', available at: http://www.eff.org/A/psychwar.primer.

De Lacy, J. (1989) 'The sexy computer', in T. Forester (ed.) *Computers in the Human Context*, Oxford: Basil Blackwell.

Denning, D.E. (1990) 'Concerning hackers who break into computer systems', paper presented at the National Computer Security Conference, Washington, DC, 1–4 October 1990, pp. 653–64.

—— (1992a) 'Responsibility and blame in computer security', in NCCV (1992), pp. 46–54.

—— (1992b) 'Hacker ethics' in NCCV (1992, pp. 59–64.

Denning, P.J. (ed.) (1990) *Computers Under Attack: Intruders, Worms and Viruses*, Reading, MA: ACM Press and Addison-Wesley.

Doctor Crash (1986) 'The techno-revolution', *Phrack* 1(6): phile 3.

Dougan, W. and Gieryn, T. (1990) 'Robert Morris: Worm? Virus? Hero?', unpublished paper, Sociology Departments of UCLA and Indiana Universities.

Douglas, M. (1966) *Purity and Danger*, London: Routledge & Kegan Paul.

Dreyfus, S. (1997) *Underground: Tales of hacking, madness and obsession on the electronic frontier*, Kew: Mandarin.

Dunlop, C. and Kling, R. (eds) (1992) *Computerization and Controversy: Value Conflicts and Social Choices*, Boston: Academic Press.

Electronic Frontier Foundation (1990) 'EFF response to the Atlanta sentencing', *Computer Underground Digest* 2(7): file 3.

Fine, D. (1995) 'Why is Kevin Lee Poulsen really in jail?', available at: http://www.com/user/fine/journalism/jail.html.

Forester, T. (ed.) (1989) *Computers in the Human Context*, Oxford: Basil Blackwell.

Forester, T. and Morrison, P. (1990) *Computer Ethics: Cautionary Tales and Ethical Dilemmas in Computing*, Cambridge, MA: MIT Press.

Gibson, W. (1984) *Neuromancer*, London: Grafton.

—— (1986a) *Burning Chrome*, London: Grafton.

—— (1986b) *Count Zero*, London: Grafton.

—— (1988) *Mona Lisa Overdrive*, London: Grafton.

Gilboa, N. (1996) 'Elites, lamers, narcs and whores: Exploring the computer underground', in L. Cherny and E.R. Weise *Wired Women: Gender and New Realities in Cyberspace*, Seattle: Seal Press.

Godell, J. (1996) *The Cyberthief and the Samurai: The True Story of Kevin Mitnick and the Man Who Hunted him Down*, New York: Dell.

Gold, S. (1990) 'Computer security', *Micro Decision* June 1990: 47–61.

Goldstein, E. (1990) 'Response to Telecom Digest's views', *Computer Underground Digest* 1(13), July 1990: file 4.

—— (1993) 'Hacker testimony to House Subcommittee largely unheard', *Computer Underground Digest* 5(43): file 1.

Goodwins, R. (1993) 'Motley bunch hack at the end of universe', *The Independent* Friday 13 August: 11.

Greenberg, D. (1988) 'Documentation accompanying "FluShot" virus cure'; available through electronic bulletin board.

Hafner K. and Markoff J. (1991) *Cyberpunk: Outlaws and Hackers on the Computer Frontier*, London: Fourth Estate.

Hannemyr, G. (1997) 'Hacking considered constructive', position paper for the 1997 Oksnoen Symposium on Pleasure and Technology, available at: http://home.sn.no/home/gisle/oks97.html.

Hansard (1990a) United Kingdom Parliamentary Debates, House of Commons, 9 February 1990.

—— (1990b) United Kingdom Parliamentary Debates, Standing Committee C, 28 March 1990.

Haraway, D. (1985) 'A manifesto for cyborgs: Science, technology, and socialist feminism in the 1980's', *Socialist Review* 80: 40–55.

Harris, G. (1993a) 'Computer hacking "addict" is cleared of conspiracy', *The Scotsman* Thursday 18 March: 1.

—— (1993b) 'Daring data raider dependent on hacking fix', *The Scotsman*, Thursday 18 March: 3.

Hawn, M. (1996) 'Fear of a hack planet: The strange metamorphosis of the computer hacker', *The Site* July 15 1996, available at: http://www.zdtv.com/0796w3/worl/worl54_071596.html.

Heim, Michael (1991) 'The erotic ontology of cyberspace', in Michael Benedikt, *Cyberspace: First Steps*, Cambridge, MA: MIT Press.

Heiman, J.D. (1997) 'Banned from the internet', *Swing Magazine* March 1997: 70–5, available at: http.www.paranoia.com/~mthreat/swing.html.

Hobsbawm, Eric (1975) *The Age of Revolution*, London: Weidenfeld & Nicolson.

Hollinger, R.C. and Lanza-Kaduce, L. (1988) 'The process of criminalization: The case of computer crime laws', *Criminology* 26(1): 101–26.

Holloway, J. and Peláez, E. (undated) 'Learning to bow: Post-Fordism and technological determinism', unpublished paper, Edinburgh University.

Independent (1993) 'Odd addiction, perverse verdict', Thursday March 18: 25.

Johnson, B. (1991) 'What the laws enforce', *RISKS* 11(32), March.

Johnston, M. and Wood D. (1985) *Right and Wrong in Public and Private Life*, London: Gower.

Kane, A. and Mason, J. (1993) 'When hacking turns into an obsession', *Financial Times* Thursday 18 March: 7.

Kane, P. (1989) *V.I.R.U.S. Protection: Vital Information Resources Under Siege*, New York: Bantam.

Kapor, M. (1991) 'Civil liberties in cyberspace: When does hacking turn from an exercise of civil liberties into crime?' *Scientific American* September 1991, available at: http://www.eff.org/pub/Legal/cyberliberties_kapor.article.

Karnow, C.E.A. (1994) 'Recombinant culture: Crime in the digital network', Defcon II, Las Vegas, July 1994, available at: http://www.cpsr.org/cpsr/computer_crime/net.crime.karnow.txt.

Keller, L.S. (1990) 'Machismo and the hacker mentality: Some personal observations and speculations', paper presented to WiC (Women in Computing) Conference, pp. 57–60.

Kidder, T. (1982) *The Soul of a New Machine*, Harmondsworth: Penguin.

Knorr-Cetina, K. and Cicourel, A. (eds) (1981) *Advances in Social Theory and Methodology: Towards an Integration of Micro and Macro Sociologies*, London: Routledge.

Konstantinou, Jeanie (1995) 'Computer hackers: Invasion of computer systems', available at: http://www.ascu.buffalo.edu/%7Ehlmeyer/Complaw/CompLawPapers/konst.html (Computers and Law website).

Landreth, B. (1985) *Out of The Inner Circle*, Washington: Microsoft Press.

Lange, L. (1996) 'Hacker Goggans: Life on both sides of the firewall', *Electronic Engineering Times* 883, January 8 1996, news section, available at: http://www.cdc.net/~x/1996/erikb.asc.

Laughlin, C. (1991) 'What the laws enforce debate', *RISKS* 11(34), March.

Leichter, Jerry (1992) 'The good, the bad & ugly facts', *CuD* 4(18): file 1.

Levy, S. (1984) *Hackers: Heroes of the Computer Revolution*, New York: Bantam Doubleday Dell.

Littman, J. (1996) *The Fugitive Game: Online with Kevin Mitnick, the Inside Story of the Great Cyberchase*, Boston: Little, Brown & Co.

—— (1997) *The Watchman: The Twisted Life and Crimes of Serial Hacker Kevin Poulsen*, Boston: Little, Brown & Co.

Liz E. Borden (1991) 'Sexism and the computer underground', *Computer Underground Digest* 3(0): file 4.

Lundell, A. (1989) *Virus! The Secret World of Computer Invaders that Breed and Destroy*, Chicago: Contemporary Books.

Lynas, M. (1993) 'Mother tells of hacker's addiction', Edinburgh University *Student* newspaper, p. 1.

McLuhan, M. (1964) *Understanding Media*, New York: New American Library.

MacKenzie, D and Wajcman, J. (eds) (1985) *The Social Shaping of Technology*, Milton Keynes: Open University Press.

Marcuse, H. (1964) *One-Dimensional Man: Studies in the Ideology of Advanced Industrial Society*, Boston: Beacon Press.

Marda, L. and Ray, D. (1990) 'Crime bytes back', *Omni* 12(11): 34–102.

Marotta, M.E. (1993) 'Online with the superhacker', available at: http://www-kzsu.stanford.edu/uwi/post/mercury.html.

Martin, J. (1996) 'Management culture – hackers and bean counters', *Information Week* 28 October 1996, available at: http://www.cdc.net/~x/1996/cybercorp.asc.

Matthews, D. (1989) 'A bug in the machine', *The Sunday Correspondent* 17 December: 37–41.

The Mentor (1986) 'The conscience of a hacker' *Phrack* 1(7): phile 3.

Metcalfe, S. (1986) *New Electronic Information Services: An Overview of the U.K. Database Industry in an International Context*, London: Aldershot Gower.

Meyer, Gordon R. (1989) 'The social organisation of the computer underground', unpublished Master's Thesis, Northern Illinois University.

Meyer, G. and Thomas, J. (1989) 'Baudy world of the byte bandit: A post-modernist interpretation of the CU', paper presented at the American Society of Criminology annual meetings, Reno, November, available at: http://www.eff.org./pub/Net_culture...nk.

—— (1990) '(Witch)hunting for the computer underground: Joe McCarthy in a leisure suit', *The Critical Criminologist* 2 September 1990: 225–53.

Michalowski, R. and Pfuhl, E. (1990) 'Technology, property, and law: The case of computer crime', *Crime Law and Social Change* 15(3), May: 255–75.

Miller, Laura (1995) 'Women and children first: Gender and the settling of the electronic frontier', in James Brooks and Iain A. Boal (eds) *Resisting the Virtual Life: The Culture and Politics of Information*, San Francisco: City Lights.

Mizrach, S. (undated) 'Is cyberpunk the counterculture of the 1990s?', available at: http://www.eff.org./pub/Net_culture...nk/cpunk_as_counterculture.article.

Molina, A. (1989a) *The Social Basis of the MicroElectronics Revolution*, Edinburgh: Edinburgh University Press.

—— (1989b) *The Transputer Constituency: Building up U.K./European Capabilities in Information Technology*, Edinburgh University PICT Research Report Series No. 1.

Moreiras, A. (1993) 'The leap and the lapse: Hacking a private site in cyberspace', in V. Conley (ed.), *Rethinking Technologies*, Ohio: Miami University Press.

Mungo, P. (1991) 'Satanic viruses', *Gentlemen's Quarterly* 20 (British Edition), February 1991: 126–30.

Murray, W. (1992) 'On computer security and public trust', in Terrell Ward Bynum, Walter Maner and John L. Fodor (eds) *Computing Security*, Research Center on Computing and Society.

National Conference on Computing and Values (NCCV) (1992) *Computing Security*, New Haven: Southern Connecticut State University.

Neidorf, Craig (1990) 'NCSC Conference report – a "Knight Lightning" perspective', *Computer Underground Digest* 2(7): file 6.

Neumann, P. (1992) 'Computer security and human values', in Terrell Ward Bynum, Walter Maner and John L. Fodor (eds) *Computing Security*, New Haven: Research Center on Computing and Society.

Newton, J. (undated) 'On the road in cyberspace – Hackers', available at: http://www.the-wire.com/newjon/hackr2.html.

Nuttall, N. (1993) 'Healthy hobby that becomes obsession', *The Times* Thursday March 18: 5.

Parrish jr., E. (1989) 'Hacking is a crime, pure and simple', *Phrack* 2(24), February: file 1.

Peláez, E. (1988) 'A gift from Pandora's Box: The software crisis', Ph.D. thesis, Edinburgh University.

—— (1990) 'Soft ware', paper for the workshop on 'Social Perspectives of Software', Oxford, January.

Petersen, J. (undated), 'Hackers in chains: Encounters with some infamous computer hackers in federal prison', available at: http://www.grayarea.com/steal2.html.

—— ('Agent Steal') (1997) 'Everything a hacker needs to know about getting busted by the feds', available at http://www.grayarea.com/agsteal.html.

Phillips, M. (1993) 'Computers turned my boy into a robot', *Daily Mirror* Thursday 18 March, pp. 1, 4.

Pithers, M. and Watts, S. (1993) 'Hacker penetrated MoD', *Independent* Tuesday 18 March: 1.

Postman, N. (1990) 'Informing ourselves to death', German Informatics Society, 11 October, Stuttgart, available at: http://www.eff.org/pub/Net culture.

Poulsen, K. (undated) 'Recidivism explained', Scales-O-Justice website, available at: http://catalog.com/kevin/returns.html.

—— (undated-b), 'Dark Dante', letter to TV producer of an edition of *Unsolved Mysteries* on Poulsen WWW site, available at: http://catalog.com/kevin/usm.html.

PR Newswire (1985) Thursday 18 July 1985, p. 2, available at: http://www.dsl.org/m/doc/arc/nws/hcknews.hac.

Quittner, J. and Slatalla, M. (1995) *Masters of Deception: The Gang that Ruled Cyberspace*, London: Vintage.

Ravetz, Jerome R. (1996) 'The microcybernetic revolution', in Z. Sardar and J. Ravetz (eds) *Cyberfutures: Culture and Politics on the Information Superhighway*, London: Pluto Press.

Rayner, Jay (1997) 'The virtual philanderer', *Observer*, life section, 1 March: 11.

Rosenthal, Pam (1991) 'Jacked in: Fordism, cyberpunk, Marxism', *Socialist Review* 21(1): 79–103.

Ross, A. (1991) *Strange Weather*, London: Verso.

Rosteck, T. (1994) 'Computer hackers: Rebels with a cause', honours thesis, Sociology and Anthropology, Concordia University, Montreal, available at: http://geocities.com/CapeCanaveral/3498/.

Roszak, T. (1986) *The Cult of Information: The Folklore of Computers and the True Art of Thinking*, Cambridge, UK: Lutterworth Press.

Roush, Wade 'Hackers: Taking a byte out of computer crime', *Technology Review* April 1995, available at: http://web.mit.edu/techreview/www/articles/apr95/Roush.html.

Russel, S. and Williams, R. (1988) *Opening the Black Box and Closing it Behind You: On Micro-Sociology in the Social Analysis of Technology*, Edinburgh University PICT Working Paper Series.

Saffo, P. (1989) 'What is cyberspace?', *Communications of the ACM* 32(6): 664–5.

Sardar, Ziauddin (1996), 'alt.civilizations.faq: Cyberspace as the darker side of the West', in Z. Sardar and J. Ravetz (eds) *Cyberfutures: Culture and Politics on the Information Super-highway*, London: Pluto Press.

Scalione, Robert (1996) 'Crime on the internet: Can the law keep up with a new generation of cyberspace hackers?', available at: http://wings.buffalo.edu/law/Complaw (Computers and Law website).

Schell, R.R. (1979) 'Computer security: The Achilles' heel of the electronic air force?' *Air University Review* XXX(2), January–February: 16–33.

Schroeder, R. (1994) 'Cyberculture, cyborg post-modernism and the sociology of virtual reality technologies: Surfing the soul in the information age', *Futures* 26(5), June: 519–28.

Seabrook, John (1997) *Deeper: A Two-Year Odyssey in Cyberspace*, London: Faber & Faber.

Shallis, M. (1984) *The Silicon Idol: The Micro-revolution and its Social Implications*, London: Oxford University Press.

Sherizen, S. (1992) 'The end of the (ab)user friendly era', in NCCV (1992), pp. 39–45.

Shimomura, R. (1995) *Takedown: The Pursuit and Capture of Kevin Mitnick the World's Most Notorious Cybercriminal by the Man who did it*, with John Markoff, London: Secker & Warburg.

Shotton, Margaret A. (1989) *Computer Addiction? A Study of Computer Dependency*, London: Taylor & Francis.

Silicon Surfer (1990) 'Playgrounds of the mind: Cyberspace', *Computer Underground Digest* 2(17): file 6.

Smith, Michael Marshall (1996) *Spares*, London: HarperCollins.

Spafford, E.H. (1990) 'Are computer hacker break-ins ethical?', *Purdue University Technical Report, CSD-TR-994*.

—— (1991) 'Three letters on computer security and society', *Purdue University Technical Report, CSD-TR-91–088*.

Spertus, E. (1991) 'Why are there so few female computer scientists?', unpublished paper, MIT.

Springer, Claudia (1996) *Electronic Eros: Bodies and Desire in the Postindustrial Age*, Austin: University of Texas Press.

Stallman, R. (1985) *The GNU Manifesto*, Cambridge, MA: Free Software Foundation.

Steele, K. (1988) 'The social construction of the software crisis', unpublished work placement report, The Centre for Research into Innovation Culture and Technology: Brunel University.

Sterling, B. (ed.) (1986) *Mirrorshades: The Cyberpunk Anthology*, London: Paladin.

—— (1991) *CyberView 91 Report*, available at: http://www.eff.org/pub/Net_culture... Bruce_Sterling/cyberview_91.report.

—— (1992) *The Hacker Crackdown: Law and Disorder on the Electronic Frontier*, London: Viking.

Stockfield, B. (1991) 'Why the Legion of Doom has little to fear from the Feds', *Business Week* 22 April 1991: 62.

Stoll, C. (1989) *The Cuckoo's Egg: Tracking a Spy through the Maze of Computer Espionage*, New York: Doubleday.

Taylor, Paul A. (1998) 'Hackers: Cyberpunks or microserfs?', *Information Communication & Society* 1(4), winter, 401–19.

Thieme, R. (1996) *Internet Underground* December 1996: 21–2, available at: http://www.paranoia.com/~mthreat/iu.html.

Thomas, J. (1990) 'Review of the *Cuckoo's Egg*', *Computer Underground Digest* 1(6): file 4.

Thompson, K. (1984) 'Reflections on trusting trust', *Communications of the ACM* 27(8): 761–3.

Toxic Shock Group (1990) 'The evil that hackers do', *Computer Underground Digest* 2(6): file 4.

Turkle, S. (1984) *The Second Self: Computers and the Human Spirit*, London: Granada.

Uitenbrauer, F. (1991) 'Computer abuse proposal gives police lot of room for discretion' (translation of title), *NRC Handelsbad* (Amsterdam) 23 April.

United Nations *International Review of Criminal Policy – Manual on the Prevention and Control of Computer-related Crime*, available at: http://www.ifs.univie.ac.at/~pr2gq1/rev4344.html.

Vallee, J. (1984) *The Network Revolution: Confessions of a Computer Scientist*, London: Penguin Books.

Vinten, G. (1990) 'The criminalisation of hacking: A boon to computer security?', unpublished paper, The City University Business School: London.

Virtual Play: Baudrillard Online, available at: http://www.eff.org/pub/Netculture... rnism.

WarRoom (1996) '1996 information systems security survey', WarRoom Research, LLC, available at: http://www.infowar.com/.

Watts, S. (1993) 'Trial haunted by life in the twilight zone', *The Times* Thursday 18 March: 4.

Weizenbaum, J. (1976) *Computer Power and Human Reason*, San Francisco: Freeman.

Wilson, Brian Scott (1991) 'An answer to sexism in the CU', *Computer Underground Digest* 3(1): no file number.

Winner, L. (1971) *Autonomous Technology*, Cambridge, MA: MIT Press.

Woolgar, S. and Russell, G. (1990) 'The social basis of computer viruses', in *CRICT Discussion Paper*, Brunel University.

Woolley, B. (1992) *Virtual Worlds: A Journey in Hype and Hyperreality*, New York: Penguin.

Zimbardo, P. (1980) 'The hacker papers', *Psychology Today* August 1980: 62–9, available at: http://www.dsl.org/m/doc/arc/nws/hackpape.hac.

Index